SPECIAL EDUCATION
AND THE
CLASSROOM TEACHER

SPECIAL EDUCATION AND THE CLASSROOM TEACHER

CONCEPTS, PERSPECTIVES, AND STRATEGIES

By

BEVERLY LIEBHERR DEXTER, Ed.D

Adjunct Professor, Western Carolina University
WCU Programs in Asheville
Consultant, Asheville, North Carolina

32831

CHARLES C THOMAS • **PUBLISHER**
Springfield • *Illinois* • *U.S.A.*

Published and Distributed Throughout the World by

CHARLES C THOMAS ● PUBLISHER

Bannerstone House

301-327 East Lawrence Avenue, Springfield, Illinois, U.S.A.

© *1977, by* CHARLES C THOMAS ● PUBLISHER

ISBN 0-398-03607-1

Library of Congress Catalog Card Number: 76-23381

With THOMAS BOOKS *careful attention is given to all details of manufac-
turing and design. It is the Publisher's desire to present books that are satisfactory as to their physical qualities and artistic possibilities and appropriate
for their particular use.* THOMAS BOOKS *will be true to those laws of
quality that assure a good name and good will.*

Printed in the United States of America
R-1

Library of Congress Cataloging in Publication Data

Dexter, Beverly Liebherr.
    Special education and the classroom teacher.

    Includes index.
    1. Handicapped children--Education. I. Title.
LC4015.D46   371.9   76-23381
ISBN 0-398-03607-1

to the children ...

PREFACE

THIS book is for teachers, all teachers. It is also written for children who have learning problems in the classroom. To give the teacher some background concerning possible causes for these learning problems, the first five chapters cover the history of special education and some of the resulting public policies and attitudes.

Nationally, the concern for children who are not succeeding in the classroom has gained momentum during the past several decades. Recent court cases and federal legislation have brought about an unprecedented awareness of these concerns. Local school systems have modified their educational programs in the public schools in an attempt to better meet the needs of exceptional children. Yet, the major responsibility for educating these youngsters rests with the teacher.

Whether she is a regular teacher or a special teacher, the educational instructor needs to be informed as to how to best teach each child in her classroom. For this, she needs expertise in many areas of learning besides that of academic education. One person should not be expected to meet all of the educational goals outlined for the exceptional child unless he or she is specifically trained to do so.

The process of teaching is also a process of learning. Teachers do not begin teaching when they enter the classroom. Rather, this is when they begin *learning*. This learning process is often drastically opposed to the type of learning required for the preparation of teaching which they encountered during their college experiences. The children obviously have not read the same textbooks as their teachers, and thus the confusion begins. This experience can be likened to the training done by a scuba diver. He can study and memorize all of the available books on diving techniques, but if he attempts to take one of these books with him on his first dive, the words on the pages may blur when he gets into the water. Experience and advice from other qualified divers will help him to better utilize the information he has gained from reading the books. The books gave him helpful information to experiment with, but they were intended only as guides for the actual experience of diving.

So it is with teachers. The books are meant as guides for actual teaching experiences. This book in particular is meant as a guide. It is the intent of the author that the teacher read this book with the children in mind. It is hoped that this book will be useful to teachers, no matter who they are, where they are, or what they teach.

How does one describe these children? Or any children? The following was written several years ago in an attempt to describe just who the children are.

CHILDREN ARE

Children are
As parents do;
Children are
As sisters do;
Children are
As brothers do;
Children are
As grandmas do;
Children are
As grandpas do;

Children are
As aunts do;
Children are
As uncles do;
Children are
As peers do;
Children are
As neighbors do.

Children are
As teachers do;
Children are
As adults do;
Children are
As heroes do;
Children are
As movies do;
Children are
As books do;
Children are
As societies do;
Children are
As legislators do;
Children are
As militaries do;
Children are
As religions do.

Children are
As others do ...
Children are
As children do ...

CHILDREN ARE!

Beverly Liebherr Dexter

ACKNOWLEDGMENTS

IT would take a second volume of this book to fully acknowledge all of the friends and colleagues who helped along the way. Instrumental in my professional growth have been three very important people: Dr. James Wolf, Coordinator of Special Education, Canal Zone; Dr. Marilyn Flynn, Supervisor of Special Education, Fulton County Public Schools, Hapeville, Georgia; and Dr. Glenn Vergason, Chairman, Department of Special Education, Georgia State University, Atlanta, Georgia. As my supervisor during my formative years in special education, Jim Wolf encouraged me to further my teaching experiences by working with autistic and multiply handicapped youngsters in the Canal Zone. Marilyn Flynn furthered these professional experiences by convincing me that Georgia State University should be my next stopping place upon arrival back in the States. It was there that I met Glenn Vergason, who has remained both a friend and a colleague during the past eight years. His continued support and enthusiasm toward my work have resulted in the development and expansion of my professional growth.

Continued support in my writing attempts has been forthcoming from Dr. Glen Arrants, Facilitator, Western Regional Education Center, Canton, North Carolina. Glen's unlimited encouragement during my doctoral studies at Duke University helped to keep my enthusiasm alive, even through the most difficult periods of those two years.

Family encouragement has also been a continual aspect of both my professional and my personal growth. Nan Liebherr, my mother, has conquered seemingly impossible odds to encourage and support me at all times. My husband, Al Dexter, deserves the biggest thanks, though. If it were not for him, I would never have gone to the Canal Zone, nor to Atlanta, nor to Asheville. His patience throughout my years of graduate school has been matched only by his understanding during my writing sprees when I have been totally absorbed in my work.

Chapter Five of this book would not have been possible without the full cooperation of "Barb" and "Jim." Although they prefer to remain anonymous, the inclusion of their letters in this book is my way of sharing their love and concern for their son "Brad."

A final thanks goes to those who helped me secure a typewriter and to Pat Russell, Secretary, Western Carolina University Programs in Asheville, who helped with the typing of the final manuscript.

Beverly Liebherr Dexter

CONTENTS

SPECIAL EDUCATION
AND THE
CLASSROOM TEACHER

Chapter 1

A BRIEF HISTORICAL BACKGROUND
OF SPECIAL EDUCATION
... IN THE BEGINNING

A FULL history of special education and its implications for education in general would be a formidable task for any professional. Several writers in the field of special education have summarized the history of mental retardation (Cranefield, 1966; Doll, 1962; Dunn, 1961; and Kirk and Johnson, 1951), yet there has been no overall composite made of all of the historical aspects of the interrelated fields of special and regular education. Such a history would make a text in itself, and therefore, only a summary of the primary aspects of these fields is given here.

Emphasis has been placed on the historical aspects of mental retardation and learning disabilities since these are the areas of special education which are most frequently encountered by the classroom teacher. Many of the educational practices of the past have been incorporated into the modern teaching techniques of the present, and in many instances such methodologies are being applied to all areas of learning.

Men such as Edward Seguin and Jean Itard were instrumental in initiating total educational programs for the retarded. Their methods of sensory stimulation have been modified somewhat, but their theories are still relevant to today's concept of teaching the *total* child to the best of his abilities. Such theories have been handed down to educators for generations, yet they are often presented as innovative concepts in the field of general education.

Techniques currently used with the learning disabled originated with studies done in language, aphasia, and brain injury in both children and adults. Similarly, teaching techniques for

3

other handicapping conditions have also been incorporated into general educational practices of the twentieth century, although historical information related to these areas is somewhat sparse. Only the most significant historical aspects related to educational achievements in these areas have been incorporated into this chapter.

A brief historical background of some of the more prominent activities in special education is given here to familiarize the reader with various aspects of the overall field. This background is also intended to give the reader an overall perspective of special education as it relates to the educational practices of today.

The Mentally Retarded

Although there are no written records prior to the year 1500, it is an almost certainty that there were retarded individuals living in the communities at and before that time. It is also logical to assume that during the very earliest days of mankind some of the higher functioning retardates survived long enough to reproduce. Those who were incapable of any reasonable amount of self-sufficiency most likely experienced very short life spans, or were possibly even abandoned during infancy or early childhood. Their parents were not advised by the local pediatrician, nor were they counseled by the school psychologist in the child-rearing practices of the day. There were very few Joneses to be kept up with, and thus the stigma of having a retarded child did not necessarily put a social blight on the family. Instead, the child was probably allowed to function as best he could and was thus found to be acceptable by the others within the local group. He was expected to do his share of the work and to work within the structure of his group.

As man's living conditions improved over the centuries, he found himself using his intellect more than his physique for survival. With such advancement, the plight of the mentally handicapped must have become more and more obvious to everyone. Response toward the mentally retarded ranged from overprotection to overt exploitation, with the majority of the population responding to the latter extreme. However, there were a few individuals, primarily those belonging to religious sects within the church, who became pioneers in the humane treatment of the retarded. Prior to 1800, the church provided the only organized humane treatment of the retarded. As early as the thirteenth century, the churches had established asylums for the less fortunate members of society, including the retarded. Food and shelter were provided, but no form of education or training was attempted.

Although there were no formal or established programs besides the sanctuary of the asylums, interest in the retarded began to appear in some of the early medical records around 1530. Paracelsus wrote the first medical report devoted to mental deficiency entitled, "On the Begetting of Fools." His writings revealed a religious and humanistic view which questioned God's meaning in allowing a human being to reproduce a "fool." Indirectly, he was the first to mention the possibility of heredity and the role of genetics in what was termed "foolishness."

In 1602, Felix Platter wrote the first detailed description of cretinism, although he did not name it as being a specific syndrome at the time. It was Platter who was the first to suggest that although deficits might be noticed during infancy, it was during the school years that specific deficits became most noticeable.

Neither of the men mentioned above appear to have been inspirational or influential upon the professionals of their day for it was not until 1672 that the actual mention of treatment came into existence. Thomas Willis, in "Of Stupidity or Foolishness," noted that some retardates were capable of certain vocational activities, even though they could not cope with the basic academics. He proposed that treatment could be feasible only through the combined efforts of the physician and the teacher, and prescribed that a trial period of training be instigated and closely supervised. If, after a given period of time there was no improvement, then a longer course of related treatment should be implemented with the retarded.

Willis, like Paracelsus, mentioned the possibility of heredity and genetics in regard to the reproduction of retardates. He was also the first to distinguish in writing between schizophrenia and mental deficiency, basing his views on the idea of thought disorders.

Jean Itard applied the principles of sensory discrimination to the teaching of the mentally retarded in 1799. Until then, such training had been used with the deaf, and this was the first attempt to teach the retarded by this method. For his subject, Itard chose a young boy who had been found living in the woods of Aveyron, France. Victor, as the boy was later named, had apparently lived all of his twelve years in the woods without any contact with humans. Determined to educate and socialize the boy, Itard bombarded him with mental training through sensory stimulation. He tried to "humanize" the boy and develop human wants and needs within him. In this respect, his efforts failed. However, Itard's impact on the field of education for the retarded has yet to be duplicated. His contributions indirectly gave the United States their first special education programs, for it was a student of Itard's, Edward Seguin, who brought the idea of the residential school to this country around 1850.

Just prior to coming to the United States, Seguin published his theories in *The Moral Treatment, Hygiene, and Education of Idiots and Other Backward Children* in 1846. His theory of education was based on known physiology, humane philosophy, keen observation, and practical ingenuity. It employed the stimulation of the muscles and senses, imitation, reflection, and synthesis. This physiological approach emphasized educating the muscular system first, then the auditory sense, and lastly the visual abilities. The focus of progress was on the child's individuality, specific limitations, and special abilities. Each child's rate and extent of progress was based solely on his original point of departure. The primary aim was comprehensive coordinated training of the whole child, physically, intellectually, and morally. As such, the program existed throughout the child's life cycle. It began with institutional supervision of home care and readying the child for adult life through a careful program of socialization and occupational training. Organized sequencing was used to develop refinement in special areas of deficity. Seguin advocated the practical aspects of such training, and emphasized the necessity of concreteness and relativity in the tasks presented. He also strongly suggested that the day's work should begin and end with tasks which were pleasant to the individual.

Concurrently, Samuel Gridley Howe's success with blind idiots led him to believe that there was also hope for idiots (the common term for all retarded individuals during the nineteenth century) who were not blind. Encouraged by such a revolutionary thought, Howe began pioneering for the rights of the retarded. He was able to convince the legislature that with their financial support, he would be able to train retarded children. On October 1, 1848, a wing of the Perkins School for the Blind in Massachusetts was opened as an experimental school for the training of ten retarded children. Financial support was allocated to last for three years, as a trial period for everyone concerned. At the end of the third year, the success of the experimental school had reached such proportions that the Joint Committee of Public Charitable Institutions recommended the facility become a permanent one, but in another location. In 1855, the Massachusetts School for Idiotic and Feeble-Minded Youth opened in South Boston.

Encouraged by the results obtained within his own state, Howe began traveling in the neighboring areas in an effort to obtain similar programs for the handicapped in other states. Kanner (1974) credits Howe with being one of the primary pioneers for obtaining institutional services for the retarded in the United States.

Most of the first schools for the retarded in the United States were started to experiment with Seguin's methods and his environmentalist theories. They were intended to be training schools, and thus the severely retarded were refused admission. Admission was also refused to the very young and to the very old. Seguin felt that he could cure retardation, and in that respect his schools failed. However, they did lay the foundation for the state residential schools of the future.

Seguin was also instrumental in organizing the original

chapter of what is known today as the American Association on Mental Deficiency. He initiated his efforts in 1866 to form an association for those who were involved in working with the retarded. Ten years later, in 1876, the Association of Medical Officers of American Institutions for Idiotic and Feeble-Minded Persons was formed at the Elwyn Training School in Media, Pennsylvania.

As the programs which had originally been inspired by Seguin increased, the training schools found that the majority of their residential students were unable to return to the community. Custodial care became prominent, and residential training centers were established on a limited basis throughout the United States. Custodial care became the major concern of the state institutions, much the same as had been the case with the early asylums in Europe centuries before. The Association of Medical Officers was working at that time toward the establishment and differentiation of institutions in all states.

By 1879, programs for the retarded had evolved through the efforts of professionals in related clinical and educational fields. The usefulness of concrete presentations for teaching the retarded was recognized not only by special educators, but by other educators as well. The Elwyn Training School implemented a kindergarten for the retarded, a concept well advanced for that time. Music was experimented with as a means for teaching the retarded some of the more difficult academic subjects. Training was also done in the areas of self help, gymnastics, and discipline, with the final projected outcome being that of at least partial self-sufficiency.

Higher level retardates were trained to help with the domestic chores at these training schools, and thus some of the expense for the upkeep of such institutions was defrayed. It was also believed that by contributing to the overall functioning of the institution, the retarded were able to experience at least some degree of ego satisfaction. Through these efforts, plus those of individual members of the Association, state responsibility for services for the retarded gradually evolved. The more severely retarded remained in the custody of the private institutions while the higher functioning retardates were trained for employment, both inside and outside of the institutions. Despite these efforts, only sixteen of the then thirty-four states had established fully functioning institutions of this nature.

The first day class program for the retarded in the United States was established in Providence, Rhode Island in 1896. Since the use of individual intelligence tests had not yet been developed, it has been hypothesized that most of the children enrolled were "problem children" who were having difficulties in the regular classroom situation.

Maria Montessori, an Italian Physician, became interested in mental defectives in 1897. She promoted the theory that the problem with mental defectives was primarily a pedagogical problem rather than a medical one, and such thinking led to the founding of the Orthophrenic School for the Cure of the Feebleminded. It was there that she initiated the first classes for training teachers of mentally defective children. During the day the school was used to educate the retarded, and in the evenings Montessori conducted special classes for the teachers.

In 1907, Montessori expanded her theories to be used with the culturally deprived when she instituted the *Case Dei Bambina* in Rome for children of working mothers. The school's activities were designed to emphasize home activities. Self-teaching was encouraged and promoted through the use of didactic materials.

Leonard Ayres made a study of educational retardation in the public schools of the United States in 1909. In this study he found that many school aged children were failing, especially during the first year of school. He found that nearly one sixth of the school population was repeating a grade, sometimes for the second or third time. The conclusion of the educators of the period was that the fault was in the curriculum rather than in the child's mental abilities. It was hypothesized that a single curriculum plan could not possibly meet the needs of all children. As a result, intensive studies began in the area of curriculum development.

While these studies in curriculum development were being conducted, other professionals in the field of educational evaluation began to suggest that the problem might be that different children have different abilities in the academic areas. Edward Thorndike developed a test for measuring reading ability in school-aged youngsters and reported his preliminary findings in 1914. The following year, Leonard Ayres developed *A Measuring Scale for Ability in Spelling*. In 1916, Clifford Woody reported his findings in a study he conducted involving achievement in the area of arithmetic.

Other factors were being related to a child's inability to learn during the early school years. Primary among these factors were speech impediments, physical disabilities, and general poor health. Hollingworth (1923) supported the theory that the primary cause for academic failure was a weakness in general intelligence.

Alfred Binet's work in France brought about an unprecedented impact in the field of education. His research in the area of intellectual functioning resulted in a renewed awareness concerning the placement, education, and training of the mentally retarded. Based on Binet's newly developed evaluation tool, new delineations were established in the areas of clinical diagnosis, classification, and the resulting educational planning. By identifying central intelligence as the essential problem of the mentally retarded, Binet initiated a new outlook for the retarded, their parents, and their teachers.

With the advancement of Binet's work, the emphasis turned toward the psychological aspects of dealing with the retarded. In 1906, the first psychological laboratory for the specific study of mental deficiency was established at the Vineland Training School in New Jersey. Henry Goddard, then Director of Research at the Training School, discovered Binet's tests while traveling in Europe. Upon his return to the United States, Goddard published a translation of the tests, and in 1910 he developed an American standardization of Binet's earlier scale. During the next several years, the refinement and restandardization of intelligence testing was conducted by others in the field. Pioneers in this area included Rudolf Pintner, Lewis Terman, and Robert Yerkes. By 1916, Lewis Terman had incorporated the intelligence quotient into the Binet-Simon test. The concept of the IQ had originally come from L. William Stern.

With the adoption and adaption of psychometric testing procedures came a new list of terms as well as classifications to be used with the mentally retarded. Although the term *feeble-minded* had gained prominence throughout the centuries, the newer terms gave specific intelligence quotients to aid in the new classifications. Of the retarded, *idiot* was believed to be the lowest functioning with an IQ below 20. The middle range of retardation, an IQ between 20 and 40 or 50, was classified as *imbecile*. The highest functioning retardates, with IQ ranges between 50 and 70, were classified as being *morons*. Today, similar IQ ranges refer to the severely, moderately, and mildly retarded individuals. Educationally, the moderately retarded are considered to be "trainable," and the mildly retarded are considered to be "educable" within the public school setting.

In 1910, Goddard presented a paper to the American Breeders Association which supported the theory that retardation was hereditary. He later did a study of the Martin Kallikak family which traced the lineage of several generations from the same paternal parentage. During the Revolutionary War, Martin Kallikak had an illicit affair with a feebleminded barmaid. Children from this illegitimate union were reported to be of lower intelligence than the average persons of that time and area. Their offspring were also reported to have lower than average intelligence.

After the War Kallikak returned to his hometown and married. His children from this union were reported to be of normal or even superior intelligence. Their offspring also tended to have a reportedly high rate of normal or above intelligence.

Since the data for this study was collected and substantiated from heresay and old records, and since no actual testing was done to determine the level of feeblemindedness or normalcy among the descendents studied, it is questionable whether Goddard's conclusions were totally accurate. Further, it must be remembered that the environments of the two groups of descendents were dramatically opposite from each other. Those offspring who survived from the illicit union were exposed to considerably inferior living conditions than were the offspring of Kallikak's legal marriage.

Despite these considerations, Goddard's paper had an impact on the professionals of his time, and heredity was considered as the total factor determining mental retardation. Widespread efforts were initiated to not only segregate the retarded, but also to sterilize them.

There still remained questions concerning the classification of the retarded and the methods employed for diagnosing individuals as being mentally retarded. William Healy, then with the Chicago Juvenile Psychopathic Institute, developed additional aids to be used in the diagnosis of delinquent youngsters being evaluated by the Institute. The purpose of these additional aids was to differentiate cultural conditions and types of learning problems which could not be detected through the use of the Binet alone. The Healy and Fernald tests, developed in 1911, supplemented the regular scales of children who either spoke a foreign language or who were handicapped.

Stanley Porteus, in 1915, developed a series of mazes which were designed to test specific abilities of the retarded. The mazes were developed to supplement the Binet in testing for mental retardation much in the same way the Healy aids were developed to help in the differentiation of youngsters from different cultural backgrounds and youngsters who were handicapped.

In 1916, Edgar Doll emphasized the total picture for use in diagnosis. He recommended that intelligence tests, form boards, mazes, a personal history, and clinical impressions should be an integral part of the evaluation. He further suggested that these evaluative aids should be fully developed within the diagnostic framework of the day.

By 1917, Walter Fernald had also added the assessment of practical knowledge and general information, social history, and reactions, economic efficiency and moral reactions to his list of relevant information needed for a thorough diagnostic evaluation of the mentally retarded.

Rudolf Pintner and Donald Paterson developed the *Scale of Performance Tests* in 1917 as a clinical aid to the heavily weighted language areas of the Binet. Form boards and puzzles constituted the majority of the subtests, thus allowing the individual to perform in another area besides language. Of the four types of norms developed for the *Scale*, the median mental age norms have been the most widely accepted.

Although a variety of diagnostic instruments were continually being developed and experimented with during the early 1900's, other considerations began to come into view. Psychologists and educators questioned the etiology of mental retardation in certain instances and further questioned the relationship between mental retardation and such factors as emotional deprivation, sensory deficits, and low motivation. Charles Davenport reported in 1936 that there were two types of development: retarded and incomplete. In 1941, Edgar Doll questioned the current concept of mental deficiency in relation to the accepted causes of the time.

The expanding development of diagnostic instruments and evaluation techniques brought an increased number of residents into the institutions. The Vineland Training Center developed a cottage program for all of its residents. Although the cottage program concept was not unique to this Center, it was unique in the fact that it was available for all of its residents. Prior to this time, several states had already initiated cottage programs, but only for those individuals who could function with a minimal amount of supervision. It was the hope of the Vineland Center to be able to improve their services through this unusual cottage program.

Despite the fact that the United States had made a great deal of progress in the areas of diagnosis and treatment, it was still considerably behind the European countries in providing educational programs for the retarded. Germany offered special classes in the public schools as early as 1859. By 1860, such classes were generally accepted by the public, and their programs began to expand rapidly during the next fifty years. The German classes for the retarded emphasized the needs of the individual child within the educational and social construct of the day. Modified academic programs were combined with social awareness and adaptability programs. By 1905, these special classes had received favorable publicity both in Germany and in the United States.

Based on the success and acclaim received by the European efforts to educate the retarded through their public schools, similar programs were initiated in the United States. Over one hundred large city school systems in the United States had implemented classes for the retarded by 1911. The University of Pennsylvania developed a model class for the retarded based on a combination of European and American teaching techniques.

Similar classes were implemented by Goddard at the Vineland Training School. Formal training of teachers of the retarded became a secondary function of the School. Meta Anderson Post, a graduate of this teacher training program, later developed a curriculum for the retarded. For the elementary curriculum, she utilized basic social and academic skills. Her methodology included training in the sense modalities along with motor development activities. At the higher levels, she emphasized structured assessment to determine abilities, attitudes, and needs of the individual in relation to vocational training and later placement. Although she advocated the teaching techniques developed by Montessori, she emphasized the use of several techniques in order to adequately educate the individual child. She did not feel that any one method would fully meet the needs of the individual child.

During the summer of 1922 Elizabeth Farrell taught a graduate course in special education at Teachers' College in Columbia, New York. These students eventually formed the nucleus of what was later to be called the Council for Exceptional Children, and elected Farrell as the first president.

The mid 1920's and 1930's brought with them experimental approaches in teaching the retarded based primarily on the current trends in regular education at that time. Alice Descoeudres (1928) developed a comprehensive educational system for mental defectives implementing the theory that the children learn by doing. She emphasized perceptual knowledge and sense training, and felt that the grouping of subjects around a central theme was beneficial. Drawing considerably from Seguin, Binet, and her former teacher, Decroly, she developed a combination of formal exercises and a modern philosophy of teaching through experience situations.

Around this same time, Annie Inskeep (1926) published a book describing a modified traditional curriculum to be used with the mentally handicapped and slow learners. Similarly, Christine Ingram (1935) began advocating her method of teaching the retarded based on the Unit Method. She listed criteria for effective unit teaching, emphasizing the individual as an important member of the group in such activities.

Occupational education for the retarded began to take hold during the 1930's and 1940's. Richard Hungerford (1944) broadened the concept to include the total educational process. As in the past, such training was delegated primarily to the higher functioning retardates.

In 1951, Samuel Kirk and G. Orville Johnson delineated the aims of education for the mentally retarded and suggested that programs for the mentally handicapped stress occupational adequacy, social competency, and personal adequacy. They emphasized that such programs should include all levels of mental retardation for which such activities would prove to be beneficial. Their suggestions have been utilized throughout modern educational programs for the retarded.

Since the 1950's, numerous books have been written concerning the education of the retarded. The trend has been toward realistic goals for the retarded, with structured, sequential teaching techniques. The underlying theme throughout modern educational strategies for the retarded has been humane treatment of the individual.

The Blind

Louis Braille, developer of the Braille system of communication for the blind, was blinded as a young child through an injury which led to a severe infection and later total blindness. His initial educational training was done through the local school system of the small village in which he lived. As a youth he convinced his parents to let him enroll in the Royal National Institute for the Young Blind in Paris. The only form of "reading" for the blind at that time was books with embossed characters of the Roman alphabet. At the Institute where Braille attended classes; there were only fourteen such books, but they were rarely used by the students because of the difficulty imposed in trying to decipher the characters. First, the student had to identify each letter of each word by its specific characteristics. Then the student had to put the letters together to make a whole word. This concentrated effort proved to be much too tedious for the majority of the students.

In 1819, the same year that Braille entered the Royal Institute as a student, a French Army officer, Charles Barbier, was challenged with the prospect of being able to communicate at night on the battle field without being detected by the enemy. He worked out a complex system of embossed dots and dashes which proved to be too difficult for the soldiers, but was quite feasible for the blind. He revised his system and called his new reading method for the blind, Sonography. Although his system still contained too many dots for the average touch reader, Barbier's efforts provided Braille with his basic concept of dot writing in the years to come. Barbier had originally had twelve dots per cell; Braille devised six dots per cell.

When Braille first introduced his original version of his dot system in 1824, his teachers at the Institute argued that it would be foolish to try to teach blind students a system that was so totally different from the configurations used by the sighted. The students, on the other hand, readily adopted the system and before long they were taking their own class notes, writing their own compositions, and even writing personal diaries, all of which had been totally impossible for them in the past.

In the meantime, Samuel Gridley Howe, a physician and educator, helped to organize the Perkins School for the Blind in Watertown, Massachusetts. As an educator, he had trained Laura Bridgman, a deaf-blind student. His techniques were used fifty years later by Annie Sullivan when she began working with Helen Keller.

Howe's interest in the blind and deaf-blind led him toward an interest in the mentally retarded. It was this interest which helped him become instrumental in the humane treatment of all handicapped individuals. His associates included Thomas

H. Perkins, after whom the Perkins School for the Blind is named, and Dorthea Lynde Dix, whose pioneering work with the mentally ill conquered many obstacles of the time. His reform activities for the handicapped carried over into his associations with men like Horace Mann and Charles Sumner who were working toward overall educational reforms.

It was 1854 before the Braille system gained official recognition at the Royal National Institute as a dot system for the blind. As such, it followed the conventional spelling and punctuation rules of the Roman alphabet. Six years later, the Braille system was introduced in America to the Missouri School for the Blind. As in other schools for the blind, until the Braille system was introduced, the students were subjected to a variety of raised-form systems, most of which proved to be too complicated for the majority of students.

Other recognized raised-form systems were introduced in the United States following the adoption of the Braille system by the Missouri School. The New York Point was published in 1868 by William Bell Wait, superintendent of the New York Institution for the Blind.

A second raised-dot system was developed in 1878 by Joel W. Smith, a blind piano tuning teacher at Perkins Institute for the Blind in Massachusetts, now known as the Perkins School for the Blind. Although this version, known as the American braille, was never officially accepted by the blind, it offered an alternative method of communication for them.

The Deaf

The first residential school for the deaf was established by Thomas Hopkins Galludet in Hartford, Connecticut. During Galludet's young adulthood, he became interested in working with the deaf. His major studies had been in theology, yet he remained interested in the deaf following his graduation from Andover Theological Seminary. This continuing interest in the deaf led him to an investigation of the oral method which was being utilized in Europe. His trip to Europe to explore this method was met with disappointment because Thomas Braidwood, the man who was using the oral method in Scotland, refused to share his techniques with Galludet. A scheduled trip to France helped Galludet learn the techniques used in the manual method of instruction for the deaf and he received special training at the Institute des Sourdes-Muets in Paris for this purpose.

After returning to the United States, Galludet founded the American Asylum for the Education and Instruction of the Deaf and Dumb in 1817. Only six students were initially enrolled in the Asylum, and Galludet served as its first principal.

Ten years after the founding of the Asylum in Connecticut, a federal law was passed to grant land access for the Deaf and Dumb Asylum of Kentucky. An extension of this law was decreed in 1847 so that the time allotted for the purchasing of this land could be extended.

Three laws were passed during 1857 and 1858 to help with the establishment of the Columbian Institution for the Instruction of the Deaf and the Dumb and the Blind. By 1864, the Institution had been granted permission to confer degrees upon its graduates. The Institution officially changed its name to Galludet College in 1954, and thus became the only institution of higher learning in the world specifically designed for deaf students.

Captioned films for the deaf became available on a free loan basis in 1958 through the Department of Health, Education and Welfare. Further expansion of this service came through federal laws passed in 1962 and 1965.

Provisions for the training of teachers for the deaf became a federal law in 1961. Speech pathologists and audiologists were also aided through this law since their professional acitivities often included the deaf and hard of hearing.

Galludet College was granted federal funding in 1966 to establish a model secondary school for the deaf. The school was implemented to expand and further develop new educational methods, technology, and curriculums for secondary school students who were deaf. Funding was also appropriated for the construction of new facilities on the site of the model school.

In 1970, Galludet College received additional funding for a

second model school program. The Kendell School serves as a demonstration elementary school for deaf children. Included in its program is a preschool program for very young deaf children. In conjunction with its model educational programs, Galludet College also operates programs in research related to deafness in individuals of all ages.

The Physically Handicapped

There has been little research done in the area of special education for the physically handicapped child. This is due in part to the fact that many physically handicapped children have other overlapping handicapping conditions, such as mental retardation. Those children who are physically handicapped but who have normal or above intelligence are often thought to be retarded because their physical involvement of the speech muscles prevents them from being able to verbalize their communications. Physically handicapped children who have only mild motor involvement are often integrated into the regular classrooms and no special educational provisions are necessary for their instruction since they are functioning intellectually on the same levels as their peers.

In the past, the physically handicapped individual often died during infancy or early childhood. Later, medical pioneers such as Winthrop Morgan Phelps and Temple Fay began developing techniques for both the diagnosis and treatment of children with cerebral palsy. Little's Disease, as cerebral palsy was originally named, was first described by William Little in the late 1800's. Little described the syndrome as including severe mental retardation. Through his studies Phelps determined that mental retardation was not necessarily a symptom or a result of cerebral palsy. Rather, he argued that the child might appear to be retarded due to his lack of speech or his inability to communicate because of his severe motor involvement. His collaborations with Temple Fay led to the development of six major classifications of cerebral palsy. These six classifications included (a) spastic paralysis (cerebral); (b) athetosis (mid-brain); (c) tremors and rigidity (basal ganglia); (d) ataxia; (e) high spinal spastic (medulla); and (f) mixed (diffuse). Currently, cerebral palsy is classified according to the different forms of neuromuscular involvement, and the five major types include (a) spasticity; (b) athetosis; (c) ataxia; (d) tremor; and (e) rigidity. Roughly three-fourths of all cases of cerebral palsy fall into the first two categories, spasticity and athetosis.

The polio epidemic of the 1940's brought new interest and research in the area of the physically handicapped. With the development of the Salk vaccine, the threat of polio became overshadowed by other diseases which physically crippled both children and adults. Drugs, especially certain tranquilizers, have also resulted in physically impaired children. Medical technology has saved many infants from almost certain death during or shortly after birth, yet it has also left many of them blind, mentally retarded, and/or physically handicapped. As a result, these overlapping handicaps have become the responsibility of various medically and educationally oriented disciplines. Educational programs for the physically handicapped are therefore geared toward the other handicapping conditions and actual treatment for the physical disability is usually structured through physical therapy, surgery, and medication.

The Learning Disabled

During the same period of time when education for the mentally retarded was becoming an important aspect of the field of education, work in the areas of language and childhood aphasia was also developing research related to the education of handicapped children. Alexander Ewing (1930) wrote about the similar behavioral and language characteristics he found among brain injured war veterans and children with severe language impairments. He attributed this phenomenon to the fact that the speech and language functions are more susceptible than any other pathological conditions affecting the brain.

Samuel Orton (1937) also studied young children in relation to language impairments he observed in the adults he treated as a professor of psychiatry at the medical school of the University of Iowa. Orton's main interest was in individuals who had reading and writing disabilities. He felt that reading problems in children were due primarily to disorders of memory, and prescribed a regimented training program which emphasized drill and repetition of paper and pencil tasks. He coined the word *strephosymbolia* to indicate the "twisted symbols" perceived by children with reading problems. His writings during the thirties were sprinkled with such medical terms as alexia (loss of reading and writing abilities), motor agraphia (inability to write), developmental alexia (inability to learn to read at the rate and with the skill which would normally be expected), and developmental agraphia (difficulty in learning how to write in relation to other intellectual accomplishments and manual skills of the individual). Orton's terminology and remedial techniques have remained within the clinical construct of remedial reading.

Alfred Strauss was the first to use the term *exogenous* in relation to brain injury in children. In his early studies he found that certain behavioral characteristics were similar among the individuals he studied who had known brain injury. He found that these same characteristics were also common to a certain population of individuals without known brain injury. He listed four main characteristics among the latter population which indicated a possible brain injury. These four characteristics included deviations in (a) language, (b) perception, (c) conceptualization, and (d) emotional control. These four characteristics later became known as the Strauss Syndrome which, in turn, became synonymous with brain injured child and even later, learning disabled.

In 1947, Alfred Strauss and Laura Lehtinen published *Psychopathology and Education of the Brain Injured Child, Volume I.* They were the first writers to recognize that brain injury did not necessarily lower intellectual abilities. Their book stressed the use of unstimulating environments, structured classrooms, and cubicles for teaching brain injured children. Along with Newell Kephart, Strauss co-authored a second volume under the same title in 1955. This second volume emphasized the theory that these children should not remain isolated, but should be returned to the regular classroom as soon as possible.

In 1958, four papers on the brain injured child were presented at the annual convention of the National Society for Crippled Children and Adults. Three of the four papers were written by medical doctors; the fourth was by an educational psychologist. *The Dallas Medical Journal* later reprinted the four articles in a special edition of the *Journal* in March, 1959.

The first in this series of four articles was written by Nicholson Eastman and was devoted to the etiology of brain damage. Contributing factors being considered by Eastman included prematurity, hyperoxia, physical trauma during birth, the Rh factor, and congenital malformations. Although Eastman was specifically describing *known* brain damage based on the resulting types of cerebral palsy observed in children, these same contributing factors have been linked with the less severe cases of cerebral dysfunction, including cases of brain damage resulting in learning disabilities.

Meyer Perlstein, in this same series of articles, also wrote about the brain injured in relation to the physically handicapped. However, he was emphatic in his statements concerning similar behavioral characteristics between *known* and *suspected* brain injured individuals. He stated that simply because an individual may display certain characteristics of brain injury such as a short attention span or distractibility, this does not prove that actual brain injury exists within that individual. He was cognizant of the fact that the line between normal and abnormal may sometimes be dangerously thin when it comes to determining who is or who is not brain damaged to at least some degree.

The third article in the series was written by Leslie Hohman. His article was primarily about the emotional needs of the brain injured child, and he introduced his article with examples of studies he had done in relation to the encephalitis epidemic of 1918. Hohman subscribed to the theory that the neurological involvement of the brain injury cannot always be detected and therefore substantiated. He also stated that the use of the term *special language difficulties* was being misused in regard to the overall concept of learning disabilities. It was his opinion that language delay was not peculiar to only brain injured children.

Laura Lehtinen, in the last of these four important papers, asked the question, "What can we do for the brain-injured child who has normal or near normal intelligence?" In order to answer this question, she had to first define her term *brain-injured* child. Her definition included children who had behavior problems as well as learning problems both in and out of school. Specifically, she discussed visual perception, auditory perception, conceptual abilities, and overall behavior as they pertained to the brain-injured child in the classroom.

These four articles, written originally in 1958, are typical of the articles written during the following decade. Arguments between the medical doctors and the educators of the time became heated, and no matter what was said to whom, it usually became controversial.

The greatest controversy in these arguments stemmed around the definitions and terms being developed to indicate the child whose classroom performance was below his expected level of achievement, although his mental abilities were considered to be well within the normal range. It appeared that the only logical explanation was some type of dysfunction related to the brain and its thinking processes.

The concept of brain dysfunction as a primary causative factor in learning and behavioral disorders of children began to receive increasing attention during the late 1950's and early 1960's. This concept attained particular prominence among medical doctors, psychologists, educators, and language specialists. The earlier studies by professionals in these fields began to be re-examined and terms were redefined throughout these areas of speciality. Terms such as *minimal brain dysfunction, brain injury, dyslexia,* and *learning disabled* were all used by the various professions to indicate disabilities in learning and language processes. Over one hundred terms were coined and used during the sixties to describe the same type of child Strauss first wrote about in the forties.

More specific behavioral characteristics were also being listed, including such behaviors as short attention span, hyperactivity, perceptual handicaps, and mixed dominance. The role of language development and its effect on the learning ability of a child was gaining new importance. Authorities in the field began to question the relationship between language and learning problems in the child who was not achieving academically in the classroom, especially in the area of reading.

This new awareness of language and learning problems was the direct result of (a) an increased refinement in diagnostic skill and techniques, (b) the necessity for more precise classification of learning and behavioral disorders in children, (c) advanced medical knowledge which resulted in an increased number of children who survived birth traumas such as prematurity, and (d) a growing dissatisfaction with the diagnosis of purely psychological reasons for any disorganized or unaccountable behavior found in certain children.

In the mid 1960's, Sam Clements became Project Director of the U. S. Office of Education Task Force I Committee, which dealt with the identification, delineation, and remediation of learning disabilities. The Task Force Committee stated that a child with near average or above IQ might display certain learning or behavioral disabilities which could be associated with deviations of the central nervous system. Such deviations could be found in various combinations of problems related to perception, conceptualization, language, memory, and control of attention, impulse, or motor functions. Causal factors included genetic variations, biochemical irregularities, perinatal brain insults or other illnesses or injuries sustained during the early or developmental years of life.

Although the Task Force Committee clarified many of the questions which had arisen concerning children with learning disabilities, it also opened up a new Pandora's Box for the field of special education. By the late 1960's and early 1970's, learning disabilities had become an area of national concern. Educators, parents, physicians, and community organizations became involved in the identification and remediation of learning disabilities in children. Early intervention programs were initiated in many school systems; volunteers were organized into groups for special training in remedial procedures;

and universities began offering specialized courses in the area of learning disabilities. The Association for Children with Learning Disabilities was formed in 1963 to help both parents and professionals learn more about children with learning problems. The Association supports a definition of learning disabilities which is similar to the one originally initiated by the Task Force I Committee. The emphasis is on normal learning abilities in regard to intellectual functioning, but with academic retardation that cannot be explained by retardation, cultural deprivation, sensory loss, motor handicaps, or emotional disorders. However, secondary emotional, behavioral, or organizational difficulties may result from the primary deficiencies.

The Council for Exceptional Children formed a professional subgroup for teachers and other professionals in the field of learning disabilities through their Division for Children with Learning Disabilities. The Division was formed in 1968, and by 1976 there were over 10,500 members.

On April 13, 1970, President Nixon signed Public Law 91-230 which was entitled, The Elementary and Secondary Amendments of 1969. This law authorized provisions for (a) research and related study pertaining to the education of children with specific learning disabilities, (b) additional professional or advanced training for educators involved in all phases of the education of children with specific learning disabilities, and (c) the establishment and operation of model centers to aid in the improvement of education of children with specific learning disabilities.

More recently, President Ford signed Public Law 94-142, The Education of All Handicapped Children Act of 1975, on November 29, 1975. An important factor of this law is the ceiling established for the number of handicapped children who will be aided through its financial provisions. Only 12 percent of the school aged children between the ages of five and sixteen may be counted as handicapped children. Of these 12 percent, not more than one-sixth, or 2 percent may be children with specific learning disabilities. The law is scheduled to go into effect on October 1, 1977.

The Council for Exceptional Children

The first meeting of the International Council for Exceptional Children was held in Cleveland, Ohio, on February 26-27, 1923. The Council had been officially formed in the summer of 1922 by teachers who were attending classes at Columbia University during the summer session. Nearly two hundred teachers joined the organization, representing both the United States and five foreign countries.

When publicity concerning the Council was made known to the public, membership applications were received from a variety of educational and other related fields. By the time the Council convened in Cleveland, there were nearly five hundred members on the roster.

The Council's primary focus was on services for all areas of handicapping conditions. A main concern was training for exceptional children who had the potential for becoming self-sufficient and productive citizens within their own communities. By acting as a clearinghouse for instructional information for teachers of the handicapped, the Council proposed to upgrade the quality of the education and training of both the children and their teachers.

By 1956, the term International had been dropped by the Council, although today their annual conferences are still termed International. Growing activity and affiliation with the National Education Association was only one of the major reasons for eliminating the term International from the title of the group. A second major reason for this action concerned their efforts to obtain federal support for programs throughout the United States. By changing the name of the organization, the Council was able to give a more clearly defined picture of their intended objectives within the national concerns being considered by the federal government. Throughout its history, the Council has maintained an advocacy for handicapped children which has encouraged groups such as the Kiwanis and Rotary organizations to help with the financial needs of the various programs for the handicapped.

REFERENCES

1. Aiello, Barbara: Especially for special educators: a sense of our own history. *Except Child, 42*:244-252, 1976.
2. Alpern, Gerald D., and Boll, Thomas J. (Eds.): *Education and Care of Moderately and Severely Retarded Children.* Seattle, Spec Child, 1971.
3. Ayres, Leonard: *A Measuring Scale for Ability in Spelling.* New York, Russell Sage, 1915.
4. Ayres, Leonard: *Laggard in Our Schools.* New York, Russell Sage, 1909.
5. Brison, David W.: Definition, diagnosis, and classification. In Baumeister, Alfred (Ed.): *Mental Retardation.* Chicago, Aldine, pp. 1-1967.
6. Clements, Sam D.: *Task Force I: Minimal Brain Dysfunction in Children.* Washington, HEW, 1966.
7. Comptroller General: *Project Head Start: Achievements and Problems.* Washington, HEW, May 20, 1975.
8. Cranefield, Paul F.: Historical perspectives. In Philips, Irving (ed.): *Prevention and Treatment of Mental Retardation.* New York, Basic, 1966, pp. 3-14.
9. Davenport, Charles B.: Causes of retarded and incomplete development. *Amer Assoc Ment Defic, 51*:208-214, 1936.
10. Descoeudres, Alice: *The Education of Mentally Defective Children.* Trans. by Row, Ernest F., Boston, Heath, 1928.
11. Doll, Edgar A.: The essentials of an inclusive concept of mental deficiency. *Am J Ment Defic, 46*:214-219, 1941.
12. Doll, Edgar A.: Foster care for mental defectives. *Train Sch (Vinel), 36*:193-205, 1940.
13. Doll, Eugene E.: A historical survey of research and management of mental retardation in the United States. In Trapp, Philip E. and Himelstein, Philip (Eds.): *Readings on the Exceptional Child.* New York, Appleton-Century-Crofts, 1962, pp. 21-68.
14. Dunn, Lloyd M.: A historical review of the treatment of the retarded. In Rothstein, Jerome H. (Ed.): *Mental Retardation: Readings and Resources.* New York, HR&W, 1961, pp. 13-17.
15. Eastman, Nicholson, J.: The brain-damaged child: why does he happen? *Dallas Med J: Special Edition* 3-7, 1959.
16. Ewing, Alexander: *Aphasia in Children.* London, Oxford U Pr, 1930.
17. Farrell, Elizabeth E.: President's address: first annual meeting of the International Council for Exceptional Children. In Kirk, Samuel A., and Lord, Francis E. (Eds.): *Exceptional Children: Educational Resources and Perspectives.* Boston, HM, 1974, pp. 16-21.
18. Fay, Temple: Cerebral palsy: medical considerations and classifications. *Am J Psychiatry, 108*:180-183, 1950.
19. Fernald, Walter E.: Sense training for low grade children. *Train Sch Bull (Vinel), 41*:170-174, 1845.

20. Gitter, Lena L.: Montessori principles applied in a class of mentally retarded. *Ment Retard*, 5:26, 1967.
21. Goddard, Henry H.: A measuring scale of intelligence. *Train Sch (Vinel)*, 6:146-155, 1910.
22. Goddard, Henry H.: *The Kallikak Family*. New York, Macmillan, 1913.
23. Hohman, Leslie B.: The brain-damaged child: what are his emotional needs? *Dallas Med J:Special Edition* 12-14, 1959.
24. Hollingworth, Leta S.: *The Psychology of Subnormal Children*. New York, Macmillan, 1923.
25. Hungerford, Richard H.: A practical program of training and service for the high grade defective and borderline group. *Am J Ment Defic*, 48:414-416, 1944.
26. Ingram, Christine P.: *Education of the Slow-Learning Child*. Yonkers, World, 1935.
27. Inskeep, Annie D.: *Teaching Dull and Retarded Children*. New York, Macmillan, 1926.
28. Itard, Jean Marc Gaspard: *The Wild Boy of Aveyron*. Trans. by Humphry, George, and Humphry, Muriel. New York, Appleton-Century-Crofts, 1932.
29. Kanner, Leo: Itard, Seguin, Howe — three pioneers in the education of retarded children. *Am J Ment Defic*, 65:2-10, 1960.
30. Kirk, Samuel, and Johnson, G. Orville: *Educating the Retarded Child*. Cambridge, Riv Ed. HM., 1951.
31. Kirk, Samuel A., and Lord, Francis E.: *Exceptional Children: Educational Resources and Perspectives*. Boston, HM, 1974.
32. Kuhlman, Frederick: Experimental studies in mental deficiency. *Am J Psychol*, 15:391-446, 1904.
33. Kuhlman, Frederick: Larger aspects of the special class. *J Juv Res*, 13:19-27, 1929.
34. Lehtinen, Laura E.: The brain-injured child: what can we do for him? *Dallas Med J:Special Edition* 15-21, 1959.
35. Montessori, Marie: *The Montessori Method*. New York, Schocken, 1967.
36. Myers, Patricia I., and Hammill, Donald D.: *Methods for Learning Disorders*, 2nd ed. New York, Wiley, 1976.
37. Orton, Samuel T.: *Reading and Writing and Speech Problems in Children in Development of the Language Faculty*. New York, Norton, 1937.
38. Pasamanick, Benjamin, and Knobloch, Hilda: Epidemiologic studies on the complications of pregnancy and the birth process. In Caplan, G. (Ed.): *Prevention of Mental Disorders in Children*. New York, 1961, pp. 74-94.
39. Perlstein, Meyer A.: The brain-damaged child: what are his physical needs? *Dallas Med J, Special Edition*:8-11, 1959.
40. Phelps, Winthrop: The management of the cerebral palsies. *JAMA*,

117:1621-1625, 1941.
41. Richards, Laura E.: *Samuel Gridley Howe.* New York, Appleton-Century, 1935.
42. Robinson, Halbert B., and Robinson, Nancy M.: *The Mentally Retarded Child: A Psychological Approach.* New York, McGraw, 1965.
43. Rodgers, Carl T.: *Understanding Braille.* New York, Am Foun Blind, 1969.
44. Smith, Robert M.: *Clinical Teaching: Methods of Instruction for the Retarded.* New York, McGraw, 1968.
45. Stevens, Godfrey D., and Birch, Jack W.: A proposal for clarification of the terminology used to describe brain-injured children. *Except Child, 23*:346-349, 1957.
46. Strauss, Alfred, and Kephart, Newell, C.: *Psychopathology and Education of the Brain Injured Child,* Vol. 2. New York, Grune, 1955.
47. Strauss, Alfred, and Lehtinen, Laura: *Psychology and Education of the Brain Injured Child.* New York, Grune, 1947.
48. Weiner, Beuma B.: Assessment: beyond psychometry. *Except Child, 33*:367-370, 1967.
49. Weintraub, Frederick J., Abeson, Alan, Ballard, Joseph, and LaVor, Martin L.: *Public Policy and the Education of Exceptional Children.* Reston, Coun Exc Child, 1976.
50. Wolf, James M., and Anderson, Robert M.: *The Multiply Handicapped Child.* Springfield, Thomas, 1969.

Chapter 2

CURRENT ISSUES CONCERNING PUBLIC POLICIES AND SPECIAL EDUCATION ...LABELING IS FOR JAR LIDS

ALTHOUGH programs for the handicapped were instituted in the public schools early in the twentieth century, there were still very few trained teachers in this highly specialized field. As some of the colleges began training teachers in the various areas of special education, the emphasis was generally on clinical teaching because the public schools were not prepared, either financially or philosophically, to serve handicapped children.

Public education was still considered to be a privilege rather than a right, and many normal children were excluded from the public schools for various reasons. In the rural areas, for example, schools were in session during the winter months only, and if the weather became too severe, there might be no school at all for weeks at a time. This time could not be made up during the warmer months because the children were involved in manual labor on the farms.

The philosophy of the early twentieth century that education was only for a privileged few automatically excluded the severely handicapped from the public schools. Those children with severe physical handicaps were not seen by the general public, but were kept hidden at home or in an institution. Children with severe mental handicaps were treated in much the same way.

It was a common belief that such "freaks" were the responsibility of the family into which they were born. A great deal of guilt was assumed by the family for having given birth to a defective human being. The burden of keeping this handicapped child at home became the penance of the "guilty" family, especially if institutional placement proved to be un-

30

feasible.

When the public schools began to admit mildly handicapped children into their programs there were still many unanswered questions. It was questioned just where the line ought to be drawn concerning the admittance of a handicapped youngster into even a special program within the public school setting. Each school system began setting up individual guidelines for admission into the special programs. Once the children were accepted into a public school program, the educators questioned and argued about which curriculum would be the best for each particular group of handicapping conditions. Each school system soon developed or borrowed a set curriculum or curriculum guidelines to use within their special classrooms. Usually, this curriculum was geared toward the handicapping condition rather than toward the learning needs of each child.

Once these special programs became operational, questions were raised by both school and community personnel concerning the appropriateness of the programs. Children who were physically handicapped were often grouped with children who were mentally handicapped. To the general public, all of the children within the special education program were there for one reason: They were different in some way from the normal children. Usually the special children were isolated from the rest of the children in the school, even during lunch and recess. Their classroom was frequently in the basement or at the far end of the school building, away from the general flow of traffic and general activity within the building.

Although these children were all grouped into one classroom, their individual learning needs were so diverse that even the specially trained teacher had difficulty meeting their educational needs. In one such classroom might be children between the ages of six and sixteen with a variety of educational abilities. Several of these children might have mild physical handicaps, but no mental handicaps. Several others might have mild to moderate mental retardation, but no physical problems. A few of the children might have various combinations of both physical and mental handicaps. The rest of the class might have been behavior problems in the regular classroom so they were "delegated" to the special education classroom because there may be fewer children to compete with for individual attention from the special teacher.

How did these children all end up in the same isolated classroom? The more obvious or visible handicaps automatically placed them there. With the not so obvious problems the decision may have been made by the principal or even the superintendent. Or, as in the later years, the children may have been given standardized intelligence tests or group achievement tests. If the child could not read, he could not do well on the written group test. If he could not do well on the written group test, he was labeled mentally retarded and placed in the special education class. Once the child was labeled retarded and placed in the special class, he was retained there for the remainder of his academic career. A child's entire future was often determined by the results of one standardized intelligence test.

Children from different ethnic groups also found themselves categorized according to the results of IQ tests. Often these were group tests which had been standardized on majority ethnic children. The results of the group tests usually showed that culturally different children ranked far below their peers from the majority group, and thus the minority group children were placed in classes for the retarded or slow learners.

Relevant Court Cases and Special Education

During the past two decades, publicity has been given to several court cases which have dealt with improper screening, educational appraisal, special education placement criterion, high ratio of minority group children in special classes, and money compensation for damages to children who have been educationally misplaced in the public schools.

As early as 1954, tracking or placing youngsters in classes according to ability grouping was brought to the attention of the courts. In the Brown v. Board of Education case, it was declared that teaching based on race and socio-economic levels was unconstitutional and that such discrimination created an inequality of educational opportunities.

Again in 1967, in the Hobsen v. Hansen case in Washington, D. C., Judge Skelly Wright ruled the tracking system as unconstitutional. Yet, as recently as 1971 a survey by Franks revealed that in eleven Missouri school systems, Afro-American underachievers were placed in classes for the retarded while Caucasian underachievers were classified as learning disabled.

One of the more recent cases on record to gain national concern was the Diana v. State Board of Education case in Northern California. In this court case, nine Mexican-American public school youngsters charged that they were improperly placed in classes for the retarded because the intelligence tests that were used to place them discriminated against them and their primary language. The case was settled in February of 1970, with the issuing of six mandates. These six mandates provided guidelines for the educational evaluation of bilingual children in California.

Intelligence testing was to include both the child's primary and secondary language if English was not his primary language. These same children were not to be given tests which were heavily weighted in the language area. Further, bilingual children who were already placed in special classes were to be re-evaluated only on the nonverbal sections of intelligence tests. Within the year, a plan was to be developed by each school district regarding the retesting and re-evaluation procedures to be used with these children.

Plans were to be developed concerning the placement of these children back into regular classrooms whenever possible, and supplementary help was to be provided to help these students make the transition from special to regular classrooms. To help with the retesting, the state psychologists were requested to either devise new IQ tests or to revise the ones in current use to meet the needs of the population being evaluated, rather than the population normally used for the standardization of such tests. Thus, the children were to be evaluated in relation to their local peers, not to the population as a whole. Lastly, each district was asked to explain any disproportionate quotas of minority children in their special classes as compared to the percentage of such children in their regular classes.

Of the six mandates issued in the above case, only one was truly educational in nature, the one directing districts to provide transitional aid to the youngsters who were being integrated back into the regular classrooms. The other five mandates dealt directly with the use of verbal IQ tests, which has been the primary issue in most litigation on minority children.

A later California case, Case v. State of California, dealt with the educational problems of a severely handicapped youngster. Case was a school aged child who had been diagnosed as deaf and autistic with possible mental retardation. She had attended special classes, both public and private, prior to her enrollment in the multi-handicapped program at the California School for the Deaf in 1970. It was questionable whether she had made any progress at the School because of the conflicting reports argued in this case. Due to her retardation and severe overlapping handicapping conditions, the question of placement became one of "if," not "where." None of the state agencies felt responsible for educational services for the child because of the nature of her multiple handicaps.

Initially, the judge ruled that Case should remain in the School for the Deaf. Later, on January 23, 1973, the judge concluded that the Education Code did not include training children of lower functioning levels in basic self-help skills such as eating, toileting, and dressing. He concluded that children with lower functioning levels who could not adequately perform these basic skills would be considered custodial, and therefore the education of such children was not within the realm of the Education Code.

As a result of this ruling, Case was totally excluded from the School. On July 16, 1974, a decision was made supporting the ruling in the lower courts that the California School for the Deaf had acted within their rights in dismissing the child on the basis of her severe handicaps and behavior problems. It was ruled that none of her constitutional rights had been violated and that the School could not provide the educational services deemed necessary for a child with these handicapping conditions.

On July 31, 1974, the plaintiffs filed a petition for a re-hearing, but the petition was denied. Again on August 26, 1974, another petition was filed, this time for a hearing in the California Supreme Court. The interesting part of this case is not the variety of outcomes decided upon by the various courts, but the fact that once the child was dismissed from the School for the Deaf she was placed in the special education program of the public schools and has been reported to be making good progress.

Another suit filed against the California School for the Deaf involved a profoundly deaf, but "exceptionally bright" ten-year-old boy who was also enrolled in the multi-handicapped unit. In the Uyeda v. Department of Education case, filed on June 14, 1972, the mother of the child stated that even though she had initially signed an agreement with the School to accept her son's dismissal should such action be taken after his initial enrollment, his dismissal was illegal in that there had been no hearing prior to his termination from the School. A preliminary injunction was denied by the trial court and the child was enrolled in a school for the deaf in Los Angeles County. His progress was reported as very good, and thus the counsel for the plaintiff did not proceed in the litigation, although the case is still on file.

The initial breakthrough for children like the ones described above was initiated in October of 1971 when action was taken by the Pennsylvania Association for Retarded Children (PARC). The PARC challenged sections of the Pennsylvania Public School Code which excluded children from the public schools who (a) were felt to be uneducable or untrainable in the public school setting, (b) were refused admission to school by the board of school directors who had the right to refuse or accept a child who did not have a mental age of five years, and (c) were exempted from compulsory attendance laws after having been examined by a mental clinic or school psychologist who felt they could not benefit from attendance in the public school. The PARC charged the Pennsylvania Public School Code with violating the equal protection guaranteed under the Fourteenth Amendment of the United States Constitution.

Major points argued in this case centered around three important educational factors. First, it was argued that systematic educational programming for mentally retarded youngsters often produces learning. Second, the learning gained through such programs should be considered educational on the basis that education should not always be defined as academically oriented experiences. Education, it was argued is the continuing process of learning to cope with the environment and learning to function appropriately within that environment. Third, it was pointed out that early detection leads to better programming designed to meet the individual needs of the handicapped child. The earlier such programming can be initiated, the greater the amount of learning which can be anticipated to occur.

A second monumental case took place in Washington, D. C., in 1971. In the Mills v. Board of Education case, the parents and guardians of seven children brought a suit against not only the District of Columbia Board of Education, but also against the Department of Human Resources and the mayor of the city. Again, the suit was filed for failure of the public schools to provide appropriate educational services for all children. Among the children being denied a public education in this court case were children with labels such as "slight brain damage" and "hyperactive behavior." Of the seven children, four were living at home, but were denied entrance into the public schools. Although their names were on waiting lists for private facilities, there were no tuition grants being provided for any of the four children and thus the total financial responsibility was being left up to the parents. The remaining three youngsters lived in residential institutions where there were no educational programs being provided for them.

The court issued an order on December 20, 1971, which consisted of four major statements. By January 3, 1972, the following actions were to have taken place: (a) all seven children in the suit were to be provided with appropriate public school placement, (b) the Board of Education, the Department of Human Resources, and the mayor were to provide to the court a list of all other children who were not currently being served by publicly supported facilities, and (c) efforts were to have been initiated concerning the identification of all other such children who had not already been identified. The final statement of the agreement provided for a liaison person to handle special questions and concerns which might result from this court order.

By January 21, 1972, the plaintiffs had filed a motion for summary judgment on the basis that the defendants in this case had failed to comply with the court order issued on December 10, 1971. On August 1, 1972, the United States District Judge issued an order and decree for implementation of the summary judgment. His rulings resulted in two major declarations concerning the constitutional rights of all children. First, it was ruled that all children, regardless of their exceptionality or handicap, were entitled to a public education. Second, it was ruled that any procedures which prevented such children from obtaining appropriate educational services without a prior hearing and a review of the placement procedures was a denial of the class rights of due process and the equal protection of the law.

Although the defendants claimed that the financial burden for implementing such a court order would be unreasonable, the court ruled that insufficient funds could not be considered as a just reason for the lack of adequate educational opportunities for an exceptional or handicapped child, and that funds would have to be allocated for these children in the public schools. The court felt that if monies were made available for the education of normal children, monies should also be made available for the education of exceptional or handicapped children.

In April of 1974, a case was brought to the Supreme Court of North Dakota regarding the rights of a child who had been placed in a state institution for crippled children. Since the child's residence was different from that of her parents, and since the child was considered a ward of the state with welfare benefits, the question was posed as to whether *any* agency was responsible for financing her education. It was determined that

the North Dakota Constitution, in providing an equal education for all children, also provided an equal education for the
handicapped. Further, the residence of the child was said to
determine the school district which should be held responsible
for the educational programming of the child, even though this
residence differed from that of the parents. In summary, the
court ruled that it was within the child's Constitutional rights
to receive an appropriate and public education within her community of residence. It was felt that if the State Constitution
did not uphold this right to a free and appropriate education,
the Federal courts would refer to the Federal Constitution and
demand that these rights be upheld.

A second court case involving the Association for Retarded
Children evolved in Maryland. The Maryland Association for
Retarded Children brought a suit against the State of Maryland
to obtain equal educational opportunities for retarded children.
On May 3, 1974, the court made thirteen statements defending
the plaintiffs in their pursuit. The court differentiated between
mental and physical handicaps in these statements and decreed
that mental retardation alone was not felt to be a justified
reason for institutionalization. However, since the Maryland
Constitution provides for the free education of all children, the
court placed the responsibility for such an education within the
realm of the public schools. It was decreed unlawful to place a
child in a non-public school setting without full funding being
provided by the state.

Interestingly enough, the court did not arrange for any financial assistance to be provided for the public schools which were
mandated to provide the educational obligations being decreed.
Nonetheless, total fulfillment of the responsibilities being decreed was expected to take effect in September of 1975. So,
although the demand for equal educational opportunities was
being delegated to the public schools, financial assistance was
not forthcoming from this particular court decision.

Who Is Responsible for the Handicapped Child?

Several very important questions must be asked concerning

the types of court cases just described. Who really is responsible for these handicapped children? Are there other means besides court action for changing the placement of a handicapped youngster who is not functioning up to expected levels of competency in his current educational setting? What are the extraneous factors, of both the child and his teachers, which cause the handicapped child to present behaviors which are unacceptable in certain educational settings? What are the alternatives if the secondary placement does not prove to be suitable for the child?

Although all of these questions cannot possibly be answered for all handicapped children through the passage of state and federal laws, many similar questions are being answered across the nation. Society is being held responsible to see that no child or adult is rejected from public educational services which are appropriate for that individual. Programs and procedures are being developed to make certain that such services are available to all handicapped individuals.

The public is just now becoming aware of the need for equal educational opportunity, and that all children can learn something. The question has been, Does equal education *equal* education? Due to the recent court rulings, excuses related to the lack of money, facilities, and/or teachers have been found to be unacceptable. If the educational planners do not provide for these youngsters, then the courts will. What the courts decree may not, in reality, be equal education. The courts can mandate programs and the allotment of funds for such programs, but before equal educational opportunities become a reality, there are four areas of concern which must be re-evaluated and improved upon. These four areas are (a) due process, (b) placement, (c) classification, and (d) descriptive data.

Due process must be taken into consideration before any child is placed into a special education class. Until recently, it was not believed that children had rights or that they were entitled to any specific rights regarding their education. Such rights, if acknowledged, were determined and executed by adults. Children who were "different" from the norm in any way were often excluded from the public school settings. State statutes even exempted "feebleminded" children from compulsory school attendance in some instances. It has been theorized that such statutes were provided because teachers and other educators found such children repulsive (Abeson, Bolick, and Hass, 1976). In 1919, a ruling by the Wisconsin Supreme Court defended the public school's right to exclude a child with cerebral palsy because of the "disgusting" physical appearance of the child and the extra burden he placed on the classroom teacher.

The Fourteenth Amendment of the United States Constitution provides for due process in Section 1 where it states that no state shall "deprive any person of life, liberty, or property without due process of the law." This has been interpreted as being a basic right for all individuals, regardless of any handicapping conditions. By refusing a child entrance into the public schools, the schools have deprived that child of his Constitutional rights. The regular classroom teacher should not be expected to be totally responsible for a severely handicapped child, however. Rather, the public school should be responsible for providing an appropriate and free educational experience for the child, whether it be in the form of a special class, a special resource program, or special training for teachers within the public school system.

Only recently has there been any legislation enacted to provide for the placement of all children with handicaps in appropriate educational settings. The placement decision is to be made with the full awareness of the child's parents or guardians; and the parents or guardians are given an opportunity to be heard by the school system.

A further implication of due process has surfaced in the legislation concerning the placement of retarded children in residential institutions. As of March, 1976, thirty-eight states and the District of Columbia allowed parents to voluntarily commit their children for treatment in state mental institutions. The lower court has said that the children must be guaranteed a preliminary hearing within seventy-two hours of their placement, and a second hearing should be held within the following two weeks. The panel elected to be present at the hearing should be made up of interested but impartial individuals. In the state of Georgia, the parents are expected to be members of the panel unless extenuating circumstances forbid their participation. The federal government is expected to make a decision concerning the lower courts' decision in the spring of 1976.

Due process is therefore being carried over into all placement activities regarding the mentally retarded. Thus far, only public school placement in special education classes implies equal educational opportunities for all areas of handicapping conditions.

Placement of a child, regardless of the setting or the handicapping condition, should be a joint decision on the part of the parents or guardians and appropriate school personnel, including the teacher. Although due process allows for the proper procedures to be followed for the placement of a child in a special education classroom, it does not guarantee that such placement will be the appropriate placement for that individual child.

Placement does not guarantee the child an education. Rather, it places him physically in an educational setting which has been deemed the best available setting at the moment. If a school system does not have a special class specifically designated for the physically handicapped, the child with cerebral palsy is often placed in the special class for the mentally retarded, regardless of his mental abilities. For this reason, it is imperative that the parents and the appropriate school personnel meet to discuss the child's educational future. By doing this, both parties are made aware of the decisions that have been made concerning the child's educational placement. Continued communication is vitally important for everyone concerned so that future decisions concerning the child may also be made through a joint effort. With both parties aware of such decisions, the responsibility for properly educating the child becomes one of mutual concern.

Classification of children has been an issue of controversy for decades. Unfortunately, the classifications utilized too often describe the physical appearance of the child, such as crippled, or his mental ability, such as retarded, without regard for further descriptions of the specific learning problem. Just as there are varying degrees of physical handicaps, there are also varying degrees of mental retardation. Not all physically handicapped children are confined to wheel chairs; likewise, not all mentally retarded children are confined to learning only minimal academic skills.

As exemplified earlier in the court cases dealing with minority and bilingual children, mental retardation may be considered to be so only under certain circumstances. A rural child who can find his way through the "bush" with ease may still be classified as mentally retarded in the classroom because of the low scores he obtained on standardized tests. Outside of the classroom he may be able to cope quite well with his environment and may even play an active role within his own small community. However, within the confines of the classroom he may find himself lost or even overwhelmed by the academic activities which are being presented to him daily. The label applied to this child is only a part-time label; it applies only to the classroom situation.

Instead of using the cumbersome categories of physically handicapped, mentally retarded, and culturally deprived, new categories or descriptions should be developed. Classification of the child should be geared toward the learning needs of the child as they relate to his home, to his school, and to his community.

Descriptive data should be made available concerning the types of programs the child is to be involved in through the public schools. These programs should be developed to provide meaningful learning experiences for the child. Community-based programs need to be made available to all handicapped children, based on the interrelated aspects of due process, placement, and classification. The right to learn and the right to treatment should be foremost when the needs of the individual child are being considered. Both the expansion of existing programs and the implementation of new programs should be ongoing educational developments within the public school systems.

Who is responsible for the handicapped child? Everyone. The majority of the reports available today focus on the mentally handicapped, although all areas of exceptionality are assumed to be incorporated in the recent decisions being made in the courts and in the public schools. Cases such as the P.A.R.C. v. the Commonwealth of Pennsylvania case have brought the attention of the public to the problems of the parents in such a situation. As a result of the 1971 ruling of this case, due process hearings are mandatory in Pennsylvania, prior to a change in educational status, for any child between the ages of six and twenty-one years who is mentally retarded. Even those children who are suspected of being mentally retarded are included in this ruling. Therefore, youngsters who previously have been excluded, placed on waiting lists, excused permanently, shifted from regular classes to special classes, and those who have never had an educational assessment come under this mandate.

A further consequence of this case was that it established that the public schools in Pennsylvania must provide appropriate programs for all children, no matter what the handicap. The court ruled that all handicapped children are equally entitled to a proper education, and that lack of funds was not a legitimate defense for the school system. The results of this ruling have been quoted in numerous states where court action has been employed to obtain equal educational opportunities for other handicapped children.

A survey conducted in 1973 by Rodriquez and Lombardi further indicated a need for more unified approaches for placement procedures involving the parents. There were forty-nine states which responded to the survey. Of these, only eight states indicated that parental permission was needed before a child could be legally enrolled in a special education class. Forty-one states indicated that parents may assume the full responsibility for educating their child in an alternative setting such as a private school rather than a special class. An alarming twenty-six states reported that children could be excluded from school by the local boards of education on the recommendation of a school psychologist or other qualified personnel who based their conclusions on the results of individualized intelligence tests.

On the surface, such results might not appear alarming to even the educated individual who is familiar with the public school setting. After all, it does cost extra money to educate the severely handicapped merely by the fact that their number is so small, and thus, a special teacher must be hired to serve only a very small proportion of the total school-aged population within the community. Yet, if the public schools do not provide educational services for these children, the responsibility falls back on the parents. Like other citizens within the community, parents of handicapped school aged children must pay taxes to support their local school systems. If, in turn, the public school system rejects their child, the parents must find a suitable alternative setting for educating their child. In most instances, the only alternative setting available is a private day or residential school. The expense of sending a handicapped child to a private school can be, and often is, overwhelming to the average parent.

As indicated earlier, it has been necessary in the past for the courts to become involved in the placement of handicapped children. Through the legal system, specific decisions have been rendered, the basic rights of the child have been protected and enforced, and private citizens have been able to justify their claims for equal opportunities for handicapped children. But how much remains to be done in this area?

In 1972, an estimated 40 percent of the nation's seven million handicapped individuals were receiving some form of special education. However, those children who were being served were often receiving inappropriate educational services due to the average federal expenditure of only thirty dollars per handicapped child per year. When funds are limited, the special education programs are usually the first to feel the squeeze. Handed down, out-of-date books are frequently used in special classes because there are no funds available for newer instructional materials. Special education teachers often resort to their own creativeness for the development of instructional materials which will meet the individual needs of the exceptional children they have in their classes.

In some instances, especially through the Education of the Handicapped Act, monies are made available to school systems to help them provide appropriate instructional programs and materials. When such monies are available, the problem becomes one of locating the proper instructional materials for the learning needs of the children in the special classes. Children who read on a first grade reading level who are fourteen years old are not exactly ecstatic about most of the books which are available on their reading level. So, even when the monies are available, the special education teacher may still have to resort to developing her own set of instructional materials.

The facilities allocated for the specific use of classes for the handicapped are also somewhat lacking in many instances. Such facilities are often located in former school buildings which have been previously vacated due to safety regulations. Older buildings often present special problems for this group of youngsters because they are not barrier free, i.e. there are many steps to climb, bathroom facilities do not accommodate wheelchairs, etc. Also, these older buildings may present specific hazards for the handicapped child because of the danger of electrical fires from old and worn out fixtures within the classrooms. The rewiring of a large building is very costly, and the special education program may have to forego the use of simple household appliances used for the training of self-help skills because the overall cost of installing such equipment is beyond their allotted budget.

Another discouraging factor is the type of programs available to handicapped youngsters. Specialized classes in the public schools have been developed for all of the major handicapping conditions, although most geographical areas prohibit the implementation of classes for low incidence handicapping conditions such as deaf-blind. The general rule is to have at least one self-contained class for the trainable mentally retarded children and a resource teacher for the educable mentally retarded and/or the learning disabled children.

The latter two categories of children include a unique group of individuals with a variety of educational needs. Children in both categories are usually able to function fairly well in the community setting following "graduation" from the public schools, providing their educational programs have met the needs of both the children and their respective communities. Generally, programs for the older students in special education classes focus on prevocational skills.

One area which has been lacking in many of these classes is that of citizenship training. The students have been taught the fundamentals of a vocation, yet they have often not been taught much in the area of their rights and duties as citizens within the community. Voting procedures, income tax regulations, and community activities are just a few of the more important areas which need to be considered under citizenship training.

Helping the handicapped child learn to become a responsible citizen should be the goal of all public education programs. Rather than merely educating the handicapped, the schools need to become more involved with "communitycating" the handicapped. This type of program should serve a two-way function. On the one hand, the child needs to learn more about his community and the role he is expected to play as a citizen within the realm of that community. Likewise, the community needs to learn more about the handicapped and whether the anticipated roles are in line with the individual child's functional abilities. The handicapped and the community both need to become more aware of each other and of the implications each group's role has on the other in the total society. Until both groups acknowledge awareness and understanding of each other, there will be little gained in the area of public education for the handicapped.

Early detection and intervention are of primary importance to the handicapped child and his community, regardless of the severity of the problem. Head Start programs have begun serving handicapped preschoolers, but unless the local school system is able to provide an appropriate follow-through program, the extra effort may be futile in terms of long-range goals.

A report assessing Project Head Start was issued on May 20, 1975, by the Comptroller General of the United States. The discouraging fact about this report was that although disadvantaged children who had been enrolled in Head Start had shown that they were better prepared for public school education than their peers, a gradual but steady decrease in educational functioning was noticed during the first few years of school. By the end of the third grade, all educational gains made as a result of the Head Start Program were lost, and the children were functioning on the same level as their disadvantaged peers who had not been enrolled in the program.

For children who are handicapped, especially in the mental area, the results are even more discouraging unless intensive follow-through is maintained within the public schools. Children from high-risk families, i.e. the intelligence of one or both of the parents is recorded as being in the retarded range, have the greatest chance of failure after Head Start because there is no learning or educational stimulation carried over into the home environment.

Rick Heber identified women with IQ's of 75 and below for his study in Milwaukee. The children from these mothers were bombarded with a variety of stimuli beginning at birth. Even as infants these children were taken by van to a central location where they received special care. Their mothers were given lessons in the care of their infants, and home visitors helped these mothers during regularly scheduled visits to the homes. The older the child became, the more involved his mother became and the more time they both spent in the learning stimulation activities. The average IQ of these children was measured as being between 115 and 120 by the time they reached school age. Their peers who had been enrolled in the Head Start Program averaged an IQ of 90 by the same age.

By maintaining the stimulation through parent and community involvement, the Milwaukee Project has been able to show continual gains in achievement for the youngsters enrolled in the program. Several interesting side effects have occurred as direct consequences of the Project. In many instances, the mothers of these children also learned basic academic skills which they had failed to learn previously. They learned these skills from the teachers and from their own children. Their self-confidence improved as their learning skills improved and they became more interested in their futures and their children's futures. Some mothers even went back to high school and then on to vocational programs for additional job training.

Another interesting factor that occurred as a direct result of this Project was the measured intelligence and ability levels of the siblings, especially those who were younger than the Project children. While the Project children were learning basic skills, so were these younger siblings. Mothers who learned how to teach their children through the Project carried these skills over into the raising of their younger children.

So, although many of the Head Start Program reports may sound discouraging, there are many indications that preschool programs in general are beneficial for all children, especially for those who are exceptional. Early detection and intervention are only two ways in which the community may help these children.

With older children, the community may help by encouraging the special classes to visit their community resources, both public and private. Later, when these students are ready for work-study programs, the community should act as a resource in the placement of these students in appropriate jobs. If the community is unfamiliar with the handicapped, employers within the community may be reluctant to hire those teenagers or adults who are "different." When this occurs, the only alternative for job training is through the public schools where such facilities are frequently quite limited, especially for the handicapped. Thus, a continuing cycle begins. The handicapped are unable to find suitable jobs due to their lack of on-the-job training. Yet, unless someone in the community hires them for such training during a combined work-study program through the public schools, they may never gain the experience needed for these jobs. Thus, they become unemployed and must depend on the community and/or the federal government to support them. Unless they are given an opportunity to work, they will never have a chance to prove that under the proper circumstances, they too can be self-sufficient.

Public Policies and Special Education

In view of the conditions stated above, the dilemma facing parents, schools, and communities is staggering. However, the solution to these special education problems is not only additional funds, but a concerted effort on the part of parents, special education personnel, administrators, state governments, and the federal government.

One group in particular, the President's Committee on Mental Retardation, serves as a quasi-governmental group to assist in the channeling of federal endeavors. They have recently recommended that the federal government improve and restructure the current testing, placement, and evaluation processes for identifying children as mentally retarded unless a comprehensive assessment of mental ability, physical health, and adaptive behavior demonstrates a handicap severe enough to justify the label. More realistically, the Committee advocates educational justice and freedom for all children through recognition of each child as a unique individual. The Committee recommends helping teachers, administrators, school counselors and staff, curriculum developers, and teacher educators to become aware of the unjust discrimination often held against children from social, cultural, ethnic, and economic backgrounds that differ from the so-called norm. The Committee also advocates and recommends equal treatment of the retarded or exceptional child. Yet even now, as in the past, it has been necessary for federal laws to be invoked before such treatment has become a reality.

Although many of the current federal laws have been enacted as a result of social pressure from representatives of cultural minorities, several laws have been instituted as a direct result of the handicapping condition itself. Ironically, the first bill related to the handicapped which actually became a law was not directly related to the education and training of the handicapped. Rather, Public Law 19-8 provided for a land grant for the development of the Deaf and Dumb Asylum of Kentucky. Although the bill was enacted on January 29, 1827, it was another twenty years before another bill appeared concerning the handicapped. This second bill, Public Law 29-11, dated February 18, 1847, extended the original time which had been granted for the selling of the land granted to the Kentucky Asylum in 1827.

It was 1855 before the first substantive law for the handicapped was enacted. This act, Public Law 33-4, decreed that an insane asylum should be established within the District of Columbia. Although the facility was to have been a hospital for all "insane" individuals, it primarily served individuals who were associated with either the Army or the Navy. Free services were offered to the lower class individuals within the District, including those in prison or those who had committed crimes and were then found to be insane. Treatment was given to the individuals, but no provisions were made for any educational services.

The first federal law to deal directly with educating the handicapped was enacted on February 16, 1957. This act, Public Law 34-5, provided for the education of the "deaf and dumb" as well as the blind through the establishment of Columbia Institute. At the same time, funds were designated to help meet the tuition costs of the students. Another important section of this act required that a survey be made in the surrounding areas of Washington, Georgetown, and Washington County to identify eligible students for this special training institution. Students from other states were also permitted entrance into the school, but the survey did not extend to other states.

It was 1864 before Columbia Institute was granted permission to confer degrees upon its graduates through Public Law 38-52. Nearly one hundred years later, in 1954, the name was changed to Galludet College, an institution of higher learning for deaf students.

In 1879, an Act to Promote the Education of the Blind was passed into law. Through this act, the American Printing House for the Blind was established in Lexington, Kentucky. The Printing House supplies educational materials and special equipment to blind and multi-handicapped children and adults as a nonprofit institution.

Nearly four decades passed before another significant bill

pertaining to the education of the handicapped was passed into law, although several bills were enacted in the meantime which either modified or amended previous educational bills. The Vocational Rehabilitation Act, enacted on June 27, 1918, was designed to help in the rehabilitation of discharged military personnel. Both World War I and World War II proved to be instrumental in the establishment of special laws for handicapped adults who were disabled as a result of combat duty.

Between 1924 and 1946, the majority of the federal laws for the handicapped centered around the blind adult. This trend toward laws for the blind has continued up to the present, but the needs for other handicapping conditions have also been made public through similar laws. Throughout the 1950's and 1960's there were several laws passed which were related to the financial aspect of the handicapped individual through the Social Security and Public Welfare Amendments.

It was not until the mid 1950's that the federal government became involved in public education in general through the passage of the Cooperative Research Act in 1954. This act was designed to merge research activities between the federal government and institutions of higher learning. Unfortunately, there were no funds provided for the implementation of this act until 1957 when Congress appropriated one million dollars to be used for research in education. Over half of this money was delegated toward research in the area of mental retardation.

The following year, 1958, saw the passage of the National Defense Education Act, an act which was designed to encourage programs for scientists and mathematicians involved in activities deemed to be in the area of national defense. For the first time, gifted and talented students were served by a federal bill, although only indirectly and only in the areas of science and math.

Two other landmark events took place as a result of the passage of federal laws in 1958. First, provisions were made for the development and circulation of captioned films for the deaf. Second, provisions were made for the development of training programs for teachers of the mentally retarded. Both institutions of higher education and state educational agencies were eligible for funds to train professionals to work with the mentally retarded through authorized programs. It was not until 1961 that funds were appropriated for the training of teachers to work with deaf and speech-impaired individuals.

President Kennedy signed Public Law 88-164 in 1963. This law provided for the training of professionals in areas which had not previously been served. Up until this time, only the mentally retarded and the deaf were covered by federal laws. Now, all handicapping conditions were to be covered, and the Division of Handicapped Children and Youth was established as the administrative unit to handle such affairs. Sam Kirk became President of the Division shortly after its inception.

The overall reorganization of the United States Office of Education in 1965 caused the dissolution of the Division of Handicapped Children and Youth, less than two years after it had been established. After the Division was disbanded, the various activities enacted through federal laws were handled under separate administrative units. During this period, the area of handicapped children plateaued in federal support, partly caused by this new administrative regulation (Martin, 1968).

The National Technical Institute for the Deaf Act of 1965 authorized the construction and operation of a residential facility for post-secondary technical training and education for deaf individuals. The National Technical Institute for the Deaf is located at Rochester Institute of Technology in Rochester, New York, and it provides specialized technical training for qualified deaf students (Bolick, 1974).

The passage of the Elementary and Secondary Act of 1965 committed the federal government to financial support for the development of improved programs for children with special education needs. Through Public Law 89-313, financial assistance was made available to state operated and supported schools for the handicapped. This law later provided further assistance to handicapped children through Title VI, Education of Handicapped Children.

As a result of Title VI, Congress established the Bureau for the Education of the Handicapped (BEH) in 1966 as a separate agency to handle all programs for the handicapped. Although the forerunner of the Bureau, the Division for Handicapped Children and Youth, had met with undisputed success under the capable direction of Kirk, there was a great deal of controversy concerning the creation of this new agency for the handicapped. The Bureau was created within the Office of Education despite concerns and arguments from the administration at the time.

Provisions for the development of model preschool and early childhood education centers for the handicapped were made through the passage of the Handicapped Children's Early Education Assistance Act of 1968. These centers were established to provide local and state education agencies with examples of programs which could be developed within the local communities to serve younger handicapped children.

The National Advisory Committee on Handicapped Children presented its first annual report on January 31, 1968, to the Subcommittee on Education of the Committee on Labor and Public Welfare of the United States Senate. In this report, the Committee selected specific learning disabilities as a priority need which deserved special consideration in the area of educational development and programming. In 1969, the Elementary and Secondary Education Act was amended through the Gifted and Talented Education Assistance Act, which also provided for technical assistance and financial aid to teachers in the area of specific learning disabilities. Further assistance was provided for all handicapped children through the development of a national media center for the handicapped in 1969. Media, materials, and technical assistance were made available, free of charge, to teachers who were working with handicapped students.

During the early 1970's numerous laws were passed to provide even further assistance to handicapped children and their teachers. The Developmental Disabilities Services and Facilities Construction Amendments of 1970 amended the Mental Retardation Facilities and Community Mental Health Centers Construction Act of 1963. The act provides for other services (diagnosis, evaluation, treatment, day care, etc.) and facilities for the mentally retarded and developmentally disabled (originating in childhood) through individual state plans.

Interestingly enough, severely handicapped individuals were still being excluded from many of the acts being passed by Congress. In 1972, Congress incorporated significant changes into the original Vocational Rehabilitation Act of 1940. Specifically, the new act was addressed to those individuals who had the most severe handicapping conditions. Although the revised act was passed unanimously in both houses of Congress, the President vetoed the passage of the act. A second version of this act was also passed unanimously by the Congress but vetoed by the President in 1973. Fortunately, the veto was sustained by the Senate and the law went into effect. The significant factor included in this act was the role which was being delegated to the individual in the determination of his rehabilitation program. It also provided for the inclusion of handicapped individuals who had previously been excluded from such programs due to their individual handicapping conditions. Exclusion from federally supported rehabilitation programs due to handicapping conditions became unlawful.

One of the most significant federal actions taken pertaining to the education of the handicapped came about in 1974 through the amendments made to the 1969 Elementary and Secondary Education Act. As amended by the Education Amendments of 1974, Title VI has seven parts, all of which are directly related to the education of handicapped youngsters. Because of the significance of each of these parts, a further description of Title VI is warranted here.

Part A, *General Provisions,* defines handicapped children as those who are mentally, physically, or emotionally handicapped and who thus require special education and related services. Children with specific learning disabilities are also defined, in accordance with the definition currently promoted by the Association for Children with Learning Disabilities.

Part B, *Assistance to States for Education of Handicapped Children,* provides grants to aid states in the initiation, expansion, and improvement of programs from the preschool level through the secondary school level. Under Part B, two new state plan requirements became effective for the 1975 fiscal year. The first requirement was the establishment of full educational opportunities to all handicapped children, with emphasis on services to children who had previously been excluded from the public school setting. The second requirement included a plan which would insure handicapped children and their parents of receiving (a) due process in any decisions concerning special class placement, (b) maximum services in the "least restrictive educational environment" when such services could not be provided through regular classroom placement, and (c) nondiscriminatory testing and evaluation procedures.

Additional new state plan requirements became effective for the 1976 fiscal year. These four requirements set forth policies and procedures to assure (a) child identification or child find activities to identify and include children who were currently unserved, (b) confidentiality of the data obtained during the child find activities, (c) the establishment of full services to provide appropriate educational opportunities to all handicapped children which include a detailed time table and description of facilities, personnel, and services necessary to meet these goals, and (d) a public notice of the plan amendment to be made available to parents and to the general public at least thirty days prior to its submission to the United States Office of Education.

Part C, *Centers and Services to Meet Special Needs of the Handicapped*, provides grants for establishing regional resource centers for the handicapped through authorization by the Commissioner of Education. These centers provide help in the development of programs to meet special needs of handicapped children along with consultative services for both parents and educators of handicapped children.

Part D, *Training Personnel for the Education of the Handicapped*, provides grants to institutions of higher education and other appropriate nonprofit institutions to aid in (a) providing training of professional personnel responsible for conducting the training of teachers and other professionals in related educational fields, (b) providing training for professional personnel currently employed as teachers, supervisors, or researchers in the area of handicapped or related educational fields, and (c) establishing and maintaining scholarships with stipends and allowances for further training of personnel in the categories listed in (a) and (b).

Part E, *Research in the Education of the Handicapped,* provides for grants for both research and demonstration purposes. State or local education agencies, higher education institutions, and other public or nonprofit education or research agencies or institutions are eligible for such grants.

Part F, *Instructional Media for the Handicapped,* provides such materials as captioned films for the deaf. Research, production, and distribution of educational media are included under Part F.

Part G, *Special Programs for Children with Specific Learning Disabilities,* authorizes programs which support research training and model centers to meet the needs of children with specific learning disabilities as defined in Part A, Section 602. Innovative and creative approaches to meeting the educational needs of these children are given special consideration when grant proposals are reviewed for possible funding approval.

The most recent act for the handicapped, The Education for All Handicapped Children Act of 1975, amends the Education of the Handicapped Act (originally entitled The Elementary and Secondary Amendments of 1969) and was signed by President Ford on November 29, 1975. This act proposes to assure that *all* handicapped children have available to them a free and appropriate public education designed to meet their specific educational needs. Through this act, the federal government has made a commitment to pay a gradually increasing percentage of the total cost of educating handicapped children. The new formula recognizes that the cost of educating a handicapped child is higher than the cost of educating a normal child. Therefore, the amount financed will be based on the national per pupil expenditure averages multiplied by the number of handicapped children ages five through seventeen who are being served in each state.

During the 1978 fiscal year, 5 percent of this total for the state will be paid for by the federal government. This percentage will gradually escalate until 40 percent of the total cost will be financed through the government by the 1982 fiscal year. Since the formula developed for this act carries with it an inflation factor, the actual money figure will fluctuate from year to year with the required adjustments in the national expenditure average per pupil. These funds may be used for handicapped children ages three through twenty-one years. However, no more than 12 percent of the children between the ages of five and seventeen can be counted as handicapped due to the nature of the formula. No more than 2 percent of this total 12 percent can be considered learning disabled for funding purposes.

In order to obtain federal monies for handicapped children after October 1, 1977, the local school district must be able to generate an allocation of $7500 for itself. Several districts may go together, however, in order to obtain the required amount. The state education agency will act as the clearinghouse for all data obtained from the local districts to determine whether they have followed the prescribed guidelines in order to be eligible to receive these special monies.

The act also requires the development of individualized instructional programs for each handicapped child who is to be served through monies obtained from the federal government. This plan is to be written with the consent, and thus the involvement, of the handicapped child's parents or legal guardians. The program is to be evaluated annually and revised as necessary for the betterment of the educational development of the individual handicapped child. In effect October 1, 1977, will be an individualized instructional plan, developed and put into writing for each handicapped child served through this act.

Another provision of this act is the supervision of other agencies by the state education agency. This is to establish one central agency as the one accountable for the education of each handicapped child. By placing such authority with the state education agency, the act is intended to secure coordination among related agencies as well as cooperation among the various state education agencies. Further, the public awareness that is anticipated through the act is expected to decrease the amount of bureaucratic "buck passing" that is currently being experienced by parents and teachers of handicapped children who are in need of a variety of educationally related services.

Fortunately, the act is expected to be an ongoing and continuing service to the handicapped since no expiration date has been attached to it. The impact of such legislation is anticipated to have long-range effects on the education system in general. If all handicapped children are authorized to receive a free and appropriate public education, then all "normal" children should retain equal rights regarding their educational provisions. To attain such goals in reality, the teacher training institutions and their colleagues in higher education institutions are going to be forced into taking a closer look at their programs. Teachers will have to be trained in all areas of exceptionality, with emphasis on areas revolving around normal child development and general learning theory.

Public School Policies and Special Education

The disturbing factor throughout the history of special education has been that in order to obtain money for the education of children who are "different," a state or federal law has had to be enacted. Such laws, although beneficial in the initial phases of such education, are often damaging in terms of long-range goals for the handicapped. Before special monies are allotted, a specific label must be placed on a child. These labels do not refer to individual learning or educational needs, but rather to grouped handicapping conditions. Categorical monies for these handicapping conditions are usually based on the prevalence of such conditions among school-aged children. If a child does not fit into a specifically delineated category, there may be no additional money to help meet his educational needs.

By placing children into categories, a stigma is prematurely formed concerning the child and his family. Even in modern times there is much confusion over mental deficiency and mental illness. Appropriate definitions for both areas are still lacking because they do not differentiate between two individuals who may have been labeled in the same category according to general symptoms or suspected causal factors.

Within general or even specific categories there are even further problems. Because human beings are human beings, there are a wide variety of individual differences, even among so-called homogenous groups. Due to human nature itself, there cannot be such a thing as a true homogenous grouping. All seven-year-old children may not be ready to read or write or even attend the public school. But the law states that unless there are extenuating circumstances, the seven-year-old in our society should already have been in school for a minimum of at least one year.

In regard to the various categories currently used in the field of special education, the question is often asked, "What *is* so special about these children?" Dunn (1968) asked whether special education classes for the mildly retarded were justifiable. He questioned the legality of labeling children on the basis of their academic functioning levels. In doing so, he questioned the generally accepted theory that IQ tests differentiate children who should be placed in educational settings other than the regular classroom. He even suggested that self-contained classrooms for the mildly retarded would soon become obsolete. Although his views have been widely quoted in articles and books which discuss the problems of labeling, his theories and suggestions have rarely been put into practice because of the structure of the educational system and the allotment of funds available for the intense training and evaluation procedures which he envisioned.

The problem, then, is not simply deciding which labels should be used or whether they should be used. Instead, the question appears to be one of which educational needs are going to be met and whether these needs are going to be met for all children, regardless of whether or not a label has been attached to their individual learning abilities or disabilities.

Just how are these learning abilities or learning disabilities of specific children determined? Usually, the child is given a series or battery of psychological tests which claim to test specific learning skills. The administration of merely one test is usually considered inadequate for determining specific abilities within the individual child. Also, the importance of teacher evaluation and observation has often been overlooked in the past by the psychologists. The teacher is with the child a minimum of four hours a day, five days a week, throughout the school year. The psychologist may spend a few hours observing the child in the classroom situation prior to administering the tests, but normally there is not enough time to allow the psychologist to fully get to know the child as an individual, and therefore, as a unique human being. He must base his opinions on somewhat limited contact with the child, and such contact is often confined to the testing situation alone.

In a few short hours, usually spread out over a two or three day period, the psychologist is expected to complete a psychological evaluation which will determine the child's strengths and weaknesses in accordance with his overall intellectual abilities. The outcome of this brief encounter with the psychologist may determine the life outcome of the child.

The comprehensive evaluation is written up by the examiner, given to the school, and placed in the child's folder. Open communication and coordination are vitally important to the child's future once his report has been typed up and placed in this file. The interpretation of that report is of primary interest and concern to the child, his parents, and his teachers because it determines the educational placement of the child, the role his parents will be expected to play with respect to this placement, and the educational procedures which will be implemented by his teachers.

The results of this interpretation are also of consequence to everyone else involved with the education of this child. Recommendations are often made by the psychologist, yet they may not be totally educational in nature since there are few psychologists who have educational backgrounds directly related to the teaching of handicapped children. Thus, suggestions may be made concerning the basic educational needs of the child without any mention being made of specific teaching methodologies which should be employed. Such recommendations often leave the child's teachers with the impression that they have learned very little applicable knowledge from the psychological evaluation. Since access to the actual tests administered is rarely available to the classroom teacher, she has only the test scores to tell her where the child was weak or strong on a particular test. Although subtest scores of certain tests at least somewhat describe the areas being tested, unless the actual test forms and test results are available to the teacher for study, the scores are relatively meaningless to her.

By looking at the actual test given to a child, the teacher may see exactly where the child made his mistakes. For example, one child may be able to complete a variety of tasks on a specific test, but he may receive the same overall score as a child who is unable to complete tasks except in one specific area. On the subtests of such a test, the teacher will be able to identify both the general strengths and weaknesses of the two children. By taking a close look at the specific items missed within each subtest, the teacher will be able to determine the specific strengths and weaknesses of each child. She will be able to see whether the child misread the arithmetic signs or whether he simply could not do the arithmetic problems given to him on that particular test.

If the teacher is able to schedule a conference with the psychologist following the educational evaluation, she may be able to gain further insight into the psychologist's interpretation of the specific test results. She should feel free to ask any questions concerning the types of tests utilized, specific tasks required of these types of tests, and the results obtained on any or all of the tests which have been administered.

REFERENCES

1. Abeson, Alan: Movement and momentum: government and the education of handicapped children. *Except Child, 39*:64, 1972.
2. Abeson, Allan, and Bolick, Nancy (Eds.): *A Continuing Summary of Pending and Completed Litigation Regarding the Education of Handicapped Children.* Reston, Coun Exc Child, 1974.
3. Associated Press: Court to rule on child rights. Asheville, *Citizen-Times,* March 23, 1976.
4. Ballard, Joseph: Active federal education laws for exceptional persons. In

Weintraub et al, (Eds.): *Public Policy and the Education of Exceptional Children.* Reston, Coun Exc Child, 1976, pp. 133-145.

5. Bolick, Nancy (Ed.): *Digest of State and Federal Laws: Education of Handicapped Children.* Reston, Coun Exc Child, 1974.

6. The Council for Exceptional Children: *A Model Law for the Education of Seven Million Handicapped Children.* Reston, Coun Exc Child, 1972.

7. DuBois, Philip H.: *A History of Psychological Testing.* Boston, Allyn, 1970.

8. Edwards, Newton: *The Courts and the Public Schools.* Chicago, U of Chicago Pr, 1933.

9. Franks, David J.: Ethnic and social status characteristics of children in emr and ld classes. *Except Child, 37:*537, 1971.

10. Gillespie, Patricia H., Miller, Ted L., and Fielder, Virginia Dodge: Legislative definitions of learning disabilities: roadblocks to effective service. *J Learn Disabil, 8:*660-666, 1975.

11. Gozali, Joav, and Gonwa, James: Citizenship training for the emr: a case of educational neglect. *Ment Retard, 11:*49-50, 1973.

12. Hollingworth, Leta S.: *The Psychology of Subnormal Children.* New York, Macmillan, 1923.

13. Keogh, Barbara (Ed.): *Early Identification of Children with Learning Disabilities.* Philadelphia, Buttonwood Farms, 1970.

14. Kidd, John W.: Issue at point: mr — the emerging dilemma. *Ment Retard, 9:*58-59, 1971.

15. Kirk, Samuel A., and Lord, Francis E.: *Exceptional Children: Educational Resources and Perspectives.* Boston, HM, 1974.

16. LaVor, Martin L.: Federal legislation for exceptional persons: a history. In Weintraub et al, (Eds.): *Public Policy and the Education of Exceptional Children.* Reston, Coun Exc Child, 1976, pp. 96-111.

17. Marinelli, Joseph J.: Financing the education of exceptional children. In Weintraub et al, (Eds.): *Public Policy and the Education of Exceptional Children.* Reston, Coun Exc Child, 1975, pp. 151-194.

18. Martin, Edwin W., Jr.: Breakthrough for the handicapped: legislative history. *Except Child, 34:*493-503, 1968.

19. MacMillan, Donald L.: Issues and trends in special education. *Ment Retard, 11:*3-8, 1973.

20. Minskoff, J. Gerald: Understanding learning disabilities. In Calkins, E. O. (Ed.): *Reading Forum.* Washington, HEW, 1971.

21. President's Committee on Mental Retardation: *Islands of Excellence, MR '72.* Washington, PCMR, 1973.

22. Rodriquez, Joseph, and Lombardi, Thomas P.: Legal implications of parental prerogatives for special class placement of the mr. *Ment Retard, 11:*29-31, 1973.

23. Ross, Sterling L., DeYoung, Henry G., and Cohen, Julius S.: Confrontation: special education placement and the law. *Except Child,*

38:5-12, 1971.
24. Sheldon, Jan, and Sherman, James A.: The right to education for the retarded. *J Educ, 156*:25-48, 1974.
25. Spicker, Howard: Address given at Georgia State University. Atlanta, February 25, 1972.
26. Taylor, George R.: Special education at the crossroad: class placement for the emr. *Ment Retard, 11*:30-33, 1973.
27. Trotter, Sharland: Labeling: it hurts more than it helps. *J Learn Disabil, 8*:191-193, 1975.
28. Vaughan, Richard W.: Community, courts, and conditions of special education today: why? *Ment Retard, 11*:3-8, 1973.
29. Weingold, Joseph T.: Issues at point: rights of the retarded. *Ment Retard, 11*:50-52, 1973.
30. Weintraub, Frederick J., and Abeson, Alan: New education policies for the handicapped: the quiet revolution. *Phi Delta Kappan, 55*:526-529, 1974.
31. Willis, Ken: Hearing is required to commit children. Atlanta, *Constitution*, February 27, 1976, p. 1-A.
32. Zelder, Empress Young: Public opinion and public education for the exceptional child — court decisions 1873-1950. *Except Child, 19*:187-198, 1953.

Chapter 3

RECENT ATTITUDES CONCERNING LABELS ... DIFFERENT LIDS FOR DIFFERENT KIDS?

INITIALLY, the specific labels for each area of deficiency were somewhat useful. When professionals gathered together, they were "tuned in" to each other's dialog because they were familiar with the terminology being used during the conversation. Familiarity with this terminology also helped form a common bond among the other disciplines and education, *when* they agreed upon the terminology and the resulting definitions.

Later, when special funding was needed for the handicapped, labels were used not only to describe the conditions which were preventing the child from receiving a public education, but they were also used to gain sympathy from the lawmakers. By labeling a child with negative-sounding labels, the promoters of special education funding were able to conjure up in the lawmaker's minds a sympathetic picture of a child who could not function without total supervision from an experienced and trained adult. This served the purpose of obtaining special funding, but in the process, millions of children were caught up in the negative results of this type of labeling.

In order to procure this funding from the federal government, school units had to provide proof that there were enough handicapped students within their districts to make the allocation of extra monies necessary. Small school units found that they were unable to secure special funding for their small groups of handicapped children. To add to the confusion, the available tests were not always administered by fully trained psychologists or psychometrists. Again, the smaller units were hurt because they could not always afford to pay the salaries for such trained personnel.

Labels Versus Learning Styles

The major controversy within the labeling syndrome has been the use of labels to describe the less visible deficiencies such as mild mental retardation and learning disabilities. With these two types of exceptionalities both the cause and the effect are intermingled with specific labels. Along with mild mental retardation, the label of culturally deprived is often assumed, especially if the child comes from an ethnic group which would be considered a minority group, both racially and culturally. Some people prefer to use the terminology of culturally different rather than culturally deprived. No matter which label is used, the stigma of being different is still there. The visibility of being in a racial minority group becomes a part of the handicapping condition.

In the field of learning disabilities, the controversy over terminology has gone from the ridiculous to the absurd. A medically oriented person will describe a child as having dysgraphia and dyslexia, both of which are actually forms of aphasia. An educationally oriented person will describe this same child as having difficulty with writing (dysgraphia) and reading (dyslexia). The medical field will classify all writing and reading difficulties using the terms just mentioned. The field of education will delineate the type of writing or reading problems in more specific terms which are often related to the child's academic functioning abilities which are in turn related to these specific problems.

A child who is having difficulty in forming the letters of the alphabet might be described by the educator as also having difficulty with his grasp in similar types of fine motor activities such as cutting and coloring. Or, if he has a tendency to reverse certain letters, he may be described as having a problem related to directionality where he confuses right and left, and therefore he confuses similar letters such as "b" and "d." Such difficulties are anticipated in a young child or even in an immature or slow child.

When such problems persist beyond the second grade, there

is reason for concern because these problems may carry over into other types of learning activities. By the time the child is in the third or fourth grade he is expected to do many of his assignments by first reading the directions to himself. If he is unable to read, he will be unable to complete the assignment. The fewer the number of assignments he is able to complete, the further behind he becomes in his academic subjects. What starts out as a minor reading problem develops into a major academic problem unless special considerations are made for the child.

If he learns best through listening, then perhaps he will succeed in the classroom if his lessons are on tape rather than in written form. The taping of lessons takes considerable time on the teacher's part, so in many instances a parent or even a student volunteer is used to help tape specific lessons. Teachers have often found that several children in the same classroom can benefit from this type of instructional procedure, whether or not these children have been specifically labeled as auditory learners.

The labeling is not so important here as the individualized approach used to meet the learning needs of the child. Elaborate diagnostic tests are not always necessary for determining *how* a child learns best. Observation of a child in the classroom will often give the teacher clues as to his particular learning style.

Learning styles, like teaching styles, vary. Learning style may be defined as the process by which the learner goes about learning a specific skill. It is the process which is important, not the final outcome or goal which is achieved. This process should be made up of logically sequenced behaviors which gradually lead to the desired response.

Each person has several learning styles which depend upon the skill to be learned. There may be an overlapping of learning styles which helps the individual learner obtain the desired goal. Two children with the same learning abilities and disabilities may not use the same learning styles for a similar task. In the same manner, two comparable adults who are trying to learn the metric system may use totally different methods. One adult may be able to remember all of the conversion tables by merely studying and memorizing them, while the other adult may have to repeat the tables aloud many times, or even practice writing them before he feels comfortable using the metric system.

In order to discover a child's learning style, the teacher should observe him in a variety of learning situations. Does the child use similar strategies for learning different skills? Does he transfer what he has learned in one situation and apply it to a new, yet similar learning situation? How does he go about accomplishing the tasks involved in learning a new skill? When he is faced with a task for which he has incomplete skills, how does he compensate for this?

Basically, there are four aspects of learning to consider when looking for the learning style of a child. The most basic of these aspects is the child's physical condition or his general health. If he is not feeling well, is tired, or is taking medication, he may be affected by this to the point that his efficiency in learning is somewhat lowered.

Next, the teacher should be aware of the psychological or emotional aspects which might affect the learner. If the child has met with continued failure in the past, he may expect to meet with it throughout the future. What sort of self-expectations does the child have? If he expects to fail, he most likely will fail. Further, if he does fail, how does he react to the situation? Is he able to control his emotions with a reasonable amount of maturity? Unless a child understands his emotions, he will have difficulty in learning to cope with them appropriately.

The next aspect to look for is the child's behavior when he is attempting to complete a task. This is commonly referred to as "on task behavior." To obtain specific information concerning each child, the teacher should work individually with the child. During the learning task she should ask herself specific questions concerning the processes the child is utilizing. Upon completion of the task, she should ask herself some basic questions related to what reinforced the child during the activity.

Does the child initiate work activities, or does he look for excuses for not completing the task? What sort of attending behavior does the child exhibit during such learning tasks? Is he concentrating on the task at hand or is he busy doing other unrelated activities? Does he plan and organize the various steps leading to the completion of the task? How long does he attend to the task, and how long does it take him to complete the task? When the task has been completed, is he able to do a self-evaluation of his work? What reinforcers were utilized successfully with this particular child? How often did he have to be reinforced, and what were the most successful reinforcers?

The final aspect of learning which the teacher needs to be aware of is the dynamics of problem-solving behavior. Almost all behavior involves some type of problem-solving behavior, whether it is general or academic behavior. Decision making is a general fact of life for administrators, yet few people realize the importance of this aspect of learning when they are working with children. When a child has a learning problem he must first recognize that a problem does exist. This sounds much easier than it is in real life situations. No one likes to admit that there is a problem, yet awareness of such problems is the beginning of the solution.

Once the child becomes aware of his problem, he must decide whether or not to engage in activities which will lead to an appropriate solution. Just *trying* to do better on the next spelling test may not be the solution. Therefore, the problem itself must be carefully analyzed. This analysis should reveal alternative approaches to solving the problem. In the case of the spelling test, perhaps the child needs to practice listening to, then spelling the words aloud while writing them. If this seems like a feasible solution, then it should be tried. Based on the final results, the next spelling test, the child has either resolved his problem or he needs to find another alternative. In academic problem solving, the teacher is an important component of the overall activity. By teaching the child about basic concepts, the teacher can help the child learn to analyze his basic problems. Children take things very literally, so perhaps the definitions of the concepts need to be altered. The concept may be defined for the child by placing it in his perspective and relating it to objects and events with which he is familiar. Working on this premise, the teacher should be able to give general rules for the concept, identify common factors of the concepts, and compare a specific concept to other concepts which the child already knows.

There are two other important factors which should be mentioned here concerning the learning style of a child. These factors relate also to how a child learns best and what are some of the underlying contributing factors involved in this learning process. First of all, it is imperative that when a child learns something, he should learn it correctly the first time. Some children can identify their spelling words when they see them listed with other words, yet they are unable to initiate the writing of these words through only auditory cues. Such children may have memory problems, which is the second factor related to learning styles.

The teacher should investigate the process by which a child remembers. How many times has it been said that a child remembers only what he wants to remember? There is some truth in this statement. If the material to be learned is useful and meaningful *to the child*, there is a good possibility that he will remember it. What a child remembers and why he remembers it are very important in the learning style he utilizes.

Learning styles can be improved. They can also be taught. Inefficient learners need help in learning to organize and retrieve specific information. If a learning style itself is inefficient, that style can be altered if the teacher knows what to look for in learning styles. She does not necessarily have to attach a label to the child or to his learning style. She can take the child where he is functioning now and work toward a more efficient style of learning according to his individual needs. Different children learn differently. Different teachers teach differently. By modifying both the learning styles of the children and the teaching styles of the teachers, the educational needs of all children will be better met by the public schools.

Labels and Learning Disabilities

A recent survey covering terminology, definitions, and identification procedures used by all fifty states revealed that all of the states included some category or terminology which constitutes a learning disability label (Gillespie, Miller, and Fielder, 1975). The majority of the states relied heavily on the definition developed by the National Advisory Committee on Handicapped Children which had been incorporated into the Specific Learning Disabilities Act of 1969. This definition emphasizes that the child must display specific behaviors related to the basic psychological processes which are involved in the understanding or use of language, either written or spoken. Learning problems which are caused by mental retardation, visual, hearing, or motor handicaps, emotional disturbance, or environmental deprivation are not included in this definition. A child must not come under these labels if he is to be included under the learning disabilities label.

Of the fifty states, only sixteen utilize interdisciplinary teams of professionals to aid in the diagnosis and placement of children who come under the label of learning disabilities. These teams usually include members of the medical, psychoeducational, and educational fields. As a team, these professionals work together, sharing their skills to better facilitate both the diagnosis and the placement of exceptional children who are suspected of being learning disabled.

The thirty-four states which do not employ interdisciplinary teams utilize a variety of diagnostic and placement procedures. Several states require that along with psychoeducational testing, the child must also have a complete physical examination. Other states place the major responsibility upon resource or other special education teachers who are involved in the educational evaluation of exceptional children within the school system. A few states place the responsibility upon the shoulders of a committee selected by the school board.

Due to the variety of definitions and identification processes utilized by the fifty states, a child may qualify for services in one state while being denied similar services in another state. Only *two* states will provide monies for services provided to children who do not qualify under the state definition of learning disabilities. In forty-eight states, a child must fit the specific definition of learning disabilities in order to receive state allotted monies for such services. Thus, a child who does not fit into the category outlined by his state may not receive any services since these special services cost money.

Nicholas Hobbs (1975), along with committee members operating under the auspices of the U. S. Office of Education, have recently investigated the problems encountered through current definition and classification processes. The general conclusion has been that the negative consequences which have resulted from current labeling practices have far outweighed the intended positive benefits. As a result of their studies, the committee has suggested that both educational and psychological testing be abolished except for research purposes. It is felt that unless specific, individualized programs are developed and implemented as a direct result of such evaluations, these tests are basically infringing upon the rights of individual children.

Hobbs and his colleagues have suggested that the emphasis be changed in psychoeducational evaluations and the programs which result from these evaluations. They feel that the major focus should be toward what they term "ecological strategy." By this they mean that all possible resources should be utilized toward aiding in the socialization process of exceptional children. Particular emphasis should be placed on the family unit as a social structure which can help the exceptional child live as normal a life as possible under the prevailing circumstances.

The Hobbs report suggests several realistic practices which can help parents effectively work with and understand their exceptional child. The report recommends that parents should be involved in the educational process from the very beginning. Along with this, any reports to the parents should use language which they can easily understand. Such reports should emphasize the child's abilities as well as his disabilities so that the parents will understand that their child is being viewed from all aspects of his functioning abilities. With due respect, the parents should be prepared for any possible inadequacy of available services which they may encounter while trying to obtain appropriate services for their child. Many times the services they may need may not be available within their local region because of the low incidence of the type of handicapping condition their child has or the lack of funds. The parents should become involved in the decision-making processes. By becoming decision-making partners with the educational team, the parents will be able to declare their rights and the rights of their child.

When home management programs are recommended to the parents, the goals should be specific as well as realistic. Usable, down-to-earth suggestions to the parents on how to cope with everyday experiences of their child at home are more beneficial and realistic than extensively diagrammed programs which could not possibly be carried out successfully in the typical home situation.

Awareness of, and Attitudes Toward, the Mentally Retarded

In 1970, Henry Gottwald conducted a study concerning public awareness of mental retardation. Through the Survey Research Service, a Division of the National Opinion Research Center at the University of Chicago, a sample of 1,515 subjects was selected from a national sample to participate in this study. Information was collected through personal interviews conducted with these subjects. The information was then placed on cards and prepared for analysis.

Initially, the participants were asked what the phrase *mentally retarded* meant to them. Nearly half of the participants (45 percent) gave answers which described the phrase in terms of mental deficiency, and many of these answers also included supplementary information related to causal factors. The second largest category of responses was classified under "miscellaneous" by Gottwald, and these constituted slightly more than 19 percent of all descriptions given by the participants. A little over 18 percent of the responses defined the phrase as meaning slow learners or people who were unable to learn. Multiple answers were given by several of the participants, resulting in a total of 1,601 responses for the 1,515 participants.

Despite this, only 421 participants attempted to define or differentiate the phrase in terms of degrees or functioning abilities which might be associated with mental retardation.

Another question which was asked of the participants was if they had heard or read anything pertaining to mental retardation within the past several months. Over half of the participants (69 percent) had been exposed to such an experience, with television being the primary means of communication experienced. Fifty percent of those participants who had been exposed to information concerning mental retardation during recent months had received their information through the media of television.

At this point, those participants who had not heard or read anything concerning mental retardation within recent months were asked if they had ever heard of mental retardation at all. A surprising eighty-four persons declared that they had never heard of mental retardation. These participants were subsequently dropped from the study and were not allowed to continue with the questionnaire.

Other questions which were asked of the participants related to factual knowledge concerning mental retardation, attitudes toward the mentally retarded, and personal experiences with mentally retarded individuals. Variables such as age, occupation, and religion were analyzed in accordance with the overall findings from the survey.

Younger participants appeared to have more positive flexible attitudes toward the mentally retarded. Although participants in professional and skilled positions were more positively oriented toward allowing the mentally retarded to function within the working world of the community, those in professional and managerial positions questioned the role of the retarded in citizenship-related activities such as voting and marriage. There did not appear to be an overall trend in attitudes which was directly related to the participants' occupations.

Religion appeared to play a significant role for the participant's response on questions related to the ability and grouping of the mentally retarded. In general, the Jewish respondents were more liberal in their statements about these areas of concern.

It should be remembered that all of the above statements have been taken out of context, and thus generalizations concerning this survey should not be made based on this limited amount of information. Gottwald himself did not try to generalize from his findings. He merely reported the facts obtained and analyzed the completed information. A thorough reading of his survey should be a must for those readers who are interested in taking their studies one step further.

Gottwald's survey barely touched the surface of the general population, yet a more extensive survey would quite possibly yield similar results. Certain aspects of the American culture impede and complicate the process of social and cultural changes concerning the mentally retarded. The emphasis on achievement through personal effort all but defeats itself in terms of the accomplishments made by retarded individuals in society.

Competitiveness for grades in school and for promotions which lead to higher salaries is also a problem for the retarded individual. Success is relative, yet the American system tends to convey that only those persons who are first in school achievement or work-related situations are successful. Idealized standards of beauty and personal appearance have infiltrated the lives of most Americans. Television commercials lead the public into believing that the use of certain vitamins or cosmetics will ultimately result in a more acceptable individual in the eye of the public. The so-called noncomformists have conformed to a specific "look" such as the wearing of faded blue jeans.

Discrimination in schools and jobs, stigmatization in the area of personal relationships, and categorical definitions which imply that the individual is inadequate or that he does not fit into an accepted category, affect the mentally retarded as a group and as individuals. Public schools place the child into a frame of reference which may follow him throughout his adult life. Jobs are limited for a person who carries the label *retarded* with him. Social reactions and interpersonal relationships are further determined by this label. Unenlightened adults may fear for the safety of their own offspring, afraid that the mentally retarded might somehow negatively influence their children. Misunderstandings often result from lack of awareness concerning the mentally retarded. As a result, the retarded may be also inclined to view themselves negatively or as a surplus to the general population.

A small study conducted in 1970 by Joav Gozali revealed that the majority of these special students resented their treatment and eventual placement in the public schools. Several years after participating in a work-study program in Milwaukee, fifty-six males were surveyed concerning their attitudes toward special class placement. Of these fifty-six young adults, 85 percent perceived their special classes as degrading and useless. Nearly all of the participants (91 percent) stated that they would never consent to having their children enrolled in special classes. A similar number of participants (87 percent) responded negatively to questions concerning continuing associations and/or friendships with peers from their special classes.

Although these young men had been enrolled in the work-study program during the 1964-65 and 1965-66 school years, their attitudes toward special class placement were still negative during 1970. No attitudinal surveys were conducted during the years when these young men were participants in the program, so it is not known exactly how they perceived the program during those years. The fact that after six or seven years these individuals harbored primarily negative perceptions of their school placement is alarming.

In 1973, Robert Titus and John Travis reported on a study done with graduates from the LaGrange, Illinois, special program. The primary focus of the study was to survey the types of jobs currently held by the graduates. All of the students had participated in the special four to five year program developed by the public schools.

In assessing the overall program, the class was divided into two groups. While one group felt that the program had been generally helpful to them, the other group felt that it was not at all helpful, considering their current job status. Several of the students in the latter group felt that they had been unjustly treated by being selected for placement in the program. The rest of the students in this group stated that the only reason they had remained in school was because of the mandatory attendance laws.

Parents of the students were also interviewed concerning their perceptions of the overall program. As might be expected, the parents of those youngsters who viewed the program as being of little use also viewed the program in negative terms. These parents specifically mentioned the fact that they felt their children had been wrongfully placed in the special classes. Such placement was felt to be detrimental to the child's future.

Since this study was completed, several new aspects have been added to the special program in LaGrange. A social worker has been employed to help with therapeutic activities geared toward the student's acceptance of himself. Individual growth and ego development have been stressed through problem-solving activities for both the students and their teachers. To help with the actual program development, a new center was established which evaluates and trains the students in relation to their individual work habits, skills, and limitations.

At the same time, additional services have been made available to the parents of these students. A series of discussions with the staff of the local mental health clinic and increased parental contact by center staff personnel have been utilized in an attempt to develop further understanding of both the program and the students by their parents.

As has been evidenced by these and other similar studies, students who have been classified as mentally retarded often have negative attitudes toward themselves and toward the special programs of which they have been a part. Although such findings may not be universal, the overwhelming negativism revealed in these studies in two different states is cause for alarm among all educators.

There are very few longitudinal studies in the literature concerning observations of teachers and children in special class settings. It seems ironic that these educational resources, initially conceived to facilitate learning in children who have been labeled mentally retarded, have sometimes come in direct conflict with that central objective. It has been felt that such programs may even be contributing to the development and extension of certain maladaptive behaviors in some children. Adverse effects of these programs are considered to be somewhat universal in one respect: they tend to intensify and complicate further learning and emotional problems in some children.

The frustrating fact is that attitudes are often directly related to the connotations which are revealed through categorical labels. As early as 1945, Ohio supported classes for educable mentally retarded students. In order to make such classes acceptable to legislators, parents, students, and the general community, the term *slow learner* was adopted to describe these students. The IQ range was set at 50-80, with the chronological age in the six to eighteen-year-old range. Similar criteria were being used elsewhere to depict mentally retarded children.

Chloe Hollinger and Reginald Jones surveyed a small Ohio community in 1969, nearly twenty years after its first special class for slow learners had been implemented. They were interested in several aspects of the community's attitudes toward individuals who had been classified as slow learners. First, they were interested in knowing how individuals within the community felt toward such persons. Next, they investigated individual's knowledge of slow learners. Last, they were concerned with the general acceptance of persons who were labeled slow learners as compared to those who were labeled mentally retarded.

Open-ended questions were used to inquire into the respondents' abilities to define the terms *slow learner* and *mentally retarded*. The results indicated that although their definitions were often incorrect, the individuals surveyed showed a significantly more positive attitude toward those persons who were labeled slow learners. Both educational and social limits were placed on persons who were labeled mentally retarded. For example, it was generally felt that a slow learner could attend college if he had special tutorial services, but a mentally retarded individual should never attempt any type of educational program beyond the public high school special education programs.

As of 1970, Ohio was the only state which had managed to avoid the issue of labeling for over twenty-five years. This was accomplished through the use of terms which were acceptable to the general public along with requirements which met the national regulations pertaining to the IQ and chronological age ranges.

On the national scene, state laws and regulations vary so much that a child's label may be changed merely by changing his state of residence. In 1971, John Kidd stated that the ceiling for trainable mentally retarded children in one state could be an IQ of 48, while in another state it could be an IQ of 60! The label a child receives, and thus the educational facilities and resources available to him, depend largely on the state in which he resides.

In 1968, the President's Committee on Mental Retardation estimated that *at least 75 percent* of all youngsters who are labeled retarded are products of social and psychological, not organic, etiologies. This means that only one out of every four children who have been labeled mentally retarded may actually be retarded. The other three have been misdiagnosed and/or mislabeled due to social or emotional factors which force the child to function on a level which would be considered retarded in academic situations. If the child is bilingual or from a minority group, the language-based intelligence tests do not allow him to function up to his ability during such an evaluation. Or, if the child has never been exposed to puzzles, crayons, or scissors, he may not be able to successfully complete the performance sections of such a test.

A large scale study of programs for the educable mentally retarded was conducted between 1957 and 1961 by the Chicago Board of Education. William Itkin reported these findings, which further confirm the findings of the President's Committee, in 1970. Nonachieving students in these special classes shared a variety of adverse commonalities. In general, these children came from lower economic levels where there was lower family interest in educational achievement. They shared backgrounds which revealed more adverse and/or multiple factors than the average child. There were more frequent diagnoses of psychiatric, speech, and neurological disorders. The majority of these students received significantly lower teacher ratings and personality scale scores. These children were also indigenous to the city.

If these same children had been products of different home environments, would they have still been labeled retarded when they entered school? Of course, no one really knows the answer to this question. The debate over nurture (environment) versus nature (heredity) in the area of mental retardation will continue indefinitely as long as professionals allow labels to interfere with the current educational concept that children need labels before they can be taught properly. Remove the label and what do you have? A child.

A Label Fable

Once upon a time ago there was a group of special education teachers who banded together to form a professional agency for the development of functional labels for the children they were working with in their teaching situations. This group of teachers had grown weary of the labels currently being used with the children, so they decided to change history and initiate a change in the labels. For many weeks they pondered their situation. One of them finally said, "Let's ask the regular classroom teachers for some help."

So they went to each regular classroom teacher in their respective school buildings to ask for opinions on a new system for labeling. The classroom teachers were very friendly and cooperative, but they could not come up with any solutions to the problem either.

No matter how hard they tried, none of the special education teachers could think of any new terms to use for their children. For many weeks they made lists and lists of terms that had been recommended to them by the various disciplines. A group of psychologists had suggested that they use *well done, medium,* and *rare* to describe the mental functioning of the gifted, normal, and retarded children. At first, this sounded like a brilliant idea, but then one of the special teachers remembered that two of her children had cerebral palsy, and she did not feel that these terms fully described those particular children.

By this time, the medical profession had heard about the special teacher's project and they, too, wanted to become involved. At a special meeting of the doctors of the county, the concept of new terminology was discussed by the twelve in attendance. They were all carrying their medical dictionaries with them to help solve the problem of terminology, and toward the end of the meeting they resorted to these dictionaries for further clarification of their newly developed terms.

On the following day, the doctors presented their list of twenty-eight terms to the special education teachers. *Aplenti dysfusia* was the term selected by the doctors to describe the general category known as special education. Under this general heading were three major terms: *alegzia, dislegzia,* and *nolegzia.* These terms meant, respectively, with good mobility, with partial mobility, and with limited mobility.

From there the terms were again subdivided according to further neurological involvement which affected the overall functioning of the brain as related to the level of mobility. The next category used the terms *hemidasplentia, homodasplentia,* and *heterodasplentia.* Respectively, these terms indicated that both hemispheres of the brain were functioning in abundance with each side doing its assigned duties, both hemispheres of the brain were functioning alike so that there tended to be confusion over which side was the boss, and both sides of the brain were functioning opposite of each other with uncontrolled differences in their overall abilities to function as a whole. On and on went the list until it came to the last term, *minimal* _____ . Here, the teachers were to simply fill in the blank.

The special education teachers accepted the terms from the doctors and agreed to use them for a trial period of time. Unfortunately, they kept confusing the terms. When they tried to explain them to the classroom teachers, their explanations were met with blank stares because of this confusion. One time the special teachers would use one term, and the next time they would use a different term which vaguely sounded like the original term. Before long, everyone was confused and frustrated again

It was nearly spring, yet the special education teachers had still not solved their problem of which labels to use for their children. They had tried a variety of labels with their children, including, *slow, slower,* and *slowest* and *dumb, dumber,* and *dumbest* as had been suggested by a high school English teacher. Still, none of the experimental labels seemed to satisfy the special teachers.

The final group meeting of the special education teachers for the year was held on the third Monday in May, and at this meeting the special teachers decided that all of their efforts had been in vain. For an entire school year they had hassled with the problem of labeling and all they had to show for it were several journal articles which some of them had published. One of the special teachers had begun collaborating on a book discussing the controversy, but after two months he had decided that the task was just too time consuming for him, and the unfinished manuscript was spread throughout the trunk of his car.

Just as the meeting was about to break up, the small son of one of the special teachers barged into the room. "Mom! Come quick!! That funny looking kid you work with just fell down out in the middle of the street and he can't get up."

With that, everyone jumped up and rushed to the rescue. It didn't take them long to solve the problem of getting Jackie, the "funny looking kid", back in an upright position and on his way back to his house.

As the special teachers were walking back into the school building, one of them commented, "You know, your son is right. Jackie is a 'funny looking kid' to the other children. His braces and wheelchair really make him, if you'll excuse the expression, stand out in a crowd."

The comment was taken lightly by most of the special teachers, but the mother of the child who had made the comment suddenly shrieked, "Eureka! If my son can give Jackie a label which pretty much describes him, maybe he can give us other labels for other children. After all, everyone else in the community has tried to come up with functional labels, so why can't my son!"

After much discussion, the special teachers brought the child, Jimmy, into the room where they were conducting their meeting. "How do you describe little Clara?" they asked him. After a little thought, Jimmy said, "Well, she doesn't *look* funny like Jackie, but she sure *acts* funny. She can't read or do her arithmetic in class. And the other day she was having trouble with trying to figure out the consequences of an unfinished story we had just read. She couldn't understand why it was wrong to run across the street without looking first. I don't think she realized that she might get hit by a car."

"What about Jon? How would you describe him?" the special teachers asked. "Oh, him! Man, he *wanders around the entire room* all day long. He just can't sit still for a minute. He's something like Ricky, except Ricky *bothers and destroys*. Those two aren't anything like Peggy, though. She must be the smartest kid in school because she always *gives outstanding output on demand*."

With that the teachers told Jimmy he could go back outside to play while they finished their meeting. After Jimmy left, the special teachers compared their notes on what he had said. It didn't take them long to come up with five functional labels for their children.

The *funny looking kid*, or *FLK*, was a child who had visible handicaps or disabilities. The *funny acting kid*, or *FAK*, was a child who had invisible or hidden handicaps which were not readily observed by the casual onlooker. Next came the *wanders around the entire room*, or *WATER*, child who was unable to sit still and attend for any length of time. The fourth classification was for the *bothers and destroys*, or *BAD*, child who had temper tantrums, agitated others, and was destructive either to himself or to the other children. Last came the *gives outstanding output on demand*, or *GOOOD*, child who excelled in all areas.

Satisfied with themselves, the special teachers called the

meeting to a close. The very next day they presented their new list of five labels to their superintendent. Although he was somewhat confused over their excitement, he allowed them to present their new categories at the teachers' meeting after school. He also gave them permission to copy and distribute the five page handout they had developed to help the regular teachers learn the new categories.

The teachers' meeting was a huge success, and by the following week everyone in the school system was using the new terms. Everyone except Mrs. Learnfield, that is. She was most adamant about this new labeling process. "All of his records say that he has minimal brain dysfunction, but now you tell me that he has *WATER!* How am I supposed to teach a child when I don't even know which category he comes under? And if you want to get down to specifics, there are days when I think that most of my children are *BAD* or most of them are *GOOOD.* So what do you propose I do about them on those days?"

Just as the special teacher was about to explain the new terms again to Mrs. Learnfield, her son Jimmy came up to her. "Mom," he interrupted, "do you remember that kid we helped the other day when he fell down in the street? Did you know that he has a collection of rocks and minerals? He just asked me to come over to see them, but I said I had to check with you first. When I told him who my mother was, he said you were a *GOOOD* teacher for working with him everyday."

As the mother nodded in approval of the after school visit, Mrs. Learnfield laughed at the situation. "I suppose now that Jimmy has put a label on you we will have to change things a bit. Perhaps we need to devise a list of categories for the teachers rather than for the kids. In fact, now that I mention it, maybe that is a *GOOOD* idea! I think we can use the same terms, just change our definitions a bit."

With that, Mrs. Learnfield dashed excitedly into the teachers' lounge to share her good news with the teachers. As the door was closing on the lounge area, she was heard to say, " ... and if we make this a multidisciplinary effort, I am certain we can settle this problem by the time school opens in the fall."

MORAL: A label in the classroom is worth two in the lounge.

REFERENCES

1. Alese, Joseph A.: Operation awareness. *Ment Retard, 11:*38-39, 1973.
2. Beatty, James R.: The analysis of an instrument for screening for learning disabilities. *J Learn Disabil, 8:*180-186, 1975.
3. Blatt, Burton: Some persistently recurring assumptions concerning the mentally subnormal. *Train Sch Bull (Vinel), 57:*48-59, 1960.
4. Edgerton, Robert B., and Karno, Melvin: Community attitudes toward the hospital care of the mr. *Ment Retard, 5:*3-5, 1972.
5. Ensher, Gail L.: The hidden handicap: attitudes toward children and their implications. *Ment Retard, 11:*40-41, 1973.
6. Gillespie, Patricia H., Miller, Ted L., and Fielder, Virginia Dodge: Legislative definitions of learning disabilities: roadblocks to effective service. *J Learn Disabil, 8:*660-666, 1975.
7. Gottwald, Henry: *Public Awareness About Mental Retardation.* Reston, Coun Exc Child, 1970.
8. Gozali, Joav: Perception of the emr special class by former students. *Ment Retard, 10:*34-35, 1972.
9. Hobbs, Nicholas: *The Futures of Children.* San Francisco, Jossey-Bass, 1975.
10. Hollinger, Chloe S., and Jones, Reginald L.: Community attitudes toward slow learners and mental retardates: what's in a name? *Ment Retard, 8:*19-23, 1970.
11. Itkin, William: The non-achieving educable mentally retarded: implications of his needs for education and the community. *Ment Retard, 8:*53-54, 1970.
12. Kidd, John W.: Mental retardation: the emerging dilemma. *Ment Retard, 9:*58-59, 1971.
13. Kidd, John W.: Some unwarranted assumptions in the education and habilitation of handicapped children. *Educ and Train Ment Retard, 1:*54-58, 1966.
14. Kirk, Samuel A., and Elkins, John: Characteristics of children enrolled in the child service demonstration centers. *J Learn Disabil, 8:*630-637, 1975.
15. Loney, Jan, Comly, Hunter H., and Simon, Betty: Parental management, self-concept, and drug response in minimal brain dysfunction. *J Learn Disabil, 8:*187-190, 1975.
16. MacMillan, Donald L.: Issues and trends in special education. *Ment Retard, 11:*3-8, 1973.
17. McGlannan, Frances K.: Learning disabilities: the decade ahead. *J Learn Disabil, 8:*113-116, 1975.

18. Neinstead, Serena: Talking with ld teachers. *Read Teach, 28*:662-665, 1975.
19. O'Such, Twila G., and Goldberg, I. Ignacy: Educators' perceptions of the american association on mental deficiency. *Ment Retard, 11*:3-7, 1973.
20. President's Committee on Mental Retardation: *MR: 67.* Washington, PCMR, 1968.
21. Taylor, George R.: Special education at the crossroad: class placement for the emr. *Ment Retard, 11*:30-33, 1973.
22. Titus, Robert W., and Travis, John T.: Follow-up of emr program graduates. *Ment Retard, 11*:24-26, 1973.
23. Trotter, Sharland: Labeling: it hurts more than it helps. *J Learn Disabil, 8*:191-193, 1975.

Chapter 4

CURRENT TRENDS IN PUBLIC SCHOOL SPECIAL EDUCATION PRACTICES ... WHO'S MINDING THE STORE VS. WHO'S TENDING THE SHOP

IN the past, educational services in the public schools for handicapped or exceptional children have been provided by special education teachers. A multitude of experimental approaches have been implemented during the past several decades. Some of these educational approaches have proven to be highly feasible and have been easily adaptable to many school systems. Other approaches have been reserved for only special school settings because of their unique characteristics.

Currently, there are a variety of special programs available to exceptional children throughout the United States whose educational needs are encompassed by the services of the public schools. Some school systems provide only one type of program with little or no flexibility, while others provide such a variety of alternative programs that the youngster may find himself shuffled among "specialists" from the time he walks inside the school building each day until the final bell rings at the end of the day. Most systems, however, provide one basic type of program with allowances for some flexibility within the program itself. A few systems are unable to provide any services that meet the specific educational needs of the individual youngster, and in some instances the state will absorb some or all of the cost required for the enlistment of outside services and resources. Some systems have even gone so far as to fully integrate their handicapped youngsters within the total public school functions in an attempt to provide equal educational opportunities for all students who need alternatives to the types of programs previously offered to them through the public schools.

When developing alternative programs for exceptional children, three issues of concern must be confronted by the administrators of such programs. First, the relationship between regular and special education must be taken into consideration. With alternative programs comes a shift in the roles and responsibilities of both regular and special education teachers.

As a result of the current emphasis on equal educational environment and least restrictive alternatives, the concept of mainstreaming exceptional children into regular classes has become widely publicized throughout the United States. Unfortunately, the implementation of emphasis has been placed on the special educators while the emphasis of implementation has been placed on the regular educators. Several states are moving toward legislation which will require all university students who are majoring in any phase of education to take at least one course in exceptional children. Needless to say, one course entitled *Introduction to Exceptional Children* will not answer all of the classroom teachers' questions concerning mainstreaming.

To most classroom teachers, the term "mainstreaming" merely implies "sink or swim" on their part. Suddenly they see themselves as having been given the major responsibility of teaching youngsters who previously were considered "unfit" for the regular classroom.

To some degree, this is true, but the majority of special educators do not view mainstreaming as "passing the buck" to the classroom teacher. Instead, they see this alternative as a method for integrating exceptional children into the society they will have to live in for the rest of their lives. It is only logical to prepare these youngsters for community living through actual experience with their communities and those individuals who comprise these communities.

A second issue concerns the terminology used to define mainstreaming. A variety of concepts are usually involved when either a regular or a special teacher uses the word "mainstreaming." Explicit definitions of mainstreaming such as those given during 1974 by Jack Birch and Jerry Chaffin are often used to help special as well as regular educators better understand the concept of mainstreaming and what it implies for all educators.

Jack Birch (1974) speaks of keeping the exceptional children within the regular classroom for as much of the school day as possible. He defines mainstreaming as "providing high-quality special education" to these youngsters whether they are in the regular classroom or in a special resource room.

Jerry Chaffin (1974) relates mainstreaming to the mildly retarded child within the regular classroom. He advocates supplemental educational experiences and instructional support as being provided by the classroom teacher.

Other definitions are readily available in nearly every current volume on the education of exceptional children. The argument concerning terminology is one which may never be completely settled. What is important in this argument is the overall concept of exposing exceptional children to the current flow of regular education within the public schools. In order to accomplish this, total involvement of the home, the school, and the community is necessary. A better understanding of the individual child and how he functions in his home, his school, and his community is the major thesis of most advocates of the mainstreaming concept.

The third issue concerning mainstreaming involves a combination or a meeting ground of the first two concerns. It has to do with the relationship of the regular and special education teachers, and the concept and terminology of mainstreaming, and how these relate to the actual implementation of alternative programs for exceptional children.

A commitment to mainstreaming does not mean that all children should be expected to function adequately in regular classrooms. It does not mean that all self-contained classes, special schools, and institutions should be abolished, nor does this commitment mean that all classroom teachers should be expected to become "one semester wonders" in learning to deal with exceptional children in their classrooms. Rather, the advocates of mainstreaming are trying to achieve as much integration as possible of mildly handicapped children into regular classrooms. They do emphasize, however, that mainstreaming and special classes are not mutually exclusive.

Similarly, most advocates of mainstreaming realize that this is only one facet of the current methodology by which exceptional children may be helped to reach their highest potential. They use the term to imply flexibility in administrative arrangements, in teacher roles, and in student services.

Just as previous research evidence has shown that open education has not been the answer for all children because some children do better in structured settings, future research may show that mainstreaming is not the answer for all children, because some children need intensive instruction in specific learning areas. Nonetheless, the concept of mainstreaming is continually gathering momentum throughout the United States, and once a school system has decided to mainstream their handicapped youngsters, the educators involved will be obligated to select a model to follow and to do their best with the implementation of such a model.

The circumstances under which a school system operates its alternative program for handicapped children will vary considerably. The extent of implementation will also vary between school systems. As a case in point, one school superintendent, after receiving numerous sarcastic comments by his administrative peers within his state, calmly solved the "problem" of mainstreaming with his own rhetoric. He admitted to the group that it was true that only 13 percent of the identified handicapped youngsters were being served directly by his special education teachers. Therefore, he concluded, the remaining 87 percent of these identified youngsters must currently be mainstreamed within the regular classes.

The Impetus for Mainstreaming

The field of special education has emerged from the "dark ages" of total care for the handicapped to the "new dawn" of educational services for all handicapped children. With this emergence has come criticism, not only of the programs, but even of the rationale for programs dealing with the handicapped.

During the 1950's and 1960's, self-contained special classes were the only continuing services provided for the exceptional child in the public schools. Professionals in the field argued over the efficacy of such classes, especially for the mildly handicapped children. G. Orville Johnson (1962) argued that perhaps too much money was being spent on the specially trained teachers who worked with small numbers of students, and on the specially designed programs which were being developed and implemented for the exclusive use of children who had been diagnosed as mentally handicapped. The primary focus of his argument centered around the fact that there were many children in the regular classrooms who displayed similar learning problems, but because there was no formal diagnosis on these children, they did not receive special educational considerations.

Further arguments arose from defenders of the minority groups of children. Children who were bilingual were discriminated against on the English versions of the standardized IQ tests, and were consequently placed in the special classes for the retarded. Kenneth Clark, in an address to the Social Science Institute of Coppin State Teachers College in Baltimore on March 15, 1963, charged the public schools with offering higher level educational opportunities to children from higher socio-economic backgrounds.

Clark went even further by stating that the current discussions of the education of culturally deprived children were based on two groups of false assumptions. He called the first group of false assumptions "well-intentioned assumptions." He argued that although the concept of teaching a child in terms of his own needs and capabilities sounds logical on the surface, it has caused confusion, misunderstanding, and injustice in the educational process. For example, it has always been assumed that children from working class families need both a different approach to the educational process and a different type of education in general than children from middle class families.

Likewise, children from lower socio-economic families have

been assumed to be unmotivated due to the lack of educational stimulation available in the home situation. Thus, educational programs for such children are lower in their level of academic emphasis, and this results in the lower academic achievement of the youngsters placed in such classes.

Concomitant to all of the above assumptions is the inevitable "IQ trap" for culturally deprived children. The children are usually tested during the primary grades before they have been exposed to the types of academic activities which are being evaluated on the test. When a child receives a low IQ score on such a test, his teachers automatically assume that he is incapable of learning, so their efforts to teach the child any academics are self-defeating. If the teacher refrains from teaching the child the academics he needs for the future, how will he learn them? If he doesn't learn them, he will never be able to improve his IQ score on a standardized test.

The second group of assumptions listed by Clark are what he calls "class and racial snobbery." Related directly to the first group of assumptions, these assumptions "prepare" a culturally deprived child for a devastating future. The educational system refuses to place much faith in such a child, so rather than training him for meaningful aspirations in the academic process, they claim that in reality only menial jobs will be available to the child once he becomes an adult, so the training is also menial.

Clark furthers his argument by discussing the consequences of such actions within the educational process. Children are treated as uneducable, and therefore they become uneducable. This process of a self-fulfilling prophecy is termed "educational atrophy" by Clark. Just as a limb of the body will become atrophied from lack of use, portions of the brain's learning capacity will also become atrophied or sluggish when they are not allowed to be used and developed. Clark feels that a great deal of human potential has been wasted due to this "atrophy" of the educational process. He also feels that this process is a denial of the child's basic rights.

At the conclusion of his speech, Clark made some specific suggestions for remediating the problems and the underlying assumptions just discussed. Among these suggestions is one asking that all children be treated equally during their first eight years of school. By eliminating the IQ tests, Clark feels that all children will be encouraged to learn to the best of their abilities, and these abilities will not be affected by a numerical rating on a standardized test.

Clark was arguing for the rights of the minority children, the ones he calls "socially rejected." Are not these same circumstances related to all children who are labeled as being handicapped?

Robert Rosenthall and Lenore Jacobson (1968) did an interesting study in California related to the self-fulfilling prophecy among children in regular classrooms. Standardized intelligence and achievement tests were done on children in the first six grades of a school in the San Francisco Unified School District. A random selection of children was made from the total group, and these children were labeled as being rapid learners with hidden potentials. At the end of the school year, all of the children were re-evaluated for intellectual gains and school progress. The gains made by the random sample of children who had been falsely labeled showed significantly greater gains than their peers. The most dramatic gains were evidenced in the first and second grades. Such results would tend to indicate that the labeling effects on a child determine the educational gains he will make in the classroom.

Lloyd Dunn (1968) criticized special classes in the public schools for creating self-fulfilling prophecies among children who were given negative-sounding labels such as mentally retarded and learning disabled. He argued that such labels had long-lasting effects on the children which were often harmful to their future roles in the public schools and later in society. Another criticism from Dunn was that the majority of the pupils in special classes came from low status backgrounds. Again, the minority groups were expected to be low achievers, and after being labeled as such, they inevitably became low achievers.

The possibility of grouping children according to their functioning levels rather than through the use of categorical labels has also been suggested. Categorical labels such as mental retardation and learning disabled do not always reveal the functioning level of the individual child, yet this is the way children are usually grouped in the public schools. It has been pointed out that children with the same categorical label or the same IQ do not necessarily have the same educational needs.

By placing children according to their functioning levels, educators could better meet the learning needs of the individual child. Burton Blatt (1973) has shown that many children placed in regular classes fail to meet the demands made upon them in the educational setting. Perhaps these children are encountering difficulties which are not totally their own fault. The implication is that the public schools as well as special education practices are in need of reform.

There is no single solution to the problem of who should teach what, and how, and to whom. However, concepts such as the *least restrictive environment* and the *cascade* system have had an unprecedented effect on the educational placement of exceptional children.

The least restrictive environment implies that any individual is entitled to an education which does not interfere with his civil liberties. In the public schools, this means that alternative programs for exceptional children need to be outlined and implemented so that they, too, will receive equal educational opportunities. These alternative programs are intended to provide the needed educational services for the child without placing undue restrictions upon his freedom. A child who is emotionally disturbed should be given an opportunity to live at home and attend public school classes rather than live in a residential institution which may not even be located within his own state of residence. If the state statutes do not provide for such placement in the public schools, the United States Constitution may be used by the plaintiffs. The impetus of the court cases thus far has been away from residential facilities and toward more community based programs which are considered to be more in the mainstream of public education.

In line with the concept of the least restrictive environment is the cascade system developed by Maynard Reynolds (1962). The cascade is intended to be used as a guideline for educational services and placement of the handicapped. It has recently been adopted by the Council for Exceptional Children as a model for special education services and delivery of these services through a variety of alternative settings.

Consisting of several alternatives, the cascade system begins by assuming that the majority of the handicapped children can be served by the public schools through only minor changes in their existing programs. Three phases are included in the regular classroom structure: (a) regular classroom with specialist consultants, (b) regular classrooms with itinerant teachers, and (c) regular classroom with a special resource room. These phases are considered to be the least restrictive alternatives among those offered within the cascade system.

The next six alternatives, in descending order include: (a) part-time special class, (b) full-time special class, (c) special day school, (d) residential school, (e) hospital school, and (f) residential hospital. The last alternative is considered to be the most expensive for the fewest number of children.

It must be remembered that the cascade is only a model, a theoretical prototype, for the development of programs for exceptional children. Mandates being handed down from the courts are requiring some school systems to develop modifications which are not included in this model. Some school systems are incorporating newly developed programs into existing programs for the handicapped. Others are developing innovative alternatives for the education, treatment, and therapy of handicapped children. Throughout the United States, special education services are undergoing a revolution for the betterment of all children.

Public School Alternatives

Self-Contained Classroom

This is the most restrictive setting for handicapped children within the public school setting. Originally, such classrooms were in the basements of the school buildings, or even in isolated smaller buildings located on the school grounds. The children were not allowed to venture into the regular mainstream of the school except under very special circumstances. When they did enter into the world of the regular school building, they were scorned or totally avoided by both the other teachers and the other children.

Currently, such classrooms are used to provide services for children who have either severe mental or physical handicaps, or for children who are unable to tolerate the larger classroom setting. In most instances, these children are encouraged to integrate with their normal peers during social activities, lunch, art, music, assembly programs, and even physical education. The extent and scheduling of this interaction is usually determined by the special education teacher, the regular classroom teacher, and the child's readiness for such activities.

Primary level self-contained classes are usually restricted to twelve students, on the average, while elementary classes may contain as many as sixteen students. One teacher and possibly an aide are utilized for this type of setting.

It is usually recommended that self-contained classes not be utilized in the upper grades except for the severely handicapped students who have been unable to adjust to the integration attempts made during the earlier school years. If there is a self-contained classroom at the secondary level, it is often a modified version of the original model in that it provides gradually increasing independence among the handicapped students. Job-related work skills and work habits are often included in this type of program.

Resource Room

Resource rooms were originally developed to help provide additional services for blind or deaf students enrolled in the public schools. Traditionally, the resource room has served students who have special learning needs but who are able to function fairly well in the regular classroom through the added services of the special resource teacher.

Resource teachers provide direct learning experiences for the youngsters while consulting with regular teachers in assessing individual strengths and deficiencies. Ideally, the two teachers work as a team and assume joint responsibility for implementing and evaluating the plan they have co-developed for the youngster. Since the child is already enrolled in the regular classroom he is considered within the mainstream of general education.

The resource teacher assesses each child's knowledge and behavior, and plans appropriate activities for each child. Assessment materials are often ordinary instructional and testing materials, rather than formal standardized tests. Assessment results help determine the content of each child's program and the way in which that content can best be taught. Some children need individual teaching while others can participate in small group instruction. Once instruction is begun, assessment becomes an integral and ongoing part of instruction, and the instructional program is always subject to change.

The results of the initial assessment may indicate that a child does not need to come to the resource room, but that he does need some extra help in his regular class. A child who does come to the resource room may also need extra help in his regular class. In these cases, the resource teacher acts as a consultant to the regular class teacher, suggesting ways to help the child.

A child may stop attending the resource room any time his resource teacher and his regular teacher decide that he no longer needs the direct services of the resource teacher. She may continue to work with his teacher or with him on a scheduled basis, however.

Resource Centers

An alternative to an isolated resource room is the use of a resource center. In some instances, only the title has changed, but in others the entire concept has been totally revised. Instead of having one teacher in one room to provide a multitude of services for handicapped children, a group of specialists are located within a center which serves all children in the school building. Special education teachers, speech therapists, diagnostic equipment, and even school counselors may be housed in this type of center.

In Bloomington, Minnesota, this type of program is being implemented at the elementary school level. Once the children reach junior high school age, the resource centers are replaced by special counselors. These counselors are assigned to specific students for special counseling sessions, yet they also serve as advocates for all students within the schools to which they are assigned.

By moving throughout the building, these counselors are able to keep an eye on the happenings inside of the classrooms. In some instances, they have even been known to sit in on lectures given by the regular classroom teachers. This is done to ask questions which might enable them to help their students better understand the concepts being presented and to help themselves better understand the needs of their students.

Block or Departmentalized Classes

At the junior and senior high school levels, the block or departmentalized class is used quite frequently. Unlike the resource room or resource center concept, the handicapped children served through this type of program are given special instruction in a particular academic area rather than in all areas of academic subjects.

This type of program recognizes the fact that some youngsters with learning problems may excel in certain academic subjects and therefore should be placed with their peers for such course work and in the "block" for subjects they are having difficulty with. In some ways, this can be compared to the tracking system since the children are grouped according to their learning abilities in specific subjects. However, the block system is intended to help with specific subjects and therefore a student is not confined to one isolated group throughout the entire school day.

Since many regular subjects are already departmentalized at the junior and senior high school levels, this type of program modifies or eliminates the stigma of being in the "dummy" class which is isolated from the rest of the school functions.

At the senior high school level, this type of program is often utilized in conjunction with work-study programs. For half of the day the students are involved in on-the-job training through actual employment in the community. The other half of the day is spent in the school's block system which is geared toward teaching the students basic academic skills which are related to the world of work. Cooperation and communication between the special education teacher, the school administrators, and the employers are of vital importance for the success of such programs.

Itinerant Teachers

Itinerant speech teachers or speech therapists are responsible for anywhere from two to five schools. Since they must travel between schools, their facilities are usually lacking due to the physical constraints within the individual school buildings. Case loads may vary from sixty to one hundred pupils, with most of the students receiving a maximum of two thirty-minute speech lessons per week.

Itinerant reading teachers share the problems of the itinerant speech teachers, as well as their facilities, in many cases. Their case load and number of schools are greatly reduced by comparison, yet the constraints upon their functioning as members of the individual schools are numerous.

Itinerant teachers for homebound students are responsible for academic subjects covered from the first through the twelfth grade. Home visits are usually made once a week, and due to the amount of driving time required between homes, such visits rarely last more than one hour. Parents are often encouraged to help with the educational needs of their youngsters in such instances, yet few are prepared to handle the responsibility involved.

When a school system is unable to provide the necessary educational services, there is sometimes financial aid available for the recruitment of such outside resources. For example, severely or multiply handicapped children in North Carolina who are unable to find appropriate education in the public schools may qualify to receive tuition grants to private or out-of-state facilities. As a result of a 1973 General Assembly appropriation, sixty-two grants, at a maximum of $2,000 each, are now available to school-aged handicapped children who meet the special State Board of Education requirements.

These requirements stipulate that the youngster must be eligible to attend North Carolina public schools, but he must have "professionally diagnosed needs so specialized that the public schools do not at this time provide facilities or programs" to meet the individual needs. The private or out-of-state facilities attended must be accredited, approved, or licensed as offering an appropriate instructional program. Information concerning these grants is made available through the local superintendent's office, and parents must apply through the school unit which would normally serve the youngster.

Diagnostic Prescriptive Teacher

The diagnostic prescriptive teacher (DPT) is a highly specific method developed to keep the handicapped child within the regular classroom during most of the school day. Although the DPT may work with a child outside of the classroom setting, it is only for the purpose of obtaining an educational prescription. Thus, the children are rarely served outside of the regular classroom except for diagnostic purposes.

The room used for obtaining educational prescriptions has often been compared to the resource room because it is also used for individual work with exceptional children. However, the DPT's room should be made available for all students in the school, and may even be used as a special study room when the DPT is not using it.

There are ten specific steps to be followed in the DPT program, including (a) referral, (b) observation, (c) referral conference, (d) diagnostic teaching, (e) educational prescription, (f) prescription conference, (g) demonstration, (h) short term follow-up, (i) evaluation, and (j) long term follow-up.

Initially, the regular classroom teacher makes a written referral outlining the learning or behavior problems of the child she wishes the DPT to observe. This is followed by a visit to the classroom by the DPT to observe the child in his normal educational setting.

After the child has been observed by the DPT, she and the regular teacher schedule a conference to discuss further information concerning the child. Following this conference, the DPT works with the child individually to determine which methods and materials are most suitable for his learning needs. A written report of these findings is prepared by the DPT for the regular teacher. Included in this report are specific teaching procedures which have been determined to be successful with the child.

Next the DPT and the regular classroom teacher confer to discuss the educational prescription which has been written by the DPT. Suggestions and comments resulting from this conference may result in possible modifications of the original prescription.

Once a prescription has been agreed upon, the DPT demonstrates these teaching procedures in the regular classroom setting. Following this demonstration, the DPT visits the classroom periodically to observe the child, confer with the teacher, and present further demonstrations if necessary.

After thirty days of following the recommended prescription, the classroom teacher fills out an evaluation form concerning the child. During the remainder of the school year, the DPT maintains an ongoing communication with the classroom teacher to monitor the progress being made. Gradually the DPT is faded out of the direct services program for the child, but only after both she and the regular teacher are satisfied with the child's progress.

Consulting Teacher

Closely related to the resource room, the special counselor, and the diagnostic prescriptive teacher, is the consulting teacher. Like the DPT, the consulting teacher works closely with the regular teacher in the classroom setting. The role of the consulting teacher is to observe the children in their regular classroom settings and then work with the regular teacher to develop individual programs which may be implemented within the existing structure of the regular classroom. Many times the consulting teacher is itinerant in that she is assigned to several schools within the same school district.

Vermont has operated an extensive consulting teacher program for the past several years. Their program emphasizes the use of instructional objectives and behavior management techniques. After the regular teacher initiates a request for help through a special form, an evaluation is completed on the child in the areas of concern as listed on the form. The primary areas being evaluated are language, arithmetic, and social behavior. Help is provided through the consulting teacher only when the child falls below a set level of competencies in one or more of these areas.

If the decision is made to utilize the consulting teacher, a parent conference is scheduled. A program for the child is not developed until the parents have given their written consent for such services. Once this permission is obtained, the consulting teacher goes into the classroom to observe the child and to make suggestions to the classroom teacher. Again the parents are brought into the situation since permission must be granted by them before any program is initiated.

The role of the consulting teacher then becomes one of aiding the classroom teacher in learning to chart specific behaviors, selecting appropriate educational objectives, and implementing a program of behavior management for the child. As with all behavior management programs, the key to success is finding the appropriate reinforcer for the individual child and implementing the reinforcement schedule to meet the goals of the desired outcome.

Survival School

Using the community as a teaching resource has often been used with classes for severely and moderately retarded children.

In Franklin, Wisconsin, this same concept is currently being used with all of the handicapped students at the Country Dale School. The primary focus of the program is to incorporate academic skills with community resources in order to teach survival to the students.

Field trips out into the community are organized by the students, and public transportation is utilized for such trips. The students plan the trips, structure the activities involved during the trip, and are accountable for implementing these activities.

Outside agencies such as the Red Cross have been invited to come into the classroom to teach simple first aid skills to the older students. Other activities related to recreation and safety have been developed through the use of other local agencies.

Within the classroom there are facilities for teaching cooking, ironing, and other basic self-help skills needed for survival within the home situation. All of the activities are planned to teach the students basic skills which they will need at home and in the community during their adult lives.

Individualized Instruction

Although the phrase "individualized instruction" has been recently overused in the professional education journals, some school systems are proving that it can be a reality without being an unobtainable goal for the regular classroom teacher. The open classroom concept readily lends itself toward this type of program since there are usually several teachers assigned to large groups of students. The students rotate around a large central area, working in small groups on specific tasks. By assigning a special education teacher to this team of rotating teachers, the children have been able to remain in the same classroom with their peers at all times.

The special education teacher may wish to designate a specific area of the open classroom as a learning center to which the children come for special help. Or, she may wish to rotate around the room herself, helping individual children or small groups of children as the need arises. Usually, only the mildly handicapped youngsters are assigned to such programs within the public school setting.

Annexes

To provide equal educational opportunities for some of the more severely handicapped students, several school systems have begun building annexes onto already existing public school buildings. These additions to the regular building bring the handicapped youngsters closer to the activities of the regular classrooms, yet somewhat isolate these children from the normal peers.

In Miami's Dade County Schools, this type of program is being utilized to help the handicapped students adjust to the public schools. The annexes are used to help integrate the youngsters during lunch and recreation periods, although for the majority of the school day the handicapped youngsters remain within the annex.

One advantage to newly built annexes is that barrier-free construction has allowed many physically handicapped youngsters to attend public school for the first time. By being given special instruction during the elementary school years, many of these handicapped youngsters are able to transfer into high school programs with only a minimum of adjustment problems.

In school districts where annexes are not feasible, a modified program has been developed through the utilization of unused portions of already existing school buildings. Remodeling several classrooms has often resulted in an annexed type of program for handicapped students. One advantage to this type of annexing is that the program is more an integral part of the overall school building. Facilities may be more readily shared by all of the teachers, and through the sharing of resources, the teachers are able to gain more insight and understanding into the educational needs of individual students.

Access Centers

Access centers are being utilized in areas where specific

resources are needed for the more severely handicapping conditions. Many times these centers are converted school buildings which have been renovated and modernized to meet the needs of the population being served. Such centers are also used as parent training centers.

There are two advantages to having an access center which is designed also as a parent training center. First, the special education teachers are able to better utilize their time by remaining in one location rather than traveling throughout a district to make home visits on a regularly scheduled basis. The teachers are able to spend their time teaching rather than traveling.

Second, parental involvement implies parental commitment. It is very frustrating and time consuming for a special teacher to travel to a distant home only to find that the child is sick, the parents are not at home, or the family is not interested in obtaining the services being offered. When the parents are required to bring their child in for services, they are more likely to become active participants in the educational services being provided for their child.

A modification of the access center program just described also involves parent training, but in a slightly different manner. The Tennessee State Department of Mental Health's Regional Intervention Program in Nashville does not assess fees to the parents it serves. Instead, the parents, usually the mother, pay for these services through an agreement to work for the program for six months. This works out positively for everyone concerned. Mothers who are enrolled in the program receive training from other mothers, and a common bond may be established among these parents which could not possibly be obtained among parents and professionals. The mothers who are acting as trainers are positively reinforced for their efforts within the program and thus they are more accepting of the program in general. When either group of mothers are feeling depressed, there is always someone there who has experienced similar doubts and frustrations. A mutual understanding combined with empathy has encouraged many of these mothers to remain with the program beyond their six month work agreement.

Vocational Centers

During the past decade, the concept of vocational centers for disabled youth has gained quite a bit of popularity. Many states have occupational and physical rehabilitation centers, yet the public schools are now beginning to create vocational and prevocational training centers for teenaged handicapped youth.

In 1969, seventeen local school districts in Minnesota banded together to form a consortium to operate a vocationally oriented high school specifically for handicapped youngsters. The Special Education Rehabilitation and Vocation Education (SERVE) is an interagency effort involving three state agencies: the state department of vocational education, the state board of education, and the state department of vocational rehabilitation. All of the high schools in the seventeen cooperating school districts have a SERVE classroom where disabled and handicapped youth participate in individualized programs related to vocational orientation and job-related academic skills.

In conjunction with the newly organized SERVE programs, the area vocational high school helps in the placement of students involved in the local SERVE programs. The ultimate goal is to either integrate the students back into the regular classrooms or place them in appropriate jobs within their local communities.

Allied Service Centers

Also called community/schools, allied service centers are building complexes designed to meet a variety of educational needs within the community. The same complex might include a nursery school, a community college extension, an adult education center, medical and dental clinics, as well as other educational and health related facilities.

By combining these allied services, the community is better prepared to meet the needs of all of its citizens. Handicapped individuals are not confronted with unnecessary transportation problems since all of the facilities are readily accessible within one general area. When such facilities include child care centers, there are opportunities for benefits to both the children being served and to those teachers who may be in training programs for working with the handicapped child. The medical and dental facilities may be used for treatment and/or for training for both the teachers and their students. Family health facilities may also be incorporated into such training.

Diagnostic/Evaluation Centers

Some local school districts have found that the easiest way for them to serve their handicapped youngsters is through a diagnostic/evaluation center. Originally, such centers were operated in conjunction with state residential facilities or other state facilities. Gradually, some of the larger school districts began incorporating the concept of a diagnostic/evaluation center into their remedial programs for mentally retarded or learning disabled youngsters.

Ideally, these centers are short-term facilities where the children are observed, evaluated, and educated. The children are referred by their local schools, and after the initial evaluation, they are either accepted or rejected for more in-depth evaluations through the center. Transportation may or may not be made available to the children, which in some cases automatically determines whether they will be able to attend the center for further observation and evaluation.

Once the child is admitted to the program, he is enrolled, usually on a trial basis, in a special education classroom within the center. When he is in this classroom, he is observed and evaluated by his teacher and other specialized personnel who work in the center. Tentative educational programs are outlined and implemented, with evaluation becoming an ongoing process.

Communication with the local school system aids in the integration back into the public school upon the consent of all parties concerned with the child's welfare. In most instances, the child is retained in the center's program for three to six months, depending on the severity of his educational problem. For some children, the process becomes more involved and thus takes much longer.

The special education classrooms designed for the diagnostic/evaluation center are often used as demonstration classrooms for teachers and students who are in training for working with handicapped youngsters. University personnel may be based in such centers to coordinate both the teaching and the learning activities of teachers and students.

Since this type of program takes the child out of his local school, it is not being utilized as much now as it has been in the past, except with some of the more severe learning problems. The problem of transportation has also been a factor in maintaining such a program on an equal educational opportunity basis. The current thinking in the field is that it is better for the child to remain within the local school to receive special services if at all possible.

Magnet Centers

Special day schools which cater to specific disabilities are often referred to as magnet centers. By definition, such centers are restrictive, yet for some handicapped children, this is the least restrictive environment in which they can function. Most of these centers serve only one handicapping condition, such as the blind. Incorporated in such centers are job training facilities and sheltered workshops. Some of these workshops are used to train severely retarded individuals for jobs within the community. Others serve strictly as employment centers for the handicapped.

New York City has recently opened a facility which is specifically for the multiply handicapped. It accepts only children who have at least two major handicapping conditions. The unique aspect of this program is the fact that Hunter College has their Institute of Health Sciences located in the same building. The multiply handicapped youngsters go to the Institute for diagnosis, physical therapy, and rehabilitation services. In turn, the Institute uses the center's special education classes for in-service training purposes. This interdisciplinary cooperation has proven to be highly successful for both groups of individuals.

Unfortunately, the process of integrating the children back into the public schools has been hampered by the lack of appropriate facilities. The public schools are currently working toward a cooperative venture which will provide adequate educational services for children who have two or more handicapping conditions.

A Prime Example

The direction of education has changed drastically in Texas during the past several years as a result of Plan A, a new concept of comprehensive special education. Plan A calls for the total integration of all handicapped youngsters throughout the state of Texas by 1976.

Plan A had its beginnings in 1968 when the State Board of Education conducted a statewide survey. The survey revealed some rather alarming facts concerning the education of handicapped children in Texas. It was discovered that fewer than 50 percent of all identified handicapped children were being served through appropriate educational services. Of all the children who were receiving special education services, approximately 50 percent were residing in seven counties. More than forty of the 254 counties within the state were providing no special education services to handicapped children.

A further study of the special education classes which were in progress revealed that the children were being stigmatized by the labels being used to describe their handicapping conditions. Also, a high percentage of the children enrolled in these classes were from minority groups. It was felt that such problems were not unique to Texas, since previous studies had shown that negative labels often cause low learning results through the self-fulfilling prophecy. Minority children in other states were also being labeled as retarded and were dropping out of school because the educational programs were not meeting their individual learning needs.

The comprehensive survey and study conducted by the State Board of Education resulted in the development of Senate Bill 230, which was passed unanimously by both the Senate and the House of Representatives in 1969. Immediately following the Governor's signing of the bill, the Texas Education Agency developed the preliminary design for Plan A.

Of the seventeen major recommendations made regarding Plan A, three were more significant than the others in respect to equal educational opportunities for the handicapped. First, it was recommended that labeling and categorization of children be discontinued. This meant that any labels which described a child's handicapping condition, i.e. mentally retarded, were to be eliminated from any descriptions made of the child.

Second, it was recommended that the emphasis be shifted from the handicapping condition of the child to the educational need of each child. The discontinuation of the use of labels was emphasized, as it had been in the first recommendation. It was suggested that special importance be placed not on labels, but on the individual needs of each child within the school system.

The third important recommendation called for the shift from self-contained special classes to mainstream or regular education facilities. It was suggested that every handicapped child should be provided with the regular school program whenever possible. Modifications of the regular programs and additional support should be implemented when necessary.

During the 1970-71 school year, five school systems were selected to participate in the pilot testing phase of Plan A. By the following school year, 1971-72, twenty-four more school systems were added to the program. By the 1972-73 school year, the program was expanded to reach seventy thousand handicapped school-aged children in Texas. Each year additional school systems will have been added to the program until all handicapped children in the state will be involved in a Plan A school system. The anticipated date for completion of this total involvement is the 1976-77 school year.

Through Plan A, several important additions have been

made to the overall concept of special services to the handicapped in Texas. Prior to Plan A, services were provided for children ages six through twenty-one. Through Plan A, a commitment has been made to provide comprehensive services to all exceptional children ages three through twenty-one.

Prior to Plan A, funding was allotted according to the number of handicapped children who had been identified. Through Plan A, funding is now allotted according to average daily attendance (ADA). For each three thousand children in ADA, the school district is allowed twenty professional instructional units, seven teacher aides, and three professional supportive personnel units. Professional supportive personnel include supervisors, educational diagnosticians, and visiting teachers. Prior to Plan A, such supportive staff positions were not available.

Funds have also been made available for evaluation purposes, consultant services, and special materials. Provisions have been made for districts to contract for additional or different services than those being provided. Specialists and supplementary services are now provided for all regular classroom teachers.

While these educational changes are being implemented, Plan A classes are being examined and evaluated by Project PRIME (Programmed Re-entry Into Mainstream Education). Project PRIME is the largest single study ever undertaken in the field of special education. It is anticipated that the findings from this project will give policy makers across the nation firm data on how handicapped children can benefit most from integration into the regular classroom. Other anticipated outcomes are the identification of strategies and climates in administration and teaching which are necessary for the accomplishment of the final goals.

Some of the primary issues being investigated by Project PRIME are those which special educators have been concerned with for the past several decades. Included in these issues are concerns related to (a) the needs of the community, (b) the most valuable educational resources within the school system, (c) which conditions are the most positive toward the successful integration of handicapped children into the regular classrooms, (d) what difference teachers make, and (e) the actual difference between handicapped and nonhandicapped children who are enrolled in regular programs.

Project PRIME is a cooperative venture of the United States Office of Education's Bureau of Education for the Handicapped, the Texas Education Agency, local school districts, and institutions of higher education. Information is currently being tabulated regarding teacher education programs. All preliminary findings from Project PRIME indicate that its results, combined with the dynamic concept of comprehensive education for the handicapped as outlined in Plan A, will have an impact on special education programs and policies throughout the United States.

REFERENCES

1. Beery, Keith: Mainstreaming: a problem and an opportunity for general education. *Focus Except Child,* 6:1-7, 1974.
2. Beery, Keith: *Models for Mainstreaming.* San Rafael, Dimensions, 1972.
3. Blatt, Burton: *Souls in Extremis.* Boston, Allyn, 1973.
4. Birch, Jack: *Mainstreaming: Educable Mentally Retarded Children in Regular Classes.* Minneapolis, U of Minnesota, 1974.
5. Brown, Lou, and York, Robert: Developing programs for severely handicapped students: teacher training and classroom instruction. *Focus Except Child,* 6:1-8, 1974.
6. Chaffin, Jerry D.: Will the real 'mainstreaming' program please stand up! (or ... should Dunn have done it?). *Focus Except Child,* 6:1-18, 1974.
7. Christopolos, Florence: Keeping exceptional children in regular classes. *Except Child,* 39:569-572, 1973.
8. Clark, Kenneth B.: Clash of cultures in the classroom. Address given to the Social Science Institute of Coppin State Teachers College, Baltimore, March 15, 1963.
9. DeGenaro, Jennie: Informal diagnostic procedures: what can I do before the psychometrist arrives? *J Learn Disabil,* 8:24-30, 1975.
10. Deno, Evelyn: Special education as developmental capital. *Except Child,* 37:229-37, 1970.
11. Dunn, Lloyd M.: Special education for the mildly retarded — is much of it justifiable? *Except Child,* 34:5-22, 1968.
12. Forness, Steven R.: Implications of recent trends in educational labeling. *J Learn Disabil,* 8:445-449, 1974.
13. Glenn, Hugh: The myth of the label 'learning disabled child.' *Edu*

Digest, 40:27-29, 1975.

14. Grosnick, Judith K.: Integration of exceptional children in regular classes: research and procedure. *Focus Except Child,* 3:1-11, 1971.

15. Hallenbeck, Phyllis: Remediating with comic strips. *J Learn Disabil,* 9:22-26, 1976.

16. Hammill, Donald, and Weiderholt, J. Lee: *The Resource Room: Rationale and Implementation.* Philadelphia, Buttonwood Farms, 1972.

17. Holt, John: *How Children Learn.* New York, Pitman, 1967.

18. Johnson, G. Orville: Special education for the mentally retarded — a paradox. *Except Child,* 29:62-69, 1962.

19. Kaufman, Martin J., Gottlieb, Jay, Agard, Judith A., and Kukic, Maurine B.: Mainstreaming: toward an explication of the construct. Washington, USOE/BEH, 1975.

20. Kaufman, Martin J., Semmel, Melvyn I., and Agard, Judith A.: *Project PRIME.* Washington, USOE/BEH, 1973.

21. Kolstoe, Oliver P.: Programs for the mildly retarded: a reply to the critics. *Except Child,* 39:51-56, 1972.

22. Landreth, Gary L., Jacquet, Willard S., and Allen, Louise: *J Learn Disabil,* 1:24-29, 1968.

23. Lerner, Janet W.: *Children with Learning Disabilities,* 2nd ed. Boston, HM, 1976.

24. Lewis, Alan: A resource room program for ld pupils. *Academic Therapy,* 10:93-100, 1974.

25. Lord, Francis E.: Categories and mainstreaming in special education: perspectives and critique. In Kirk, Samuel A., and Lord, Francis E. (Eds.): *Exceptional Children: Educational Resources and Perspectives.* Boston, HM, 1974, pp. 419-424.

26. Lord, Francis E.: The open classroom and individualization of instruction — reinforcing practices. In Kirk, Samuel A., and Lord, Francis E. (Eds): *Exceptional Children: Educational Resources and Perspectives.* Boston, HM, 1974, pp. 466-471.

27. MacMillan, Donald L.: Special education for the retarded: servant or savant? In Jones, Reginald L. (Ed.): *Problems and Issues in the Education of Exceptional Children.* Boston, HM, 1971, pp. 400-417.

28. Molloy, Larry: *One Out of Ten: School Planning for the Handicapped.* New York, Educ Facil Labs, 1974.

29. Quay, Herbert C.: The facets of educational exceptionality: a conceptual framework for assessment, grouping, and instruction. *Except Child,* 35:25-32, 1968.

30. Reger, Roger, and Koppmann, Marion: The child oriented resource room program. *Except Child,* 37:460-462, 1971.

31. Reynolds, Maynard C.: A framework for considering some issues in special education. *Except Child,* 28:367-370, 1962.

32. Reynolds, Maynard C.: Reflections on a set of innovations. In Deno, Evelyn N. (Ed.): *Instructional Alternatives for Exceptional Children.*

Reston, Coun Exc Child, 1973, pp. 179-186.
33. Reynolds, Maynard C., and Balow, Bruce: Categories and variables in special education. In Kirk, Samuel A., and Lord, Francis E. (Eds.): *Exceptional Children: Educational Resources and Perspectives.* Boston, HM, 1974, pp. 425-439.
34. Rodriguez, Joseph, and Lombardi, Thomas P.: Legal implications of parental prerogatives for special class placements of the me. *Ment Retard, 11*:29-31, 1973.
35. Rosenthall, Robert, and Jacobson, Lenore: *Pygmalion in the Classroom.* New York, HR&W, 1968.
36 Rosenthall, Robert, and Jacobson, Lenore: Teachers expectancies: determiners of pupil's IQ gains. *Psychol Reports, 19*:115-118, 1966.
37. Sheldon, Jan, and Sherman, James A.: The right to education for the retarded. *J Educ, 156*:25-48, 1974.
38. Taylor, George R.: Special education at the crossroads. *Ment Retard, 11*:30-33, 1973.
39. Yates, James R.: Model for preparing regular classroom teachers for 'mainstreaming.' *Except Child, 39*:471, 1973.

Chapter 5

BUT WHAT ABOUT LEARNING DISABLED CHILDREN? ... A PERSONAL GLIMPSE

THE controversy over learning disabilities has grown during the past decade. Each group of persons involved with learning disabled children has strictly delineated their own set of terminology, diagnostic proposals, and remedial procedures.

Despite the controversy involved with this area of special education, many improvements have been made concerning the educational services being provided for youngsters who have learning problems in the regular classroom. Teachers everywhere are receiving better training in the areas of child development, learning theory, and classroom management. Still, learning problems exist in certain instances which are not totally the fault of the child or his teacher.

When the school system proves to be inflexible in allowing teachers to use a variety of teaching approaches, or when the teacher herself shows such characteristics, the focus usually switches to the child and it becomes *his* learning problem. Children who are caught up in this type of controversy may be labeled incorrectly *and* unfairly. Their parents have little to say concerning the matter. Caught up in this bind, the child and his parents soon find themselves wondering where they have failed. This type of dilemma may cause further problems within the structure of the family unit.

The parents, wanting the best for their child, follow the advice of the specialists who are involved in the educational process of their child. They are often willing to try almost anything in order to satisfy their own needs to succeed with their own child.

The child, unable to experience success in the classroom,

labels himself as a failure early in his academic career. He eventually reaches a point where he is either unwilling or unable to try any longer because of his repeated failures. His self-concept slowly deteriorates, and he begins to think of himself as hopeless where academics are concerned.

The teacher, confronted with this type of child along with twenty-five or thirty other youngsters in the classroom, also feels the emptiness associated with failure. She is only one person, and she cannot possibly be all things to all people, especially when there are so many diverse personalities for her to deal with in the classroom. Her training and common sense tell her that *something* ought to be done to help this child, but her resources may be quite limited. She may have no special teacher within the school to help her learn how to deal with those children who are different from the norm, so she may be left to her own resources for educational development and implementation. Not all teachers are endowed with either the time or the expertise to cope with the variety of learning problems which may arise within the regular classroom.

It is difficult to explain to others how all of these factors may affect an individual family. The interrelationships between the child, his parents, his teacher, and the school system often determine the outcome of the child's future. His present life is also deeply affected by these circumstances.

The following series of letters has been condensed from actual correspondence which took place during a two year period. Names and places have been changed, but the contents are factual. The parents' reactions and feelings have been used to convey some of the frustrations encountered by parents who have children with learning problems. It is hoped that the reader will take into account the fact that the child discussed in these letters is a unique individual who is his own person. It is also hoped that the reader will recognize that portions of this child may exist in many other children who also deserve to be considered as unique individuals who are trying to live up to the overall expectations which have been set by their parents, their teachers, and themselves.

Letters to a Friend

October, 1973

Dear Bev,

Well, we had good old school conferences this week, and the teacher hit me with Brad may have a learning disability. Well, at first I was really taken back. It seems Brad reads by sight not sound, and she said he could have "auto-bul" (misspelled and not sure what it is or what it means) problems.

Don't really understand it at all. But Brad will go two days a week to the learning disability teacher for a half hour. They don't feel he needs any testing, and this will be a short time thing.

So I guess it's not a big problem. His grades are good and most all of his papers are stars.

The teacher said if they teach him to read by sound now while he is just learning to read, it will be much easier.

Love,

Barb and Jim

November, 1973

Dear Barb and Jim,

I wish I could sit down right now and talk with you about your recent letter. My interpretation of your interpretation of your parent/teacher conference has me somewhat baffled. And, since we can't sit down and chat over a cup of coffee, I am going to write to you, as a friend, and as a professional with a graduate degree in learning disabilities.

Knowing Brad's development as I do, I find it difficult to believe that all of a sudden he has a learning disability. I am more inclined to think that there may be a problem in the way he conforms to the school situation. He is primarily a visual learner who is being taught to conform to an auditory (phonic) approach to reading. Since he hasn't been able to make the adjustment to using his auditory channel more readily, he has been labeled as having a learning disability.

When a youngster has difficulty in learning, everyone is inclined to focus in on the child rather than the teacher or the school system. They forget that it may be the teacher who is using the wrong approach with the child, rather than the child being unable to learn. As for Brad's being a visual learner ... what is so wrong about that? He hasn't neglected using his auditory channel for learning, as can be evidenced by his advanced verbal abilities and the absence of any defective speech patterns.

Being primarily a visual learner becomes a handicap only when the method of teaching is so narrow that it calls on only the auditory channel for learning. Contrary to popular belief, there is *no one* best method for teaching reading. The learner himself should be the one who determines which learning method is best for him, not a textbook committee who must purchase the books nearly one year in advance of their actual use.

Again, I want to get back to the label this teacher has placed on Brad. I question professional ethics in that the school is unwilling to even test Brad at this time. It is bad enough to stick a label on a kid after administering a battery of standardized tests, but to do so without the benefit of any test results is a disgrace to the field of education.

Although I have never met his teacher, I can guess that she is fairly frustrated by the challenge of teaching a classroom of eager first graders their first real academics. In this, I empathize with her. With access to a special teacher who will help youngsters learn, I am sure she feels that this is the best approach for working with a bright little character like Brad. It is not easy to individualize to meet each child's particular learning needs, and if the majority of her students are learning through a phonic approach to reading, it is only natural for her to single out the others as having learning problems. But I still question just who it is who has the problem!

Brad is a bright little guy who does not readily conform to the regimented routine set up in the normal public school system. He is inquisitive, alert, sensitive, and mature for his age in many respects. You know this much better than I do. How else could he have entertained himself for three days with only a few toy cars, some string, and a shoe box when you visited us in Atlanta? Why, we hardly knew that he was there! He wasn't withdrawn into his own little world, he just enjoyed making up new games with those few toys. I think it was a challenge for him to see how many games he could invent.

And when we took him to Six Flags Over Georgia, he was so much fun! He was barely four years old at the time, yet if he had been seven years old I would have been amazed at his exceptionally good behavior. If he hadn't shown up for meals, I may have forgotten that he was there! These sort of experiences with Brad hardly indicate a youngster with a learning disability who characteristically has a short attention span, is clumsy, is restless, and is impulsive.

The best way for you to help Brad now is to go along with what the school suggests. As his teacher indicated, this will be a short term thing. He will probably have very little difficulty learning phonics, and everyone will be able to pat themselves on the back for doing such an excellent job of "remediation." Next year he will fit right in with the other second graders and no one will remember that he used to be primarily a sight reader.

Love,

Bev

December, 1973

Dear Barb and Jim,

Last week I had a meeting with several people from the State Department of Public Instruction. The State Assistant Superintendent was there and he asked me to put into writing some of the thoughts I had just shared with him concerning learning disabilities. Our program is just getting started, and there is a lot of controversy going on right now concerning terminology and remedial procedures. I thought you might like a copy of what I just sent to him, although it is really geared more for the classroom teacher than for parents. At best, it is fairly vague about specific remedial procedures because these would take a book to describe but it may help clarify some points for you about learning disabilities in general.

Love,

Bev

Some Personal Thoughts Regarding Learning Disabilities

While driving back from our meeting last Wednesday, I began trying to formulate my ideas concerning the information you had requested. I had made all sorts of notes and was trying to make some sort of sense out of them. My mind began to wander back to my final internship for my graduate degree in learning disabilities, and I could not help but remember the turning point of that delightful quarter's experience in a classroom with six, seven, and eight year old children with learning disabilities.

I started the quarter off with a bang by trying to follow in my supervising teacher's footsteps. My background had been in speech therapy, and I guess I was trying to impress Mrs. Jones. Whatever she did with the children, I did twice as much . . . but of the very same thing!

After nearly three weeks of this I just threw up my hands in despair at the way the children were performing. Luckily, they had not regressed, but on the other hand, their progress was not anything to brag about. I was discussing this with my husband one night, and made the comment that these kids just could not learn, and there was no hope for any of them. His reply to me was, "What are you doing wrong?" His statement hit me like a bolt of lightning. I thought the kids were at fault for not responding to my lesson plans, but it was me who was not responding to their needs. I had been treating them like normal first graders instead of realizing that although they could not read very well, most of them had Verbal IQ's on the WISC of 130 and above. This point really hit home the day I mentioned the spots on a picture of a jaguar and six year old Michael corrected me with, "Mrs. Dexter, the correct terminology is rosettes."

Since these children had already been diagnosed as having learning disabilities through a diagnostic team evaluation, part of my problem was solved for me when it came to structuring for individual needs. Unfortunately, few children with learning disabilities receive such thorough diagnostic evaluations and follow-ups. Therefore, it is up to us as educators to become familiar with the characteristics of a child with learning disabilities.

There are many terms currently used to describe this type of child, including minimal brain dysfunction, brain-injured, and dyslexic. The Association for Children with Learning Disabilities defines the child as having normal or above average intelligence with learning problems of a perceptual, conceptual, or coordinative nature. The President's Advisory Committee on Learning Disabilities states that the learning disabilities may not be due to malnutrition, deprivation, emotional disturbance, or severe cerebral damage. These are working definitions, but what about the practical translation?

The learning disabled child is one who appears to be blind at times, yet his eyes are perfectly normal in their structure. He may appear to be deaf or retarded, but he is neither of these either. His intake of information gets muddled and this affects his output. It all gets mixed up once it enters his brain and he has difficulty sorting things out and putting them in the proper perspective.

How do you recognize such a child? Look around the classroom for one or more of these ten most visible signs:

1. *Hyperactivity*: While the rest of the kids are walking down the hall in an orderly manner, he is jumping, hopping, or skipping.

2. *Perceptual-Motor Impairments/Eye-Hand Coordination*: If the child is a girl, you just know she will never make it as a teenager. The first time she puts on that magenta lipstick, it will probably end up on her forehead or even on her ear.

3. *Emotional Lability*: The child overreacts to new situa-

tions and any changes in routine procedures. If the gym period is changed at the last minute, he may cry or throw a temper tantrum, although the rest of the children calmly accept the change.

4. *General Coordination Deficits*: The child stays away from most sports and active games, especially when competition is involved. He may act the part of the clown when he is involved in such activities because he knows that he must look like one.

5. *Disorders of Attention*: While you are working with the class on a particularly motivating activity, he suddenly gets up to look out the window or sharpen his pencil. He cannot stick to a task for any length of time.

6. *Impulsiveness*: He cannot pass another child without hitting, pinching, or kicking. You turn your back for one minute and he has gotten into at least two fights, both of which he claims are not his fault.

7. *Disorders of Memory or Thinking*: He forgets what you have taught him from one day to the next or from one moment to the next. He does not seem to retain anything that he seemingly has learned in the classroom.

8. *Unable to Conceptualize or Organize Thinking*: The child is unable to coordinate his thoughts or things that he should know. Deductive reasoning is beyond him.

9. *Specific Learning Disability*: The child is academically two years behind his projected abilities in the academic areas of reading, writing, spelling, and arithmetic.

10. *Disorders of Speech and Hearing*: Usually, this presents itself in an articulation problem. The child may reverse words, sounds, and/or syllables in his connected speech.

Have you ever had a child who nodded his head when you asked him if he understood the directions, yet he failed to follow them on the given task? Or one who eagerly raised his hand to answer a question, but forgot both the question *and* the answer when you called on him? Better yet, a child who could spell a word but could not read it in his text? The child with a severe learning disability suffers from a malfunction of the input (seeing, hearing) or output (speaking, writing) channels of learning or both, and the inner processes involved in the functioning of the brain.

Basically, there are five major categories of learning disabilities as diagnosed on the original Illinois Test of Psycholinguistic Abilities or the ITPA. The first is the *Auditory Learner*. Here there are problems in the visual-motor channels. The child reverses "p" and "q," "u" and "n," etc. past the chronological age of seven or eight. He often has mixed laterality, being left handed and right footed. He trips over his own feet, bumps into things, seems to fall off a chair for no apparent reason. He may be able to do well in verbally answering test questions, but fails on written exams. Handwriting and other fine motor activities such as drawing and cutting are unusually poor for his age. He does poorly on group IQ tests because they are usually in written form. He gets lost easily, and often cannot tell time.

Some techniques you might use with such a child include a phonetic approach to reading using flash cards and auditory clues. Tape lessons whenever possible and let the child answer questions on the tape. Show the child how to use line markers for reading to help him focus in on only the word(s) he is to attend to.

The *Visual Learner* has problems in the auditory-vocal channel, and thus he relies on his vision for clues to learning. An articulation problem may be present, and he may confuse sounds or syllables of words such as saying "pasghetti" for spaghetti. Even with small words he has difficulty in sequencing, and thus he often responds in one word sentences. He has great difficulty with rote memory such as the alphabet and number combinations. He often seems to be less intelligent than his IQ score indicates.

Since he is a visual learner, he often watches the speaker's face for clues to the meaning of what is said. He learns better if you show him how to do something rather than tell him. Therefore, he needs all the visual aid possible during the initial stages of remediation. The look-say method of teaching reading works best, and he does well with sight words on flash cards. His auditory channel is weak, so intensive work is needed in the area of auditory discrimination. He may need to start out at a level where he identifies the difference between a horn and a bell, with a gradual progression toward identifying different horns and bells. He also needs work in sound blending (C-A-T) to learn the sequencing of sounds. This may be done through the use of the Language Master or the Audio Flash machines.

A *Decoding Disability* can be either auditory or visual. When the problem is *Auditory,* he cannot translate what is said to him. He hears, but it literally goes in one ear and out the other. Short sentences with only one central idea should be used with him. Questions should be short and to the point. Gestures should be used to give added clues to the context of what you are saying. Visual aids of all types should be used to support auditory materials that are presented to him.

When the decoding problem is *Visual,* the child shows little interest in picture books. He is unable to form a story from what he sees in the pictures. Here again the phonic reading method works best. He also needs plenty of opportunity to talk and to express himself. Comprehension should be checked in several different ways since it is difficult to know for sure just how much he understands. Tapes, records, and other auditory materials should be used in conjunction with visual aids to help this child.

The child with *Poor Association* does not relate what he sees and hears with what he has previously seen or heard. He raises his hand frequently, but often gives an unrelated answer. When given directions, he may start to follow them, then stop as if to contemplate his work, then begin doing something entirely different.

One-concept instructions with plenty of opportunity for response are necessary for this child. Short responses should be accepted initially, with a gradual increase in the demand for longer answers. Work on his ability to find similarities among shapes, colors, animals, and objects he sees every day. Sorting by similarities or differences is also good. Buttons, poker chips, and steel washers may be used for this activity. Tell him stories with inconsistencies and help him to recognize them. As progress increases, so should the level of difficulty in the task you give him. He can help at home by sorting the laundry, the silverware, or even the groceries (what goes in the cabinet, what goes in the refrigerator etc.)

The child with an *Encoding Disability* has trouble relating in words something he has seen or heard and knows quite well. If this is *Vocal*, he either talks very little or else he talks a lot, yet he actually *says* very little. He needs to work on complete sentences, such as through the use of various language development kits which are available commercially.

When the problem is *Motoric*, handwriting and drawing are poor. You cannot tell if he knows the answer or not, because you cannot read what he has written! He usually has trouble with imitative games like Follow the Leader, and Simon Says is a complete disaster for him.

By tracing letters and pictures he can learn the fine motor control necessary for handwriting and drawing. Work on having him imitate simple movement. Simple finger plays and charades are good, providing they are on his level of competency. Failure with these activities should be avoided at all costs.

After reading over what I have written, you probably found yourself thinking that this type of child resembles (a) the slow learner, (b) the unmotivated child, (c) the emotionally disturbed child, (d) the culturally deprived child, (e) the mentally retarded child, or (f) the just plain spoiled brat. This is because a child who has a specific learning disability may *also* have additional problems. But you must approach them differently. The lack of motivation disappears when the proper stimulus is found, and learning becomes normal. Psychiatry and special education have methods for helping the emotionally disturbed child. The culturally deprived child often responds to enrichment and follow-through programs if the intervention is made early enough. The spoiled brat ... well, a pat on the back, just a little bit lower and a little bit harder often helps!

Even the mentally retarded and slow learner can be helped to maximize their learning potentials with the proper teaching methods. But, the child with a severe learning disability *must* be approached on the basis of his individual learning patterns.

January, 1974

Dear Bev,

Well, we got Brad's first report card this week. I am enclosing a copy of it along with the special education teacher's report. As you can see, the reading level is marked three. They use the Houghton Mifflin Readers and Level Three is in three parts. They just started *Dinosaurs*, which is the last of that level, then they go to *Rainbows* which is Level Four. They should start *Rainbows* before school is out. So far as I can tell, that would be average.

I understand the check marks under Reading, and this is what the special education teacher is helping him with. The Exercises Self Control check is for talking. He often comes home telling me, "The teacher got after me for talking again." I look for this to happen. He talks all of the time. But he has had darn good teachers with Jim and me!

We really weren't upset by his report card. We told him we were pleased and hoped on the next one he would do just as well. And we hoped he would listen to the teacher a little better. I just didn't have the heart to get on him about all the checks under Work Habits. After all, he's a boy in the first grade. I think boys have a case of worms until third or fourth grade. Maybe I am wrong, but it always seems to me that girls settle down to busy seat work much sooner. Boys seem to look around the room and think about the Matchbox® cars in their pockets and who or what they will play with at recess.

On the Learning Disabilities Progress Report ... I don't understand it. The last we heard, Brad was going to be going only two times a week for thirty minutes each time. I didn't know that he went every day. As you can see, I underlined some of the teacher's remarks on the development of his vocabulary. I really don't understand how he can be considered low in that area. If Brad were asked what happens when his finger is cut, he could give you a complete description of the entire circulatory system, and understand every word of it!

I did want to tell you that your letter regarding Brad was a good shot in the arm. Parents can really feel bad when a teacher drops a bomb like that on them. I think all parents feel they have let their child down. In some way, they feel they have done something wrong, like not giving their child everything he needed. Most parents pour their hearts and souls into a child and want everything in the world for that child. Bev, should I buy some audio-visual equipment and multi-media learning kits like they are using in school so we can help him at home?

Brad brought a book home last week to do a book report. Well, he read the book as soon as he got in the door, then I helped him with the report. He could read every word! He paused on the word *find*, but was able to sound it out. He was very proud that he could read the whole book. I wrote a note to his teacher and expressed hope that Brad would be able to do more of this type of work. I feel it would be a help to him, and he enjoyed it so much.

Love,

Barb and Jim

February, 1974

Dear Barb and Jim,

Thanks for the update on Brad's progress in school. I hope you can read more into his report card than I can! It sure didn't tell me much about a kid who is supposed to have a learning disability. A check under any area showing a weakness can mean so many things. Too bad the teacher's comments didn't indicate the manner or degree of weakness Brad has in these areas.

Let's look at all the areas where he *didn't* receive a check. Two major pluses are that he reads with comprehension and shows an interest in independent reading. Under Work Habits, Attitudes and Social Growth he had only four checks within the thirteen areas outlined. The remaining nine areas have no marks at all. Does this mean his progress is satisfactory in all of these areas? If so, I would say he has plenty to be proud of for a first grader. I do wish someone would burn this form and develop one you could read and understand! As it is now, it appears that the negative is stressed and the positive is ignored! How can the kids develop decent self-concepts under these conditions?

As for the comment by the special education teacher, indicating that Brad needs to respond to questions with shorter answers rather than with conversations, I would be interested in the content of these "conversations." He may be using the conversation to give himself more time to sort out the answer. Or, he may be bringing in relevant information concerning the answer. Usually the commercial teaching kits contain a Teacher's Manual which has specific responses recorded. If a child strays from these answers, the teacher may panic. She is looking for one answer: *the* answer. Any extraneous information will not allow her to complete the lesson in the allotted time period. Luckily, kids aren't built like little robots who spout forth only what is requested of them. Unfortunately, though, many teachers would prefer the robot type kid who goes along with the answers listed in her guide book.

Knowing Brad as I do, and considering his experiences and verbal skills, I have the feeling that he is making sure he gets his two cents worth in when the special education teacher calls on him. As she said, he is eager to learn and is enthusiastic about new learning experiences. This may cause him to get a little carried away at times and "tell it all." But since I haven't seen him under these particular circumstances, I can only make an educated guess about these "lengthy conversations."

Love,

Bev

April, 1974

Dear Barb and Jim,

I am so glad you called last night ... but the next time please try to remember the time zones when you are dialing your friends who live outside of your geographical area. Just kidding, of course. Call any time.

Actually, I am relieved to know that Brad is finally going to have some psychological testing done. After all, he has been in the special resource room for nearly a year, and I think it is about time they tried to find out what makes him tick. Of course, you have to realize that these standardized tests must be taken with a grain of salt. They are *not the* answer, nor are they to be sneered at. Hopefully, the tests Brad will have will try to get at the way he learns best and how he can be helped in the classroom situation.

I can appreciate your concern over the term *psychological.* What the school system means is that he will have tests related to the psychology (the how and the why or the why not) of learning, not necessarily tests related to his mental health or yours. There may be some questions for him which are related to how he gets along with his peers, his family, his teachers, etc. but these are used to find out more about Brad as a total human being.

Be prepared for at least two sessions with the school psychologist. In order for him to get to know Brad better and to establish rapport, he will need several hours alone with Brad. Also, many of these tests are quite lengthy and Brad may be fairly tired by the time he finishes all of them. I won't go into any long details about the tests because I don't know which tests will be used. Most likely, there will be a basic intelligence test, some achievement tests in the academic areas, and some specialized tests developed for detecting specific learning problems. Brad will probably come out and tell you that all he did was play some games. This technique is often used to make it interesting and motivating for the kids. It also helps the examiner look at the way the child approaches new learning tasks.

Jim, I appreciate your request for me to test Brad, but I am afraid that I would be too emotionally involved with him to do a fair evaluation at this point. You know how much I love him, and my letters to you concerning him have indicated my biased opinions about why he is having problems in school. Also, since the school system has a psychologist, they might look upon me as an intruder ... know what I mean? And if they discovered that we were also close friends, they would burn the test results! One code of ethics I strictly adhere to is to never evaluate children of close friends, except in the case of speech problems. There are just too many instances where the results have been devastating to everyone concerned. It just presents too many problems which cannot be seen on the surface.

Love,

Bev

May, 1974

Dear Bev,

Thanks for reassuring us about Brad's psychological testing. We have decided to go ahead with it, but we are discouraged because it will be late summer before the psychologist will have time to see Brad.

At least the school year is nearly over for *all* of us. This has been such a rough year, especially for Brad. He still seems to like school, but I can't help feeling sorry for him. I wonder if I could hold up under the same sort of pressures he is exposed to every day? Let's hope we have a good summer!

Love,

Barb and Jim

July, 1974

Dear Barb and Jim,

Too bad you have to wait so long for the psychological testing. I guess I should have warned you that it might be several months before the psychologist would be able to see Brad. You are quite fortunate to be living in an area where they employ a school psychologist. There is such a need for qualified professionals who can not only administer the tests but who can also interpret the results and make suggestions to both the parents and the teachers.

I feel encouraged by the fact that at least you are able to have these services available to you within the local school district. When I look back over the past ten years as a professional educator, I cringe because of all the dumb mistakes I made either because I didn't have the proper training and/or there were no special services in the local school systems. Of course, during my first year as a speech therapist, *I* was *the* special service for the entire school system and I had just received my undergraduate degree! I am so glad that I taught for at least three years before going back to school to try to learn some of these special teaching skills, though. In fact, it was those three years that made me decide to go back for further training. There were many children who had severe learning problems then, but as a speech therapist, I had no opportunity to do much other than "explore" with the child and give him supportive help in any way that I could.

One particular child comes to mind while I write this. His name was Gary, and he had only a minor speech problem. But when I discovered that he was having difficulty in the classroom, I decided to enroll him in one of my smaller speech therapy groups. He was also receiving remedial reading, so I worked quite a bit on his auditory discrimination skills. The fact that he was bilingual really didn't strike me as being unusual because most of the children I worked with at the time spoke both English and Spanish. But it never dawned on me that Gary did not have a strong enough background in either language to allow him to function adequately in the English-speaking classroom.

For not being able to read, and thus being the brunt of many painful classroom experiences, Gary was usually a happy little guy. For the two years that I knew him, he remained in the third grade, much to the discontent of the third grade teachers. They were team teaching in the subject areas, so each of the three teachers had him every day for at least ninety minutes. As I recall, all they ever did about him was complain, first to the reading teacher and then to me. The reading teacher finally began seeing him individually two days a week, which seemed to thoroughly delight him.

It wasn't that he demanded individual attention, he merely wanted to learn how to read. He would often come in after school to reread what he had read in his session with her during the day. And if she wasn't there, he would pull up a chair and read to me. Honestly, if you could only have heard him struggle to read even those preprimer books, you would have cried for him. Yet, he *was* reading, I suppose, and to him that was all that mattered.

If success was determined only by the amount of honest effort, Gary would have been reading on grade level within a few months. Instead, he struggled for a whole year on the preprimer and primer books. Amazingly enough, he never seemed to become very discouraged. He always had a genuine smile on his face. You would never suspect the frustration that he suffered almost constantly as he sat in his classroom unable to complete any of his assignments because he could not read. Naturally, he took home a report card full of failing grades.

At the end of my second year with Gary, I realized that he was still showing very little progress in reading. He was gradually becoming aware of the same thing. I knew that I would be leaving the school system at the end of the summer to attend graduate school. When I told Gary that I would be leaving and would not be back, he merely said, "If only I could be a frog." Of course, I had to ask him why he wished such a thing. "To walk on the lily pads," was all he said.

"To walk on the lily pads." Of course! Why hadn't I thought of that? If you can walk on the lily pads, you won't drown! And you can hop from one lily pad to another without worrying about sinking, no matter what! You could "live dangerously" yet still be safe if you were a frog. All because you could walk on the lily pads.

You could be your own "person" as a frog, leaping from one lily pad to another all day long. You could leap only on those pads that were a certain size, or you could leap from one size lily pad to another without ever giving it a second thought! Or, if you wanted to stay on one particular lily pad all of your life, you could do that, too. So long as there was enough food in the area to keep you alive, that is. But one thing would be for sure, as long as you could walk on the lily pads, you wouldn't have to worry about drowning.

In retrospect, I think Gary was trying to tell me that he felt like he was drowning. He was slipping deeper and deeper into the depths of the unknown. Above him he could see daylight and all of the wonderful plants and animals on the surface of the land. But just below him lay only darkness and the unknown.

He was afraid of what was going to happen to him in the future. During the past two years of speech therapy he had felt success; he had seen the daylight, the wonderful familiar objects. He *had* walked on the lily pads! Now summer was coming and I would be leaving. I had been one of the few friends he had ever had. He did not know what lay ahead of him. Neither did I. My only consolation was the fact that he had been an active and successful member of his speech therapy classes. He would have been dismissed the first year if I hadn't decided to take him individually to "help with oral reading."

Actually, we had used those sessions to build up Gary's confidence in himself. He knew where his weaknesses were, and I vaguely knew some teaching approaches that coincided with his general learning problems. I guess I helped Gary build up his self-image, but how I wish that I had had the training then that I have now! I honestly feel that with his desire to learn and my current knowledge of teaching we could have walked on those lily pads forever.

It has only been lately that I have been thinking back on our experiences together. If only Gary could have had some educational testing other than the yearly achievement tests given in school which he promptly failed every year. If only someone had shown me how to work more effectively with Gary. If! If! If!

The last I heard, which was shortly before I came back to the States, Gary's mother had decided to send him to Honduras to live with some relatives there. I don't imagine the move was easy for Gary. He was just beginning to conquer the English language and in a few weeks he would be attending a new school where everything would be taught in Spanish. I often wonder if he eventually became so frustrated that his delightful personality became completely obliterated with hatred.

I guess the real reason I am writing to you about a child you have never met is because I am concerned about the frustrations so many children have to face in their everyday lives. I often wonder how any child survives the rigors of growing up, especially when so much emphasis is placed on learning academics in the same way, at the same time, and on the same level as everyone else. The amount of pressure we exert on kids in the classroom is unbelievable. Thank goodness someone came along and said that adults could have a little more choice about their lives and they could pursue careers or whatever else they wanted to, within reason, of course. I wonder why the same opportunity, somewhat modified of course, is rarely available to a youngster in the classroom?

Love,

Bev

August, 1974

Dear Bev,

Well, Brad finally had his psychological tests. It took two 3 hour sessions, but Brad didn't seem to mind. In fact, he was quite positive about the whole thing.

We aren't too happy with the way the testing was handled, though. First of all, the psychologist put Brad in a large padded swivel chair for all of the testing. Brad thought that was really neat, just like Daddy's! Of course he took a few whirls in it. What eight year old boy wouldn't? But the psychologist said this indicated that he was hyperactive. He wants Brad on medication, but only on school days.

After all of the testing was finished, the psychologist asked Brad if he had any questions. Would you believe that Brad all but got a case history on the guy? As you might have expected, this turned up on the psychologist's report as "too verbal and too inquisitive."

Back to the medication. We are totally against it. The psychologist recommended a tranquilizer. Do you know anything about them? What do you think about drugs for children?

By the way, we found out later that this was the psychologist's last week with this job. I honestly feel that he didn't care very much about testing Brad because he knew that he was leaving.

Love,

Barb and Jim

September, 1974

Dear Barb and Jim,

Your last letter really concerned me. I can't believe that the psychologist recommended medication only on school days. To me, this indicates a problem with the school system, not with the child. As I said in a much earlier letter, they are doing their darndest to make Brad fit the system rather than make the system fit him. Why don't you make an appointment with your pediatrician and find out what he has to say about this. Medication should be prescribed by a medical doctor, not a school psychologist.

I had to chuckle when I read about Brad being placed in that padded swivel chair during the testing. I really can't imagine *anyone* holding still for three hours under those circumstances, breaks or no breaks. And I would loved to have seen the look on the psychologist's face when Brad gave *him* the third degree! The fact that these circumstances resulted in a negative report for Brad is not a laughing matter, though. It makes my head swim to think of the possible number of kids who receive similar psychological reports under similar circumstances. No wonder there is such a surge in the number of "learning disabled" kids nowadays!

Brad reminds me of a bright youngster I tested several years ago. One of the questions was, "A man may be a king, a woman may be a _____ ." James came back with "governor." Naturally, that answer was nowhere to be found in my testing manual. So, I repeated the question to make sure that he had understood me. Sure enough, he came back with the same answer, "governor."

I couldn't resist the temptation to ask James to explain his answer. Would you believe that he had heard on the morning news that since Governor Maddox was inelligible to run for another term of office, he was nominating his wife to run for the position in his place? Well, I thought James' answer made more sense than the ones listed in the manual, so I gave him credit for it. After all, what do kings and queens mean to a six year old who lives in Atlanta, Georgia? The fact that he could transfer the meaning of "king" and "queen" to his state's governing power meant that he was no dummy. In fact, his explanation of the whole procedure was quite informative. I think he understood it better than I did!

The point is that standardized tests must be taken with a grain of salt, as I explained in an earlier letter. The youngsters selected for the standardization are not always representative of the kids who will be exposed to the test at a later date. They (the test designers) try to make up for these differences, but I personally find it unrealistic to expect a child living in New York City to respond to a question in the same way as a child living in Sandy Mush, North Carolina, to respond.

The first child lives in an urban area, the second child lives in a rural, mountain area. Surely these youngsters cannot be expected to have had the same learning experiences or even the same opportunities for learning, no matter what the skill area is. This is why mere test scores mean very little to the educated eye. Instead, we need to see the complete test results so we can see exactly which questions were missed on which tests or subtests. Then we have a better idea of where to begin our teaching procedures with the individual child.

Unfortunately, this takes a lot of time and skill in interpreting test results. Very few classroom teachers have either one. They do not have the time because the *system* does not allow them any free time during working hours for such activities, and once the teacher is at home, she has personal needs there that must be met. As for skills in interpreting tests results, this comes from course work and experience. Only if a person wants to become a psychometrist or psychologist does he receive much training in this area. This, I feel, is a fault of the universities. They seem to be caught up in the same dilemma as the public schools. They force-feed the masses, and those who don't get through are failures because all the University can do is try. If a student does not meet the course requirements, *he*, not the University, is to blame. I personally cannot buy that, but it has become a fact of life for students of all ages.

Love,

Bev

October, 1974

Dear Bev,

We took Brad to our pediatrician last month. He is really a great guy. It seems he also feels that there is something wrong with the school system if they want Brad on medication only on school days. But he also feels that if we do as the school suggests, Brad may have an easier time of it this year merely because the teachers will react more positively toward him when they discover that we have followed their suggestions. We are against medication, but we want to do what is best for Brad. What do you think? We will begin the medication this week.

Love,

Barb and Jim

November, 1974

Dear Barb and Jim,

You asked what I thought about your pediatrician's recommendation concerning the medication. I think he is the kind of doctor I would like to have if I had a child. I especially liked his theory about how the teachers will react to Brad now that you have followed all of their suggestions. It is true that we live up to what is expected of us, and that if we expect something of others it will usually turn out just as we expected. As an example from my own experiences, I would like to tell you something that happened recently. Just don't breathe a word of this to Al.

He wasn't happy with the way that I was hanging up his

shirts after I ironed them. Honest! He said that it made the collars look funny, and when he put on a tie the collar got all messed up. Well, as you know, I really couldn't care less about shirt collars right now with trying to work full-time, finish my dissertation and keep up with all the household duties that a woman has. But I let him think that I was genuinely concerned.

He spent about fifteen minutes showing me how to "properly" hang his shirts. Then I did one just to show him that I had been paying attention. I passed the test, and he left me alone to finish the ironing. Now, if you think that I am going to spend fifteen minutes hanging up each shirt, you are crazy! Especially when they look the same to me after spending only a few seconds hanging them up. However, I would be the last one to tell Al that! As long as he thinks that I am hanging them up the way he showed me, he thinks his collars look better than they ever did before.

You see, he *expected* the collars to look better because he *expected* me to spend fifteen minutes on each shirt after I ironed it. Since he expected those results, those were the results he found. With Brad, if his teachers *expect* him to be calmer from the medication, they will most likely observe these results in the classroom. So follow your pediatrician's advice, and keep me posted.

Love,

Bev

December, 1974

Dear Bev,

Thanks for your letter. We promise not to breathe a word to Al about his shirt collars.

After we read your letter we got to thinking about what you had said. We think you are right about the expectation idea. Although we have not noticed any difference with Brad since he has been on the medication, his teachers seem to think that he is a new little boy. We talked it over with our pediatrician and we have decided to take Brad off the medication. He was so irritable the first three weeks on the medication that I didn't think I was going to survive. Once he leveled off, he didn't seem to rattle as much, but we still didn't notice enough difference in his overall behavior to make it worth the three weeks of torture we all endured.

Even Brad didn't like it. He would suddenly burst into tears over the littlest things, and we were helpless because nothing we did or said seemed to console him. The pediatrician said that this is to be expected. I wonder if they ever consider prescribing some sort of medication that acts as an antedote for parents while their children are going through this phase with the medication they are on?

Love,

Barb and Jim

January, 1975

Dear Barb and Jim,

Smart move! I can't wait to see how Brad's teachers react to him without the medication. Maybe your pediatrician can suggest some sort of medication for his teachers. Ha Ha!

We thoroughly enjoyed seeing all of you at the airport last week. Brad has really grown into quite a handsome young man. And the relationship he has with little Chris is a delight to behold.

After spending a few days with my cousin who is only two weeks younger than Brad, the few hours with Brad were a welcomed relief. Not that Ned is a bad kid, he's just *all boy* according to everyone who comes in contact with him. I sure would like Brad's teachers to try to handle Ned for a day or two! Then they would know what "hyperactive" really is!

Ned is like a wild Indian compared to Brad, yet there has never been a report from any of his teachers that would indicate a problem in school. I do know that his present teacher now has placed his desk up in the front of the room right next to hers, though. She appears to be doing an excellent job of meeting the kids' needs in the area of learning channels. She has also found a productive way for Ned to use up some of his energy.

Mom couldn't believe that Brad was the child I had been telling her about (I told her about our continuing correspondence regarding his "learning problems" and my theories about the basis of some of his problems). She thought Ned was at least a year younger than Brad! And she spent quite a bit of time around Ned during the period when they lived close to home, so she knows him pretty well. I wish you could have heard her compare the two boys on the flight back home! I told her it wasn't fair to compare them because they are two different little boys who should be compared only with themselves. Too bad that isn't true in reality. I even compared them in this letter!

I received some rather disturbing news in one of my Christmas cards from a friend I worked with several years ago. Do you remember the little boy I wrote to you about last year? The one who was bilingual and couldn't read, who wanted to walk on the lily pads like a frog. Gary was sent to Honduras to study, and remained there until the hurricane hit this past year. He is presumed dead. His body has not been found. You can't imagine the empty feeling I had when I read her letter. I realize that you can't expect to win them all, but poor Gary never really had a chance to spend much time walking on the lily pads he had dreamed about. I wonder how many Garys there are in this world?

Love,

Bev

February, 1975

Dear Bev,

We were so sorry to hear about little Gary. God has his reasons, I am sure.

Well, Brad has been off the medication for several months now and none of his teachers seem to have noticed. I guess you were right about their expectations. I thought you were, but now that I have experienced it through Brad it sort of scares me. What if this is true for other kids on medication? Could this be possible?

Love,

Barb and Jim

March, 1975

Dear Barb and Jim,

You really touched on a "dynamite" subject when you questioned the use of drugs and whether children who are on them really need them. Definitely, there are some youngsters who benefit from the use of specific drugs which act as tranquilizers for them. There are some youngsters who simply cannot control their impulses to be constantly moving. This movement, added to the distractibility it causes, makes it difficult for the child to learn. The medication is used to slow down or inhibit this movement so the child can attend to the task at hand. It helps him become more receptive to what is being taught because his attention is more easily focused on what the teacher is saying, what he is reading, etc. Thus he is not so easily distracted by activities going on around him that are not relevant to what he is supposed to be doing. Also, he is not being distracted by his own movements.

Other children benefit from medication because they are "uptight," just like some adults. The pressures are too much for them and they are unable to learn because of this tenseness. They are overanxious about everything. Although there aren't many youngsters who receive this type of diagnosis, the facts are there. Some of these same kids develop the same outward appearances as the kids I described in the first paragraph. They just cannot sit still.

When you consider the pace that many Americans keep, it is no wonder that their children are affected by it. Our society demands success. When you fail, *you* are a failure. Yet how can anyone be expected to succeed at everything? Is failing the same thing as being a failure? To me, a person may fail at a task, but that does not necessarily make him a failure. Do you see what I mean? I may fail in my attempts to make chicken gravy exactly the way Grandma does, but I don't consider myself a failure in the kitchen just because of this one example.

I used to be fairly strong in my beliefs toward the use of medication. But then I started hearing reports about the use of medication for every child who was labeled hyperactive. So how do you define hyperactive? To some people it means a child who fidgets in his seat. To others it means a child who all but bounces off the wall constantly. And I have worked with my share of those kids! My definition leans more toward the latter, a child who is in constant, overt, disruptive motion. He doesn't just fidget in his seat, he takes the whole chair with him!

There have been numerous articles published during the past few years that have raised the question, "Are we unnecessarily drugging our children?" Supporters of these articles use scare tactics when they argue against the use of drugs. Perhaps this is a good idea because at least they are drawing attention to the issue. As I have stated before, I think it all depends on the child *and* the situation.

In Brad's case, I really question the use of medication only on school days. If he is truly hyperactive, he is going to be hyperactive in *all* situations, not just the school situation. Of course, there is a possibility that Brad is affected by having thirty other youngsters in the classroom with him. The other children may be causing a distraction to Brad that may not be considered a distraction to other children. However, if this were really the case, the special education teacher would have noticed a distinct difference in his behavior in the classroom compared to his behavior in the resource room prior to the medication. Also, Brad's teachers would surely have noticed a change in his behavior by now. He was on the medication for two months and they all said that he was "a new little boy." Although they are not aware of it, he has been off the medication for two months now and they haven't seemed to notice. It will be interesting to observe their reactions when you tell them that he is going off the medication at Easter.

Love,

Bev

April, 1975

Dear Bev,

Right before the Easter holidays we told Brad's teachers that the pediatrician had recommended that we take him off the medication. They were quite concerned, to say the least. "And he has been doing so well all year with the help of the medication!" We told them we were going to try it just until the end of the year because we had already promised the pediatrician. You know, they (meaning everyone who has ever worked with or tested Brad) think nothing of tearing us parents apart in a situation like ours. Who are we supposed to believe? You know we want to do what is best for Brad, but we are being pulled in so many directions!

If we didn't have you to write to, we wouldn't have anyone to really talk to about it. We sure wish you lived closer to us. We realize now why you couldn't test Brad, but maybe you could at least talk to some of the "experts" and come to a decision that everyone could agree upon. We are so tired of this indecision! Do other parents go through this same type of frustration when their child is labeled "learning disabled"?

Love,

Barb and Jim

May, 1975

Dear Barb and Jim,

Have the fireworks started yet with demands for Brad to go back on the medication? On second thought, maybe I shouldn't even bring up the subject.

You asked in your last letter if other parents went through this same type of frustration. Unfortunately, yes. But the experiences are never exactly the same for any two sets of parents. Some parents refuse to believe that anything is wrong with their child, when in fact there is a serious learning disorder that is quite obvious even to the casual onlooker. Such parents will either ignore the consistent advice of the specialists, or they will go to the other extreme and go to every specialist they can find trying to find one who will tell them that their child is "normal." There are parents who refuse to believe it even when several specialists come up with the same diagnosis time and time again.

There are also parents who actually brag about their child having a learning disability because in some social circles it is the "in" thing to have such a child. Among this group are parents of children who are actually slow, lazy, or even retarded, but the "in" term is learning disabilities, and as such, it is a more "respectable" label.

Then there are parents like you two. Brad may have a problem, but it has been caused partially by the school system because they tried to fit the child to the curriculum rather than the curriculum to the child. You are willing to help in whatever way you can, but you are being torn in many directions by the conflicting reports on Brad.

No matter what category a parent falls under, the frustrations are there and they are for real. Unless a person has experienced this with his own child, he cannot fully appreciate or understand what you have been through for nearly two years. The Association for Children with Learning Disabilities (ACLD) is a national organization for parents and other persons interested in learning disabilities. I believe we talked about this group during one of our phone calls right after you were told that Brad was going to be seeing the special education teacher. Anyway, although all of the members are somehow involved with children who have learning disabilities, even these members cannot fully agree on a definition. Of course, there is the national definition which the Association advocates. But many of the local Associations do not fully agree with it. Many of them focus in only on reading problems, and only one type of reading problem, such as dyslexia. To me, this is a case for the remedial reading teacher, not the learning disabilities teacher. The learning disabilities teacher is usually looking for learning problems which are more in line with those stated in the definition given by the National Advisory Committee on Learning Disabilities (see my letter and article of December, 1973).

The definition is not that important unless it prevents the child from receiving the proper educational services. If the definition is so narrow that it will not take into consideration the total child and his learning style, then there should be some concern. But as long as the children are receiving appropriate services through the public schools, then why quibble about definitions and such?

Love,

Bev

June, 1975

Dear Bev,

I did want to tell you that the last six weeks of school the special education teacher asked if we would put Brad back on medication. Yet, on his report card, he had all Satisfactory Progress for the entire year. And on his last report card he had Commendable Progress in Reading and Mathematics.

I just don't get it. And you know how we feel about medication. So I took him to a specialist at the University. I had his tests from school, the special education teacher's reports, and our pediatrician's health report. Well, the man spent the grand total of ten minutes with us. He checked Brad's reflexes, had him read, asked him to stand on one foot, etc. Then he charged us $50 and said his diagnosis was Minimal Brain Dysfunction, which is so slight that there is no need for treatment ... but he does feel that medication would help Brad.

Brad reacted negatively to the suggestion that he go back on the medication. He still remembers how fretful it made him those first few weeks. Not only that, he is starting to give us lectures about how harmful drugs can be to his body! I guess he has gotten that from TV and all the publicity about the "hooked generation." I can understand his confusion over harmful drugs and helpful drugs, but it sure is difficult to explain all of this to a second grader.

At the end of the year we got a very nice note from his second grade teacher. She said she was very impressed by Brad's sensitivity toward others, his willingness to help others and to share with others. We felt this was very nice to hear since Brad is a first child and was the only child for so many years. Children can often become self-centered and won't share with others when they are the only one.

Love,

Barb and Jim

July, 1975

Dear Barb and Jim,

Here we go again with the medication! I almost wish the pediatrician had asked you not to tell the teachers anything about taking Brad off the medication. It's my theory that they wouldn't have said a thing about any changes in his behavior if you hadn't told them anything. After all, no one said anything until Brad had been off the medication for *six months*! And then it was only after you mentioned it to them that they realized any change.

I have the feeling that the specialist you visited at the University is a very rich person. He ought to be, at the rates he is charging for the little bit of work he is doing. And now we have a new label for Brad: Minimal Brain Dysfunction. Arg! That term is now obsolete in most professional circles because no one can define *minimal*. And, if there is no need for treatment, why is he suggesting drugs? That's a form of treatment, isn't it? It sounds to me like he read the records you brought for him and decided to go along with some of the things he saw written there. How in the world could anyone diagnose a child in only ten minutes?

I guess you have no other choice than to go along with the recommendations he made, though. I can't see taking Brad all over the place for diagnoses, especially when each "specialist" appears to be spending only a few minutes with him. Hopefully, the school system will let him "outgrow" this problem in another year or two. This often happens when the kids reach fourth or fifth grade.

Love,

Bev

September, 1975

Dear Bev,

After our visit to the specialist this summer, Brad started back on the medication. This fall he is going to the special education teacher for two hours every day. We also have a tutor for him to help him with phonics, blending skills, and long and short vowel sounds.

Think we have gone about as far as we can go with this. I don't want Brad to get the idea that he really has a big problem and feel bad about himself. He asked us if there was anything seriously wrong with him because of all the testing he has had. If we continued to have him tested, he might get the wrong idea and then we really would have a problem on our hands.

My sister-in-law works with a learning skills program in another state. She said that there Brad would not qualify for the special education teacher because he is not behind the other children in his class. I guess they have to be a year behind before the state will fund the teaching of such a child with the special resource teacher. So I guess we should just be thankful he can get the extra help he needs now so he won't fall behind.

Yesterday we discovered yet another factor that may be affecting Brad in school. We just realized that he has to deal with *five* different adults and their individual personalities *every day* that he is in school. Then he has to come home and cope with two other adult personalities. The kids change classrooms just like we did in high school. I would think that would be very confusing for a youngster. This year in the third grade they are doing the same thing. Thank goodness he likes all of his teachers!

Love,

Barb and Jim

November, 1975

Dear Bev,

Enclosed is a copy of last June's report card for Brad, his special education teacher's report, and a copy of his Stanford Achievement Test for this year. You will notice that he received Commendable Progress in both reading and math for the final grading period, and Satisfactory Progress in social studies, science, penmanship, art, music, and physical education.

Brad ended up going to the special education teacher for two hours every day last year. Mainly she worked on his auditory skills because this is where his weakness seemed to be when she tested him. He has been doing most of his skill work and workbook pages from his reading group downstairs with her because he seems to pay more attention to what he is doing when he is with her. She says that he knows the material, but she feels better about it when he does it downstairs with her.

This week during parent teacher conferences his teacher showed me Brad's results on the Stanford Achievement Test given in September. His highest scores were in Vocabulary and Listening Comprehension. And his highest overall score was in Auditory Skills. After reading the special education teacher's report and then looking at the Stanford Test results, I am a little confused. The special education teacher says that his biggest problem is in his auditory area, and that his vocabulary is lower than it should be. So why are these areas the highest on the Stanford Achievement Test? Also, his regular teacher said the test covered addition, subtraction, multiplication, and division, but the kids have learned only the first two math processes! He didn't always look at the signs or he would have done much better with that part of the test.

I also found out that the specialist from the University who evaluated Brad this summer sent a *full* report to the school, but all we ever received was a bill! One of the things that the special education teacher couldn't understand was that the specialist said that Brad had a visual perception problem. She said she had Brad do twenty sheets of this type of exercise and he made no errors. The visual thing is a new one to all of us.

Anyway, I am going to have that specialist send me a copy of his report. After all, it cost us $50 and he only spent ten minutes with us, including his testing time with Brad! I could only understand every third word he said, and then *I* was expected to explain all of this nonsense to Brad!

It is unreal how the school psychologist says one thing (that Brad is hyperactive), his special education teacher says another thing (that he has auditory perceptual problems), the specialist says yet another thing (minimal brain dysfunction with visual perceptual problems), and now the conflicting results on the Stanford Achievement Test! That test didn't tell me anything I didn't already know. I know Brad is an average student, and that is fine with me. I've always felt he had a large vocabulary. When he was three and four he could use a lot of big words correctly. But most important, he is well rounded. And a well rounded student can go far in this world.

He is a good boy. It's to the point that it's a little sickening to hear from his teachers, den mothers, and friends what a wonderful child we have. My biggest concern with all this messing around is that we just might ruin a nice little boy. Bev! Brad has so much going for him! He is very social, outgoing, kind, loving, well mannered, well behaved, and good looking. Plus he has many friends. To me, these things are more important than whether he is an "A" or "C" student in school.

Love,

Barb and Jim

December, 1975

Dear Barb and Jim,

To be quite honest with you, I don't know how to answer

your last letter concerning Brad and his "learning disability." I only know that I feel empathy for you as his parents, disgust for the field of education, and helplessness for me as a friend and a professional in the area of special education.

For the past two years you have shared with me your feelings and experiences with Brad once he became labeled "learning disabled." In your first letter, you said that the special education teacher found that he had an auditory perceptual problem, that testing would not be necessary because his problem was so minor, and that it would be a short term thing. She said his main problem was that he was a sight reader and the reading series used in the school was phonics oriented. Everyone felt that if Brad had help then, this would not turn into a major problem in the future. However, during that first year he "graduated" from two half hour sessions per week to one full hour every day in the special resource room. And still there was no testing done on Brad.

Then the teacher recommended that Brad be evaluated by the school psychologist. This took four months to arrange, which is to be expected when the request is made toward the end of the school year, I suppose. Anyway, the school psychologist had Brad sit in a padded swivel chair for the entire testing, which took a total of six hours. At least he had the decency to break this up into two sessions for your seven year old son! But that padded swivel chair! How Brad enjoyed whirling around and swinging his legs from that marvelous perch! Naturally, the psychologist labeled him "hyperactive" and recommended that he be put on medication, but only on school days!

Your trip to the pediatrician brought further doubt into your minds because he felt there was something wrong with the school system because they were recommending medication only on school days. Brad had not displayed anything other than normal distractability during his earlier school days, and now this was being blown up into "hyperactivity," all because of the psychologist's reaction to Brad playing in the padded swivel chair. As I recall, the psychologist also said that Brad was too inquisitive, which brought a chuckle from the pediatrician. Nonetheless, the pediatrician suggested that you follow the school's recommendations and he placed Brad on medication when school began in the fall.

Those first three weeks on the medication were very trying for all of you. Brad would burst into tears at the slightest provocation and then cry again because he was so sorry he had cried in the first place. He seemed to have no control over these emotions and was frustrated by this fact. Then he leveled off and the crying lessened, yet there was no real difference in his overall behavior. You mentioned that he "rattled" less, that he was not as talkative. But his teachers were convinced that he was "a new little boy" and that he was not "hyperactive" anymore.

You took Brad off the medication several months before school let out for the summer, but you didn't advertise the fact. Those last few months of school his grades improved and so did his behavior. He received Commendable Progress in his two major subject areas, reading and math, for the first time all year. Then the special education teacher found out that Brad was not taking the medication any longer and asked that he be placed back on it the next fall.

That summer you decided to have Brad evaluated by another person in the field of special education. You asked if I would fly up to visit you and then evaluate Brad, but I refused to do it because of professional ethics. Brad is close to me and my emotional involvement with him would prevent an objective evaluation of his true abilities. Besides, I felt the school system would not approve of me testing Brad and then turning in a report to them on plain typing paper. They wanted to see something from a clinic, hospital, or university. I had the training and the qualifications, but I was not working for any of these professional organizations at the time.

So you went to the university near you. The medical doctor who saw Brad tested his reflexes, had him read, looked at his school records, and then talked with you. And all of this took a grand total of ten minutes, but it still cost you $50! All you found out was that Brad now had a new label: Minimal Brain Dysfunction (MBD). And this term is now considered passé by many professionals in the field of education because no one can adequately define "minimal." Even the Food and Drug Administration does not recognize the diagnosis of MBD as a valid reason for administering the drug that Brad was on. The "specialist" said that the damage was so slight that there was no reason for treatment. Then he prescribed a specific drug. To me, that is a treatment.

In the fall, Brad entered third grade, doing his work on the same level as the other students, but attending the special resource program for *two* hours every day. His special education teacher said that he was capable of doing the assignments in the regular classroom, but that she felt better when he did them with her in the resource room. So he took all of his skill work and reading worksheets there to do with her.

Your sister-in-law had told you that in her state Brad would not qualify for the special resource program because he had never been behind in his academic work. You wrote to me to ask about this. Yes, in most states the child must be at least one or two years behind his classmates in order to receive special help. We both rationalized by saying that maybe it was a good thing that Brad was receiving so much help this early in life, before any "real" learning problems developed. We agreed that it was better to prevent the serious problem than to overlook the minor one.

Then you had your first parent conference of the school year last week. Everyone who has evaluated Brad during the past two years has come up with a different label for the poor kid. They have tried their darndest to place the blame on Brad for being a visual learner. Rather than try to revise the curriculum to meet his individual needs, the school system decided that since he does not fit the curriculum, he *must* have a learning problem. They refuse to believe that they could be doing anything wrong. After all, look at all the extra effort that is being expended to help Brad in the resource program!

But I still can't buy that. My personal experiences with Brad contradict all that has been said about him by the school system. He is bright, creative, alert, and no more hyperactive than the rest of the boys in this country who are eight years old. No, Brad does not fit into the definition of learning disabilities any more than he fits into that curriculum they have forced upon him during these past two years. He may have a learning problem, but I think there are some teaching and evaluation problems also involved in this particular instance. Didn't you tell me that last year there were five other boys in his class who went to see the special education teacher with Brad? That's over one fourth of the class being sent out of the room for special help every day since there are only twenty-two children in the class. Surely that indicates a problem in the classroom, not in the children.

But where do we go from here? For the past two years I have said that part of the problem was the teachers' approaches to Brad. The lack of substantial evidence indicating a learning disability proves this. A little disagreement concerning terminology might be expected in a true case of learning disabilities, but when the diagnoses are so drastically opposed to one another, such as a visual perception problem versus an auditory perception problem, I can't help but wonder what in the world is going on in the field of education.

Why are we so prone to slap a label on a kid before we even evaluate him? What school psychologist in his right mind would have a seven year old boy take a battery of tests while sitting in a padded swivel chair that only invites movement? Why are teachers so enthusiastic about a child's good behavior when they *think* the child is on medication? What right does anyone have to give a "diagnosis" after spending only ten minutes with the child? Where are the laws restricting the overcharging by "specialists" for services *not* rendered? Why are some special education teachers so insecure that they are afraid to let the children complete their class assignments in the classroom rather than in the resource room? And where are the teachers who can teach a child according to his individual learning needs rather than to the school's needs?

The professionals who have supposedly evaluated Brad have each gone their separate ways over the years. But Brad is still your child and you are still his parents. He is your twenty-four hour child, and you are his twenty-four hour parents. When are the professionals in the field of education going to realize this about *all* children and their parents? When are they going to realize the potential of the consequences with their incomplete diagnoses and evalution procedures with children like Brad? When are they going to stop all of this nonsense and get down to work on the education of children like Brad? After working with hundreds of children in three states plus a foreign country, I still don't have the answer to any of the questions I have just asked. I have been asking them for over ten years now without receiving any viable answers.

Maybe there are no answers to such questions. Maybe we are caught up in some sort of educational trend that will not allow us to find the appropriate answers. I do acknowledge the fact that there are children with learning problems. But I am more inclined to believe that these "problems" do not always result from disabilities within the child or his parents. Once we educators acknowledge the fact that many of these learning problems may be caused by our educational systems, we will be well on the road to recovery from a severe case of incorrect emphasis on the causes of learning problems which has become malignant over the past ten years.

Love,

Bev

REFERENCES

1. Arena, John I. (Ed.): *Meeting Total Needs of Learning Disabled Children: A Forward Look.* Pittsburgh, ACLD, 1971.
2. Bailey, Evalyn James: *Academic Activities for Adolescents with Learning Disabilities.* Evergreen, Colorado, Learning Pathways, 1975.
3. Frierson, Edward C., and Barbe, Walter B. (Eds.): *Educating Children with Learning Disabilities: Selected Readings.* New York, Appleton-Century-Crofts, 1967.
4. Gearheart, R. B.: *Learning Disabilities: Educational Strategies.* Saint Louis, Mosby, 1973.
5. Gross, Mortimer B., and Wilson, William C.: *Minimal Brain Dysfunction.* New York, Brunner/Mazel, 1974.
6. Hammill, Donald, and Wiederholt, J. Lee: *The Resource Room: Rationale and Implementation.* Philadelphia, Buttonwood Farms, 1971.

7. Johnson, Doris J., and Myklebust, Helmer R.: *Learning Disabilities: Educational Principles and Practices.* New York, Grune, 1967.
8. Johnson, G. Orville: *Education for the Slow Learners.* Englewood Cliffs, P-H, 1963.
9. Kephart, Newell C.: *The Slow Learner in the Classroom.* Columbus, Merrill, 1960.
10. Kirk, Samuel A., McCarthy, James J., and Kirk, Winifred D.: *The Illinois Test of Psycholinguistic Abilities,* revised ed. Urbana, U of Illinois Pr, 1968.
11. Kirk, Samuel A., and McCarthy, Jeanne McRae: *Learning Disabilities: Selected ACLD Papers.* Bostom, HM, 1975.
12. Lerner, Janet W.: *Children with Learning Disabilities: Theories, Diagnosis, Teaching Strategies,* 2nd ed. Boston, HM, 1971.
13. McCarthy, James J., and McCarthy, Joan F.: *Learning Disabilities.* Boston, Allyn, 1969.
14. Myers, Patricia I., and Hammill, Donald D.: *Methods for Learning Disorders.* New York, Wiley, 1969.
15. Reger, Roger, Schroeder, Wendy, and Uschold, Kathie: *Special Education: Children with Learning Problems.* New York, Oxford U Pr, 1968.
16. Sapir, Selma G., and Nitzburg, Ann C. (Eds.): *Children with Learning Problems: Readings in a Developmental-Interaction Approach.* New York, Brunner/Mazel, 1973.
17. Wallace, Gerald, and Kauffman, James M.: *Teaching Children with Learning Problems.* Columbus, Merrill, 1973.
18. Wallace, Gerald, and McLoughlin, James A.: *Learning Disabilities: Concepts and Characteristics.* Columbus, Merrill, 1975.

Chapter 6

HINTS FOR AUDITORY PERCEPTUAL LEARNING PROBLEMS . . . YES I HEAR YOU, BUT I DON'T UNDERSTAND YOU

FOUR major areas are covered under Hints for Auditory Perceptual Learning Problems. *Auditory Attention* problems are usually characterized by the child who does not appear to hear a thing the teacher says to him. As the saying goes, "Once you get his attention, you can teach him." Therefore, the major emphasis under this category is in the area of classroom management in relation to structuring the learning environment for success.

Auditory Comprehension refers to the ability of the child to understand what is heard through listening. The child's hearing may be perfectly normal, but he may be unable to comprehend spoken language or the meaning of auditory stimuli that are coming in to him through his listening channel.

Auditory Discrimination may involve gross discrimination problems where the child is unable to distinguish the difference between the sound of a large bass drum and the sound of a coin dropped on a glass surface. If he is unable to detect a difference between these two diverse sounds, he will most likely have difficulty in hearing the difference between speech sounds such as those emphasized in a phonic approach to reading.

Auditory Memory and Sequencing problems are found in the child who is unable to remember simple directions given to him orally. In remembering what is said to him, he usually must also be remembering the sequence in which it was said. This child becomes easily confused when all of his classroom assignments are given to him orally without any visual clues as

155

to their intended meaning. He may not complete simple tasks merely because he cannot remember the sequence of the tasks to be completed.

Before any conclusions are made concerning a child's possible auditory perceptual learning problems, a thorough screening for hearing impairment should be made by a qualified professional. Either the school nurse or the speech therapist should be consulted for the administration of specific screening and diagnostic tests of this nature.

Auditory Attention

Associated Classroom Behavior

1. Does not attend to verbal directions and/or comments.

Structuring the Learning Environment

1. View the length of attention as a level of skill development much the same as a level of skill development in the academic areas.
2. Determine the child's present length of attention and work on increasing it gradually. If the child cannot attend to a task for more than five minutes, then begin with five minute segments of the learning task.
3. Set aside specific times and places for specific learning tasks.
4. Never allow the child to terminate a task unless he becomes so frustrated that he cannot possibly benefit from its completion.
5. Make all tasks and instructions short, simple, and related to the completion of the task.
6. Be firm but gentle. Speak slowly, firmly, and clearly. Use a quiet, yet authoritative voice.
7. Provide appropriate and adequate reinforcer or reinforcing events.

OBJECTIVE

To positively modify attending behavior.

Suggested Teaching Techniques

1. Set the stage for acceptable responses to occur since positive consequences produce the most productive forms of attending and responding.
2. See that positive consequences, especially teacher attention and teacher approval, follow acceptable forms of behavior.
3. Avoid setting the stage where unacceptable behaviors are most likely to occur.
4. Avoid giving attention to unacceptable behavior.
5. Remove the child from a setting when his behavior is disruptive, destructive, or overtly aggressive, and place him in an isolated area for a short duration of time. Sometimes merely removing the child from the "action" to another area of the room will accomplish this goal.
6. If necessary, add tactile stimulation by placing the child bodily into the task, by placing a firm hand on his shoulder, or by steadying his hand to reassure him.

OBJECTIVE

To provide activities which require auditory attention.

Suggested Teaching Techniques

1. Alert the child as to when his attention is required by ringing a bell, tapping on the desk, saying a key word such as "listen", etc.
2. Play games such as "Simon Says" where the child is required to pay close attention to what is said.
3. Purposely make absurd statements that encourage the child to react. It may be necessary to act out the absurd statements such as, "I am going to take a drink of this book," to gain the attention of the very inattentive child.

Related Instructional Materials

An Empirical Basis for Change in Education (Science Research Associates, Inc.)
Behavior Modification: The Human Effort (Dimensions Publishing Company)
Changing Children's Behavior (Prentice-Hall, Inc.)
Child Management (Ann Arbor Publishers)
Help! These Kids Are Driving Me Crazy! (Research Press)
How to Use Contingency Contracting in the Classroom (Research Press)
Let's Try Doing Something Else Kind of Thing: Behavior Principles and the Exceptional Child (Council for Exceptional Children)
Modifying Classroom Behavior: A Manual of Procedure for Classroom Teachers (Research Press)
New Tools for Changing Behavior (Research Press)
Parents are Teachers: A Child Management Program (Research Press)
Positive Classroom Performance Techniques for Changing Behavior (Love Publishing Company)
Structuring the Classroom for Success (Charles E. Merrill Publishing Company)

Auditory Comprehension

Associated Classroom Behavior

1. Does not understand what he hears (responds with a "blank" expression on his face).
2. Often seems to be too attentive when oral instructions are given. Strains to "see" what is being said.
3. Prefers to work at tasks which require little listening (note whether there is a significant difference in the child's functioning when he is presented with auditory information compared to when he is working on tasks which do not require listening skills).

4. Has poor receptive vocabulary. Does not seem to comprehend spoken words (may recognize the word separately, but not in connected speech).
5. Cannot follow through on a series of verbal directions given by the teacher or by another child.
6. Does not seem to listen to daily classroom instructions. Asks to have directions repeated while the rest of the class begins working on the assignment.
8. Does not get the meaning of words from the context or from the tone of the speaker's voice.
9. Does not laugh at the right time when a story is read or a joke is told.
10. Has difficulty determining the main idea from materials given orally.
11. Has difficulty understanding what is said to him orally, especially when one of the following concepts is involved: time, quantity, orientation concerning direction in space.
12. Does not comprehend adjectives signifying relationships: big-little, full-empty, etc.
13. Does not comprehend quantitative words (more-less), numbers, or directional words (up-down, left-right).
14. Does not understand abstractions such as "beauty," "joy," etc.
15. Is unable to identify familiar sounds.
16. Is unable to learn phonetic associations between letters and their sounds.
17. Does not consistently differentiate between similar sounding words such as pen-pin, map-nap.
18. Is unable to retell a story, especially the main idea, by speaking, drawing, or acting it out.
19. May have an articulation problem or use common words incorrectly.

Structuring the Learning Environment

1. Use short, one-concept phrases at first.
2. Ask short questions that require short responses at first.

Later, ask questions which require several short answers.

3. Give increasingly more difficult oral directions which in turn require more complex verbal responses from him.

4. Give ample time between your verbal communication and his responses.

5. Accept concrete answers, but gradually supply more abstract clues.

6. Provide listening periods for him. Let him retell what he has heard.

7. Use the Language Master or pre-recorded tapes for individual practice with auditory training activities.

8. Use visual aids and provide visual clues (gestures, pictures, written materials, etc.) whenever possible.

9. Whenever possible, have the child watch the speaker's lips and face so he can utilize both his auditory and his visual channels for obtaining clues as to the meaning of what is being said.

OBJECTIVE

To teach awareness of and differentiation between different sounds.

Suggested Teaching Techniques

1. Make a tape of familiar sounds such as sneezing, coughing, barking, etc. Play the tape while showing pictures that match each sound being made. Pantomime the pictures while the child listens to the tape and watches you. Ask the child to imitate your actions, first with you as a model and then by himself. Be sure to listen to the tape carefully before you play it for him because sounds may become distorted on smaller tape recorders unless great care is taken during the original recording.

2. Make a tape of the child making sounds similar to those used in #1 above, then have him match pictures or act out the sounds he hears.

3. Encourage the child to imitate the sounds of an airplane, train, car, clock, animals, etc. Make a tape of the sounds he makes, and use pictures or word cards to identify the object when the tape is replayed for him.

4. Play games or tell stories that require different types of voices — a baby voice with a tiny, high-pitched voice, a father with a low, deep voice. Relate these voices to the child's own family members or to characters in other familiar stories.

5. Have the child close his eyes while a sound is made in another part of the room. When he opens his eyes, ask him to point to where the sound came from. Gradually ask him to identify the sound and to tell rather than point to where the sound came from. For even finer discrimination, the child may be taught to identify a particular child's voice through the same process.

OBJECTIVE

To teach auditory comprehension.

Suggested Teaching Techniques

1. Let the child experience verbal descriptions by having the actual objects available for him to touch, smell, etc. while you describe them. Use simple, concrete sentences. Later, give the object to the child and take turns telling about it. Work toward more abstract concepts through the use of pictures and then word cards in place of the actual object.

2. Describe a familiar object in the room or on the child's person and ask him to identify it.

3. Cut a hole in the bottom of a large grocery bag, then let the child draw a picture of an object or animal on the bag. Let the child wear the bag and pretend that he is the object or animal pictured on the bag. Ask the child simple questions about the object or animal that require only "yes" or "no" answers. At first use basic, factual

questions, then add more absurd questions like, "Do cows fly?".
4. Arrange several children in a circle. In turn, ask each child a question related to an experience he has had recently in the classroom or on the playground. If the child is unable to answer the question, he goes to another circle and "helps" the others when they are asked simple questions. The questions asked may initially require only a "yes" or a "no" answer, then simple one-concept answers.
5. Have the child identify nonsense statements from factual statements. Ask the child to complete the statement correctly using simple sentences. If you say, "Johnny has green hair," the child is asked to respond with, "Johnny has black hair." Examples should be given to help the child understand the concepts being taught in the activity. The use of more complex sentences, paragraphs, or even short stories may be used as the child advances in his ability to identify the nonsense statements.
6. Read a short story to the children and let them act out the story using dress-up costumes or puppets.

OBJECTIVES

To teach vocabulary development.

Suggested Teaching Techniques

1. Play games where visual cues are used to add meaning to the spoken language used.
2. Develop imitative vocabulary using action words and concepts that require the child to follow simple directions. Simple sentences such as, "Sit down" and "Touch your nose" may be used initially.
3. Develop pragmatic vocabulary by using pictures to portray persons and common objects.
4. Develop symbolic vocabulary by having the child arrange a toy farm while naming all of the animals and objects

(the farm is just an example of the many "group" objects that can be used).

5. Use large cards to print vocabulary words on with magic markers. Begin with a basic word list of words commonly used by the child. Use tracing on rough surfaces or in sand to reinforce the learning of these words. Transfer these procedures to simple sentences, choral responses, and poems. Use a picture dictionary to help in the defining of words.

6. Have the child work alone or in a group to make a scrapbook of pictures related to his word list in #5 above or a specific topic he is interested in, such as horses. Talk about the pictures he has selected for his scrapbook and encourage him to tell you about the pictures.

7. Have the child participate in meaningful conversation through imitating a telephone conversation, show and tell activities, or the scrapbook in #6 above.

8. Have the child supply simple endings to short stories. "One day the bear cub decided to take a nap under a big tree while all of his friends were playing hide and go seek. When he woke up. . ."

9. In a small group, have the children tell a story while you write down their statements. Begin the story for them if they need help in getting started. Individual children are called on to add another sentence to the story that compliments the sentence just used. When each child has given a sentence, they have "written" a story that may be used to reinforce the language development lesson.

10. Encourage the children to dramatize a familiar story by acting out the various parts. Retelling a story in this manner is also good for reinforcing what they have just heard.

11. Have the children take turns making up sentences from three or so "key" words. Each child is given a separate list of words and the other children are asked to tell whether his sentence is correct or not. Sample words might be: boy, school, today. The words should initially be given in a logical sequence, then scrambled up for

later lessons.

12. Build concepts of likenesses and differences by showing and telling how objects are alike and different. At first, use obvious clues, then work toward more subtle ones.

13. Ask the children to complete simple sentences that describe opposites or relationships. For example, "Candy is sweet but pickles are _____"; "The sky is up, the ground is _____."

14. Teach problem solving by working on anticipating needs for a variety of situations. Ask questions like, "If you were going to play baseball, what would you need to hit the ball with?" Work from one-word answers to short lists of equipment or items needed for the activity.

15. Ask questions that have obvious answers that will be funny to the child, then ask him for the correct answers. "Would you put an ice cream cone in your pocket?", "Why not?"; or "What would happen if you put an ice cream cone in your pocket?"

OBJECTIVE

To teach categories/classification of objects.

Suggested Teaching Techniques

1. Help the child with relationships by naming two items with which he is familiar and telling and/or showing him why they are alike (in the same category). Then give the child a third object and ask him to tell you why it belongs in this category.

2. Tape record sounds and ask the child to tell you if they are animal sounds, machine sounds, classroom sounds, etc. Be sure to listen to the tape first to make certain that all of the sounds are easily identifiable.

3. Using pictures or actual objects, ask the child to classify them according to size, shape, color, use, etc.

4. Ask the child to name items that belong in specific categories. "Tell me the names of some foods you like to eat,

toys you like to play with, etc." Provide visual clues during the initial activities, then gradually phase out these clues.

5. Say three words the child knows and ask him which two go together: ball, cow, bat.
6. Say two words that may or may not go together. Ask the child to tell you if they belong together and why or why not.
7. Say two words that go together and ask the child to give you a third word that goes with the first two.

OBJECTIVE

To teach abstract concepts.

Suggested Teaching Techniques

1. Using sample pictures such as "happy" and "sad," ask the child to sort a series of pictures into the proper categories. At first, he may be asked to simply match the faces, then words may be used to describe the faces. Ask him to pretend that he is happy, sad, afraid, etc. by imitating the faces on the pictures.
2. Use simple games of "Mother May I" or "Simon Says" to show the properties of verbs such as hop, walk, skip, and jump.
3. Use games such as "Mother May I" and "Simon Says" to show the concepts of prepositions such as under, over, in, and behind.
4. As you put an object *under* the desk say, "I put the _____ on *top* of my desk," and see if the child can "catch" your mistake. Take turns trying to "fool" each other by sometimes giving the wrong verbalizations for the actions being performed.

Related Instructional Materials

Advantage (Prentice-Hall, Inc.)

Association Picture Cards, I, II, III (Developmental Learning Materials)

Auditory Training: Familiar Sounds (Development Learning Materials)

Auditory Training: Rhythm Band (Developmental Learning Materials)

The Classification Game (Instructo Corporation)

The Clown Family Speech Workbook (Charles C Thomas, Publisher)

Discovering Opposites (Instructo Corporation)

Distar Language I: An Instructional System (Science Research Associates, Inc.)

Expressive-Receptive Skills Program (Knowledge Aid)

Helping Young Children Develop Language Skills: A Book of Activities (Council for Exceptional Children)

The Junior Listen-Hear Program (Follett Educational Corporation)

Language Building Cards (Interstate Printers and Publishers, Inc.)

Language Experiences in Early Childhood (Encyclopedia Britannica Educational Corporation)

Language Experiences in Reading (Encyclopedia Britannica Educational Corporation)

Language Instructional Activities (Love Publishing Company)

Language Motivating Experiences for Young Children (Children's Music Center, Inc.)

Listening Skills for Pre-Readers (Classroom Materials Company)

Listening Skills Program II-A (Science Research Associates, Inc.)

My First Picture Dictionary (Scott, Foresman and Company)

My Pictionary (Scott, Foresman and Company)

My Second Picture Dictionary (Scott, Foresman and Company)

Peabody Language Development Kits, Levels P-3 (American Guidance Service, Inc.)

Picture Sequence Cards, Sets I and II (Speech and Language Materials, Inc.)

The Sesame Street Learning Kit (Time-Life Books)

Sounds and Patterns of Language (Holt, Rinehart, and Winston, Inc.)

Speech Through Pictures (Expression Company, Publishers)

Stories for Listening: Learning Speech Sounds (McGraw-Hill Book Company)

We Listen and Learn (Society for Visual Education, Inc.)

What's Funny Cards (Speech and Language Materials, Inc.)

Who Said It? (Educational Activities, Inc.)

World of Sound (Society for Visual Education, Inc.)

Auditory Discrimination

Associated Classroom Behavior

1. Cannot identify sound effects accurately.
2. Seems unable to identify unusual or usual sounds correctly.
3. Speaks in a monotone or unnatural pitch.
4. Cannot consistently differentiate between similar sounding words such as "pen" and "pin."
5. Does not seem to be able to recognize differences in similar phonic sounds such as "k" and "t."
6. Cannot detect differences in the sounds of words or letters.
7. Cannot distinguish speech sounds in words.
8. Is unable to learn the sounds of letters.
9. Seems to have special difficulty with the discrimination of the sounds of "f-v," "s-z," "sh-ch," "th-t," "t-d," "p-b," and "k-g."
10. Cannot identify and/or supply words that rhyme with other words.

Structuring the Learning Environment

1. Ear training is really training in listening and interpreting sounds or speech. If possible, do this training in a quiet corner, that is free from visual as well as auditory distractions. First, work on awareness, then on the dis-

crimination of gross sounds.

2. Motor responses to auditory stimuli may be used throughout the training sessions. Such activities as raising hands, jumping, pointing, or picking up objects help to reinforce the auditory stimuli and its relationship to the concept being taught.

3. Teach gross awareness first, then the finer discrimination of specific sounds.

4. Provide auditory training activities which involve (a) discrimination of sounds, (b) auditory closure, (c) blending sounds, and (d) rhyming.

5. Work toward having the child concentrate on the teacher's face for visual cues as well as auditory cues.

6. Make it a habit to initially have the child repeat back to the teacher all oral instructions that have been given.

OBJECTIVE

To teach awareness of intensity of sounds.

Suggested Teaching Techniques

1. March to music, stomping loudly when the music is loud, tiptoeing quietly when the music is soft. Children enjoy the physical activity of this game and it may first be played with the whole group, then later with individuals who need additional help.

2. While the children march to the music, suddenly stop the music and ask, "Was the music loud or soft when I stopped it?"

3. Hunting for a hidden object may be directed by hand clapping. As the child gets closer to the object the clapping becomes louder; as he moves away from it, the clapping becomes softer. Letting the youngsters participate in the clapping reinforces the concept being taught.

4. Compare the ticking of a clock with that of a wrist watch; the sound of a person whistling with the sound of a police siren, etc.

OBJECTIVE

To teach the differences between high and low pitched sounds.

Suggested Teaching Techniques

1. Compare the sounds made by ringing a large bell and a small bell, or by blowing a big toy horn and a small toy horn.
2. Use instruments of different frequencies (a bell, a drum, a horn, a whistle) and let the child tell which makes the highest or lowest sound after he has experimented with each one. Later he may be asked to arrange the instruments in order from highest to lowest sound.
3. Play games which involve both identification and discrimination of pitch. Use the piano to strike various notes — high, low, and in between. Have the child stand tall with his arms above his head when a high note is struck; squat down low when a low note is played. Various notes in between may be responded to with varying positions relative to the highest and lowest positions. This game can be used as a "quickie" reprieve from seat work activities.
4. Observe differences in pitch during the story hour with younger children. *The Three Bears* is a favorite story because of the different voices used throughout the telling of the tale. Let the children imitate the voices used by all of the characters. Stories of elves and fairies or of animals who are personified also give the children a fun way to practice auditory discrimination of voice pitches.
5. For older children, role playing or simple plays may be used to help them imitate a variety of voice pitches.

OBJECTIVE

To teach quality of sounds.

Suggested Teaching Techniques

1. To develop awareness of different sounds compare such items as wooden beads dropped into a can, small glass beads dropped into a jar, pebbles dropped into a box, the squeak of a toy animal, a spoon stirred in an empty cup, the rustling of papers, the jangling of coins, etc. Do this first while the child is observing and participating in the activity of making the sounds. Then blindfold the child and ask him to identify the sounds being made. At first there should be gross differences between only two or three sounds. As the child becomes more successful, make the activity more challenging for him by adding to both the degree of differentiation and the number of sounds to identify.

2. Play games where children try to identify who is speaking just by listening to the voice quality. The listener may be blindfolded or he may stand with his back to the rest of the group.

OBJECTIVE

To teach sequencing and rhythm of sounds.

Suggested Teaching Techniques

1. Using a toy drum, beat out a simple pattern, then ask the child to repeat the pattern.

2. Using a large ball, bounce it a specified number of times, then ask the child to imitate the bouncing pattern.

3. Play rhythmical games of all types using skipping, galloping, marching, and dancing to music to emphasize the rhythmical pattern of "keeping time" to the beat.

4. Use rhythm band instruments or empty coffee cans with plastic lids to beat time to music.

5. Use the hands to clap time to the music.

OBJECTIVE

To teach likenesses and differences of sounds.

Suggested Teaching Techniques

1. Play two notes on the piano and ask if they are alike or different. If the child has difficulty, let him strike the same two notes on the piano. Show him where the keys are in relation to the tones just played.
2. Use the activities under the first two objectives mentioned in this section, but ask if the sounds are alike or different rather than if they are soft or loud, or high or low.
3. Call attention to the names of children in the group which begin alike, sound alike, or rhyme.
4. Select a number of word pairs on the basis of some gross similarity in the sound of the total word, such as "feather-father," "desk-nest," "chickens-children," "puddle-puppy." Ask simple questions like, "Which grows on birds, feathers or fathers?", "Where do birds lay their eggs, in a desk or in a nest?", "Which have wings, chickens or children?", "Can we pet a puddle?" If the children have difficulty with this activity, first make sure that you are pronouncing the word correctly the way they are used to hearing it pronounced. If necessary, use pictures and/or word cards to emphasize the words being spoken.
5. Select a number of word pairs that have fine differences in their total sounds such as "dog-fog"; "shush-slush." First say the two words while the child watches your face. Ask him if the two words are alike or different. Do the same activity while his back is toward you. Later, give him words that are also alike to see if he is listening carefully.
6. Have the child identify words containing the same sounds after listening to three or four words in a row.

OBJECTIVE

To teach rhyming sounds and words.

Suggested Teaching Techniques

1. Have the children listen, first with their eyes open and then with them closed, while a rhythmic pattern is played on a musical instrument. Ask them to repeat the pattern they have just heard.
2. Teach short jingles or poems with rhyming words. Let the children supply the rhyming word once they are familiar with the jingle. Children are often able to do this long before they can repeat the entire jingle or poem from memory. Call the children's attention to the fact that rhyming words sound *and* look alike by using flash cards to reinforce their visual cues.
3. Have the children complete orally very short rhymes begun by the teacher. Encourage the children to take turns being "teacher" and starting rhymes for the others to complete.
4. Use action poems that rhyme to help reinforce the concept through bodily movements.
5. Have the children listen for rhyming words in new jingles, poems, or songs.
6. Have the children listen for the nonrhyming words in a series of three or four words. Give three rhyming and one nonrhyming word. Have the children raise their hands, stand up, or clap once when they hear the nonrhyming word. Be sure to vary the position of the nonrhyming word in the sequence so the children do not become misdirected by always listening for the second, third, or other positioned word.

OBJECTIVE

To teach the position of a sound in a word.

Suggested Teaching Techniques

1. Using simple three letter words, have the first sound be the engine of the train, the middle sound be the passenger car, and the final sound be the caboose. Use pic-

tures of these train cars if necessary to stress the position of the sounds. Words with double vowels making one sound may also be used for this activity.

2. The same activity as mentioned above may be used for simple syllabication for older children.
3. Have the children identify sound placement by listening to a word while looking at it printed on a flash card. Remove the card from their sight and give the same or a similar word for them to use for sound placement by listening only.
4. Call attention to the names of children in the group which begin or end with the same letter(s) and sounds.
5. Have the children line up at the door for recess, lunch, etc. by saying, "All children whose first names begin with _____ may line up." Use different beginning sounds until all of the children are lined up. Vary the sequence of the sounds from day to day.
6. Follow the same activity as listed above except say, "All children whose last names begin with _____ please line up."
7. Again use the same activity except say, "All children whose first names begin with the same sound as the word _____ please line up." Do this also for their last names.

Related Instructional Materials

Auditory Discrimination Game (Speech and Language Materials, Inc.)
Auditory Discrimination in Depth (Teaching Resources Corporation)
Auditory Perception Program (Follett Educational Corporation)
Auditory Perception Skills (Tapes Unlimited)
Auditory Training: Familiar Sounds (Developmental Learning Materials)
Auditory Training: Rhythm Band (Developmental Learning Materials)

Fun With Rhymes (Instructo Corporation)

Galloping Sounds (Expression Company, Publishers)

A Guide to Speech Improvement with the Mike and Cindy Stories (Steck-Vaughn Company Publishers)

The Junior Listen-Hear Program (Follett Educational Corporation)

Let's Listen (Stanley Bowmar Company)

Listen! And Help Tell the Story (Abingdon Press)

Listening Games: Building Listening Skills with Instructional Games (Teacher's Publishing Corporation)

Listening Skills Program (Science Research Associates, Inc.)

Louie the Lazy Listener (Children's Music Center, Inc.)

The New Linguistic Block Series, Set 1-L (Scott, Foresman and Company)

Sound Out: Listening Skills Program (Academic Therapy Publications)

Sounds and Patterns of Language (Holt, Rinehart, and Winston)

Sounds for Young Readers, Vols. I-VI (Classroom Materials Company)

Sounds I Can Hear (Scott, Foresman and Company)

Sounds Like Fun (Interstate Printers and Publishers, Inc.)

Speech Correction Through Listening (Scott, Foresman and Company)

Speech Lingo (Speech and Language Materials, Inc.)

Stories for Listening: Learning Speech Sounds (McGraw-Hill Book Company)

Stories for Quiet Listening (Children's Music Center, Inc.)

Think, Listen, Say (Eye Gate House, Inc.)

Who Said It? (Educational Activities, Inc.)

World of Sound (Society for Visual Education, Inc.)

Auditory Memory and Sequencing

Associated Classroom Behavior

1. Often seems to be "too attentive" when oral instructions

are given. Strains to "see" what is being said, then does not follow the instructions.

2. Seems unable to maintain interest or attention during orally presented lessons.
3. Cannot seem to follow through on oral directions. Does not seem to listen to daily classroom instructions or directions (often asks to have directions repeated while the rest of the class goes ahead with the assignment).
4. Cannot remember what he hears.
5. Cannot repeat the sequence of a tune played on melody bells.
6. Does not know the alphabet by heart.
7. Cannot remember short sentences.
8. Cannot remember songs or poems or simple nursery rhymes or jingles which other children know by heart.
9. May not know his address or his phone number.
10. Cannot count by memory.
11. May be unable to learn the days of the week or the months of the year.
12. Shows signs of immature speech patterns.
13. Cannot pronounce common words.
14. Reverses words and letters in reading and spelling.
15. Transposes words (aminal, emeny), compound words (flybutter, belldoor) or phrases (What there are?).
16. Cannot repeat a sequence of numbers he has heard.
17. Cannot memorize the multiplication tables.
18. Cannot read or write numbers from dictation.
19. Has difficulty sounding out words; cannot seem to blend sounds or to remember the sequence of sounds in a word.
20. Has difficulty in analysis and synthesis of words. Cannot break words into syllables or into individual sounds.

Structuring the Learning Environment

1. Permit the child to use visual clues. Provide these clues when necessary.
2. Use visual aids such as pictures and gestures when giving directions.

3. Use short one-concept sentences, especially when giving directions.
4. When giving directions or instructions, give them in small units or only one at a time.
5. Encourage the child to speak in short, well-constructed sentences.

OBJECTIVE

To teach memory of sounds.

Suggested Teaching Techniques

1. Have the child close his eyes and listen to sounds inside of the room for thirty seconds. Ask him to listen to the sounds to see if he can identify them. After thirty seconds, ask him to tell what sounds he heard.
2. Use the same method as described above except have the child listen to sounds going on outside of the room.
3. Let the child experiment with two or three rhythm band instruments to see what sounds they make. Ask him to identify the instrument by the sound it makes. When he is successful at naming the correct instrument and its sound, ask him to close his eyes or to turn his back while a sound is made with one of the instruments. See if he can correctly identify the instrument.
4. Record familiar sounds on a tape recorder. Go over the tape with the child to make sure that he is familiar with the sounds. Mix up the sequence of the sounds and again ask him to identify them. Later ask him to tell where he could find the source of the original sound. For example, if the sound is a vacuum cleaner, he could find it inside of the house. Work from inside/outside sources to specific rooms of the house or areas outside of the house.

OBJECTIVE

To teach memory of spoken words.

Suggested Teaching Techniques

1. Ask the child to repeat a short series of digits. Begin with two digits and work toward seven digits (the same number as is used for phone numbers.).
2. For older children, the same task as described above may be used except they may write down the numbers as they repeat them verbally. Then have them turn the paper over and either write or say the numbers from memory again.
3. Teach the child simple rhymes, poems, and songs. Use choral speaking for small groups to encourage those children who lack the confidence to speak alone.
4. Using simple rhymes, poems, and songs that the child is familiar with, leave out key words and let him say them in the appropriate places.

OBJECTIVE

To teach auditory sequential memory.

Suggested Teaching Techniques

1. The teacher and the child have duplicate sets of noise-makers (such as bells and drums) in front of them on a table. The teacher first rings the bell and then strikes the drum. The child is asked to repeat the same pattern. When he can repeat the sequence after both hearing and seeing the teacher make the pattern, the teacher hides her noisemakers behind a screen or under the desk. Another pattern is given by the teacher with the child listening but not seeing the objects being touched. He is then asked to repeat the pattern with his own instruments. Increase the difficulty of both the pattern and the number of instruments used as the child's ability with this task increases.

2. Tap on the table several times, asking the child to listen, count mentally, then repeat the taps. If he has difficulty, tap his hand or knee rather than the table. If he still has some difficulty, tap out the sequence using his hand as the tapper.

3. Use the same method as above except ask the child to count the number of taps rather than duplicate the sequence. Then ask him to tap out the same number of taps on the desk.

4. Use musical songs with several repeated sections or refrains. Tap out the rhythm along with the song, then tap it out without the words to the song. Encourage the child to listen for different patterns within the same song.

OBJECTIVE

To teach auditory sequencing of numbers.

Suggested Teaching Techniques

1. Use flash cards with the numbers written on them in large print. Say the number as you place it in front of the child, then have him repeat what you have just said. Begin with two numbers in the proper sequence, beginning with the number one. Ask the child to close his eyes while you mix up the cards. Then ask him to say the numbers while he puts the cards in their proper order.

2. Use the rhyme "Ten Little Indians" on a tape recorder. Let the child make pictures to go with each segment of the rhyme. As he hears the segments of the rhyme on the tape recorder, ask the child to point to or hold up the appropriate picture. Gradually leave out one segment of the rhyme and ask the child to fill in the missing part. Later, mix up the order of the segments being left out of the rhyme so that the child will have to listen more carefully.

3. Have one child say his house number and the second

child repeat it. The second child has two chances to give the correct number. If this proves too difficult at first, use visual cues to help the second child.

4. Have one child give his phone number, then ask the next child to repeat it. If the second child has difficulty, use visual cues such as flash cards to help him.

5. Use a rhythm to teach phone numbers to children who seem unable to remember their phone numbers. Tap out the rhythm with hands or pencils as the numbers are spoken.

6. Play a game of "Echo." One child says a series of numbers, then a second child repeats them softly. This same technique may be used for children who do not know their numbers. Instead of repeating a series of spoken numbers, they may be asked to repeat a specific rhythm that has been tapped out by another child. By gradually placing the children farther and farther apart during this activity, they will be forced to listen more attentively to each other.

7. Jumping rope and counting may be used to reinforce auditory sequential memory. Use simple counting rhymes to the rhythms of the jumping.

OBJECTIVE

To teach sequencing of words and phrases.

Suggested Teaching Techniques

1. Use rhyming words in sequence. Begin the sequence and let each child add to it with a rhyming word. Increase the difficulty of the words as the children's abilities increase.

2. Begin with two words having related meanings such as "bird" and "chicken." Say the words and have the child repeat them. As his ability to do this increases, add unrelated words to the sequence.

3. Read a short poem to the child and ask him to retell it in his own words. If he has difficulty in the beginning, use

pictures or word cards for visual cues. Gradually fade out the use of visual cues.

4. Have the children seated in a circle. The first child says a short phrase, then selects another child to repeat it. The second child is given two chances to correctly repeat the phrase. By having the person who initiates the phrase select the next child after the phrase has been spoken, the group learns to listen to each other more closely.

5. Have the child follow verbal directions involving one, two, three, or more activities. Begin with one activity and have the child repeat the directions aloud and then follow them. Work toward having the child follow the directions without having to repeat them aloud.

6. Read a short story to the children and let them act it out in the proper sequence.

7. Play the game "Going on a Trip." The first child says, "I am going on a trip and I am going to take _____ with me." The next child repeats the sentence and adds an article that he is going to take with him. Continue until one of the children cannot repeat the sequence in the proper order. Various categories may be specified before the game begins. For example, the children may be asked to take only clothing or food on the trip. This adds variety and also narrows down the choices a child may have when deciding what to take with him on this imaginary trip.

8. Ask one child to tell how to do something such as bake cookies. Have the other children listen to make certain that the sequence is correct. Then ask another child to repeat the directions in the proper sequence.

9. Read a story that has a short series of events. Ask the child to retell the events of the story in the order they occurred.

10. Ask the child to tell about an event that happened an hour ago, yesterday, a week ago, etc. Events in the classroom or at home may be used. TV shows are also a good source for this type of activity.

11. For any of the above activities, the teacher may also play

along as a participant. However, she may want to make obvious mistakes on purpose to see whether the children are listening carefully to what is being said. Later, more subtle mistakes may be made.

Related Instructional Materials.

Auditory Memory Tapes (Tapes Unlimited)
Concept Clocks in Color (Teaching Resources Corporation)
Configuration Cards (Teaching Resources Corporation)
Fun With Words (Barnell Loft & Dexter Westbrook, Ltd.)
Hand Rhythms (Rhythm Record Company)
Helping Young Children Develop Language Skills (Council for Exceptional Children)
I Try (Noble and Noble Publishers)
Language Lotto (Appleton-Century-Crofts)
Learning to Think Series (Science Research Associates, Inc.)
Let's Learn Sequence (Instructo Corporation)
Listening Skills for Pre-Readers, Vols. 1-5 (Educational Activities Inc.)
Ordinal Placement Board (Teaching Resources Corporation)
Peabody Language Development Kits, Levels P-3 (American Guidance Service, Inc.)
Reading Readiness and Number Readiness (Rhythm Record Company)
Reading Readiness Workbooks (Follett Educational Corporation)
Riddle, Riddle, Rhyme Time (Barnell Loft & Dexter Westbrook, Ltd.)
See and Say Puzzle Cards (Teaching Resources Corporation)
Sounds I Can Hear (Scott, Foresman and Company)

Chapter 7

HINTS FOR VISUAL
PERCEPTUAL LEARNING PROBLEMS
... YES I SEE IT, BUT
I DON'T UNDERSTAND IT

HINTS for Visual Perceptual Learning Problems includes four major areas of concern. *Visual Attention* problems are usually associated with the child who does not attend to visual stimuli. He is often very distractible in the classroom because his attention is focused on the auditory stimuli going on within the room such as other children talking, chairs being moved, and papers being shuffled. Since this is basically a problem of general attention, the major emphasis in this area is one of classroom management in relation to structuring the learning environment for success.

Visual Comprehension involves the ability to understand the information that is taken in through the eyes. The child may be able to see the material adequately, but he may not be able to associate a comprehensive meaning with its intended purpose. He may see a sporting event such as a football game as an individual activity rather than as a group or team effort because he does not visually understand the relationship between one player on the field and the roles of the other players. It is difficult for him to put it all together to obtain a comprehensive understanding of the game as a whole. In the classroom, this child may be unable to gain meaning from pictures or written words unless they are presented in conjunction with auditory clues.

Visual Discrimination problems are indicated by a child who is unable to differentiate between two objects when they are presented visually. Again, he may be able to see them adequately, but he may not be able to visually determine what, if any, difference there is between the two objects. With more abstract figures such as pictures and printed symbols, the child may become totally confused unless he is allowed to use his tactile and/or kinesthetic skills to trace or outline the figures when trying to distinguish the difference between them.

Visual Memory and Sequencing involve complex skills primarily in the memory area. When the child has been shown a simple pattern of objects to study, he may be unable to reproduce that pattern once the original stimulus has been removed from his sight. He may also have difficulty putting a simple set of pictures together to complete a story because he does not remember the correct order of the pictures in relation to the story. Serious reading and spelling problems may develop because the child is unable to remember the correct order of the printed symbols. Although he may be able to orally spell a word, he may not be able to read it or write it because he does not associate the printed symbols with the spoken ones and therefore he is unable to remember a logical sequence for these symbols.

Conclusions concerning a child's possible visual-perceptual learning problem should not be made until the child has had a complete visual examination by a qualified professional.

Visual Attention

Associated Classroom Behavior

1. Is easily distracted by visual stimuli; responds to every visual stimulus.
2. Is easily distracted by other activities in the classroom.
3. Is more interested in what is going on around him than in getting his work done, and will do his work only if the teacher stands over him and refocuses his attention.
4. Needs reduction, change, or modification of visual stimuli in order to perform adequately.
5. Is more upset by physiological distress (hunger, physical distress, etc.) than are other children. Is more inattentive just before lunch and late in the afternoon.

Structuring the Learning Environment

1. Arrange the child's immediate environment so that visual distractions are minimized. Use learning carrels, refrigerator cartons, etc. to provide isolation from visual stimuli. Use these methods with caution so as not to totally isolate the child for long periods of time.
2. Place the child in that part of the room where there are the fewest number of children, in a smaller group, or in a specially designed group.
3. Place the child away from windows and other sources of stimuli competing for his attention.
4. Help the child to clear his own desk of unnecessary items before he begins working on a specific task.
5. Make all tasks or instructions short, simple and related to the task.
6. Set aside specific periods of class time for specific tasks so that the child knows that "now" he is to perform a certain task.
7. Avoid excessive tactile stimulation by making certain that chairs are comfortable and fit the child properly.
8. Avoid excessive internal stimulation by providing morning and afternoon snacks, i.e. something to eat at critical stages of the day.
9. Remember that patterning, structuring, and routinizing are three essentials in dealing with inadequate attention, hyperactivity, or lack of control.
10. Provide appropriate and adequate reinforcers or reinforcing events as these have been demonstrated as the most powerful environmental conditions for changing behavior. In addition to choosing the most appropriate reinforcement techniques, the teacher must be consistent in her own behavior.
11. Follow these principles of behavior modification:
    a. Set the stage for acceptable responses to occur, as positive consequences produce the most productive forms of attending and responding.
    b. Avoid setting the stage where unacceptable behaviors

are most likely to occur.

c. See that pleasant consequences, especially teacher attention and approval, follow acceptable forms of behavior.

d. Avoid attending to unacceptable behavior.

e. Remove the child from a setting when his behavior is very disruptive, destructive, or aggressive and place him for a *short* duration of time in an area where no reinforcement is possible for him. Quietly return him to the classroom after a brief period of isolation.

f. Provide attention to other forms of reinforcement to a child based on the pattern of his behavior which occurred. Reinforcement should *not* be based on your feelings at the moment.

OBJECTIVE

To help the child maintain visual attention.

Suggested Teaching Techniques

1. Use color to indicate any changes in directions, to point out blanks that are to be filled in, to indicate a new line in reading, to show columns that are to be used in matching exercises, or to give correct examples of the work to be done.

2. Make booklets rather than worksheets. Using the same material, divide the sheet(s) into quarters and put only one or two items on each smaller sheet.

3. Using booklets described in #2 above, put the correct answer on the back of the first page in another color or in a box on that page. This gives immediate reinforcement, but it also encourages looking ahead for answers before completing the work.

4. Always present easier problems first and work toward more complex ones to reinforce success and encourage motivation to continue the exercises.

5. Keep all worksheets clear of extraneous artwork and

"clutter."

6. Use a dark piece of paper to make a "window" for the worksheet. Cut an opening in the paper that will allow the student to view one sentence or problem at a time. Paper may be slid through the viewer as the child progresses.

7. Give short assignments and use a timer for each one. This must be used with caution because (a) a timer may become a distractor for some children, (b) the pressure of being timed may cause too much frustration with some children, and (c) those children who need more time to complete assignments will become frustrated.

8. Questions which present vital information in the body of the statement (matching, multiple choice, etc.) are more easily understood than open-ended questions. Each question should also make a complete sentence.

9. Auditory distractions, especially in the form of verbal instructions, should be kept at a minimum. Verbal directions should be given only at the very beginning of each exercise.

10. The printed material should be legible, and the spacing between each line should be adequate. Ditto masters should be as dark as possible. Some children may even need to have their work done with a black marker to help them attend to the written material.

11. A short review of the lesson both before and after its completion helps some youngsters to attend more carefully.

12. Above all, remember to keep all visual assignments within the child's ability level. Begin at a level where he can function with ease and feel successful, then gradually present more difficult learning tasks.

Related Instructional Materials

An Empirical Basis for Change in Education (Science Research Associates, Inc.)

Behavior Modification: The Human Effort (Dimensions Publishing Company)

Changing Children's Behavior (Prentice-Hall, Inc.)
Child Management (Ann Arbor Publishers)
Help! These Kids Are Driving Me Crazy! (Research Press)
How to Use Contingency Contracting in the Classroom (Research Press)
Let's Try Doing Something Else Kind of Thing: Precision Teaching (Council for Exceptional Children)
Modifying Classroom Behavior: A Manual of Procedure for Classroom Teachers (Research Press)
New Tools for Changing Behavior (Research Press)
Parents are Teachers: Child Management Program (Research Press)
Positive Classroom Performance Techniques for Changing Behavior (Love Publishing Company)
Structuring the Classroom for Success (Charles E. Merrill Publishing Company)

Visual Comprehension

Associated Classroom Behavior

1. Does not comprehend or correctly interpret what is seen.
2. Is unable to focus attention on visual stimuli for long periods of time.
3. Prefers to work on tasks that require little visual concentration.
4. May be able to correctly sound out words in a reading lesson, but does not comprehend what he reads.
5. May see only parts rather than wholes when he observes sporting events, i.e. does not see the third baseman as a part of the whole team, but rather as an individual who is out on the playing field.
6. Does not learn from filmstrips unless they are accompanied by taped cassette or other auditory stimuli.
7. Does not understand the pictures in a comic book, comic strip, etc.
8. Does not gain from visual cues given along with written materials.

9. Does not see differences in visual stimuli.
10. Seems to learn best when materials are presented orally and/or through gestures.

Structuring the Learning Environment

1. Provide auditory clues whenever possible.
2. Allow the child to first trace over the correct response, then write his own response.
3. When teaching a child the visual characteristics of an object, it is important to present only one characteristic at a time. The use of color clues, tactile clues, and verbal clues helps in the initial stages of teaching visual perception of an object.
4. When teaching a color, use another color with it that is very different from the first color. Do not always present the same color in the same order or with the same object.
5. Before teaching the names of objects, teach the qualities of the objects. An intermediate step between simple sorting or matching and understanding the meaning of such qualities is that of attaching the correct meaning to the name when it is spoken. For example, a child will probably be able to "point to the green one" before he can actually respond to the question, "What color is this?"
6. Toys that move, such as tops, balloons, balls, and pull toys may be used to teach as well as motivate the child in exploring his visual environment.
7. Allow the child to use records, a tape recorder, or other auditory methods as these make for a strong channel of learning visual comprehension and meaning.

OBJECTIVE

To teach visual comprehension.

Suggested Teaching Techniques

1. Buy two copies of a short story book. Use one copy to

read the story to the child. Cut the other book up so that the pictures may be placed on cards for the child to use while retelling the story in his own words.

2. Mount short comic strips on cards. Tell a brief story to describe what is happening, then mix up the cards and let the child retell the comic story using his own words. When he has learned this activity, show him a new set of cards and let him tell a story while he places the cards in a sequence to match his story.

3. Make several sets of matched pairs of pictures. Keep one of the pairs and distribute the rest of the cards to the children. As the teacher holds up a card, the children are asked to look at their cards and see who has the matching card. This may also be done with similar rather than with exactly matching cards.

4. Simple puzzles may be used to help the child associate the parts with the whole they will make when the puzzle is completed.

5. Using a series of comic strips cut into squares, add an unrelated comic strip square and ask the child which square does not belong in the series. This may also be done with pictures from familiar stories.

6. Ask the child to match black and white pictures of objects with the actual objects. Also use line drawings or abstract representations for the child to match with the actual objects.

7. Use pictures with mistakes in them and ask the child to find what is wrong in the picture.

8. Give the child an envelope containing cutouts of various animals. Have him match the picture cutouts to make a complete animal. Later, use only ears and tails and have him match these with corresponding pictures of the animals. At first, the entire animal may be used as a stimulus, then the ears and tails may be hidden from view or cut off the original picture.

9. Show the child a partial picture with obvious clues as to what the entire picture really is. Have him tell what the partial picture represents. Gradually increase the diffi-

culty by making the clues less and less obvious.
10. Show the child dotted outlines of the letters of the alphabet or numbers. Ask him to identify what he sees. If necessary, have him connect the dots to complete the figure. Gradually make the spacing between the dots farther and farther apart. Later go to whole words spelled out in this dotted manner.
11. Select words that the child is familiar with, such as his name. Omit one letter from the word and ask him what the word is and what letter is missing. If the cards used are laminated, the child may fill in the missing blank with a wax pencil or water base marker.

Related Instructional Materials

Alphabet Cards (Developmental Learning Materials)
Association Picture Cards, I, II, III (Developmental Learning Materials)
Clear Stencils (Developmental Learning Materials)
Colored Inch Cubes (Developmental Learning Materials)
Colored Inch Cubes — Designs in Perspective (Developmental Learning Materials)
Concept Picture Puzzles (Harcourt, Brace, Jovanovich)
Counting Picture Cards (Developmental Learning Materials)
Design Cards for Large Parquetry (Developmental Learning Materials)
The Fitzhugh Plus Program: Perceptual Learning and Understanding (Allied Educational Council)
Frostig Program for the Development of Visual Perception (Follett Educational Corporation)
Games Make Spelling Fun (Fearon Publishing Company)
Headstart in Reading — Look and Listen (Filmstrip House, Inc.)
I Want to Learn (Follett Educational Corporation)
Junior Listen-Hear Books (Follet Educational Corporation)
Lite Brite (Educational Progress Corporation)

The Mott Basic Skills Program (Allied Educational Council)
My Alphabet Book (Charles E. Merrill Publishing Company)
My Kindergraph Program (Follett Educational Corporation)
My Puzzle Book, I and II (Garrard Publishing Company)
Peabody Language Development Kits, Levels P-3 (American Guidance Service, Inc.)
Pegboard and Colored Pegs (Developmental Learning Materials)
Pegboard Designs (Developmental Learning Materials)
People Puzzles (Developmental Learning Materials)
Readiness in Language Arts (Behavioral Research Laboratories)
Reading for Meaning (Houghton Mifflin Company)
Sequential Picture Cards, I, II, III (Developmental Learning Materials)
Shapes Puzzles (Developmental Learning Materials)
Sound Phonics (Educator's Publishing Service)
The Useful Language Program (Continental Press)
Word Analysis Program (Continental Press)

Visual Discrimination

Associated Classroom Behavior

1. Cannot recognize objects presented visually.
2. Cannot recognize differences in figures presented visually.
3. Avoids work requiring concentrated visual attention.
4. Confuses and/or reverses letters.
5. Does not copy fluently from the chalkboard.
6. Is slow to finish work (does not apply self, daydreams a lot, falls asleep in school).
7. Confuses words with similar visual patterns ("rat" for "rut," "bat" for "but," etc.)
8. Is overactive, cannot sit still in class, shakes or swings legs.
9. Displays variability of performance from day to day.

Structuring the Learning Environment

1. Shorten assignments, if necessary. If it is apparent that the child cannot complete the usual assignments in the same period of time as the rest of the children, it is better to shorten the assignments at the beginning than to have him continually turn in partial assignments. Once this is begun, the child is expected to complete his assignments according to the same instructions as the other children in the class.

2. Stress auditory modes of presentations rather than visual modes. Accompany all written assignments with verbal instructions.

3. Allow the child to take oral examinations rather than written ones. Gradually work toward a combination of written and oral tests.

4. When it is required that the child work with visual materials, try to provide other aids such as multi-media presentations for him.

5. Always begin working where the child can succeed.

6. Be sure that the child understands what is expected of him. Demonstrate the directions if necessary.

7. Use the child's strengths to help build up his weaknesses, and supply the types of aid he requires.

8. Use a tachistoscope or controlled reader for visual training.

9. Even after a skill has been taught and a new one begun, continued practice on the first skill should be provided. Tapering off should be done only when mastery of the older skill has been obtained.

OBJECTIVE

To teach visual classification.

Suggested Teaching Techniques

1. Select categories according to use, size, shape, color, etc.

to teach the skill of sorting objects or pictures into categories. Use simple objects at first and have the child match similar objects with the original one. Then go to pictures for the matching activities.

2. Have the child find one object that is different from several others. Ask him to find (a) a square button in a box of round ones, (b) a green block in a group of yellow blocks, (c) a rough piece of fabric among a group of smooth fabric pieces, (d) a small ball among a group of larger balls. Encourage the child to use his tactile skills to reinforce his visual skills, i.e. to touch and feel the objects when the size, shape, or texture is different from the other objects.

3. Have the child match or sort dominoes according to the number of dots.

4. Use pictures in groups of three or four with one picture totally unrelated to the other three. Have the child name and describe the pictures. Ask the child which picture does not belong and why. If the child has difficulty with this, point out the unrelated picture and tell why it does not belong with the others. Ask the child to tell why it does not belong, using his own words.

5. To sort pictures, use line drawings and ask the child to hold up the picture that is being described according to its function, color, size, etc. "Hold up the picture that has straight lines," (pictures of a circle, a square, and a flower).

OBJECTIVE

To teach visual likenesses and differences.

Suggested Teaching Techniques

1. A series of cylinders, balls, squares, etc. is placed in front of the child. He is asked to match the actual object with the corresponding line drawing of the object. Cutting the proper sized grooves in heavy cardboard will aid the

child during the initial phases of this matching activity.

2. Nail a series of different sized jar lids, face down, onto a piece of masonite or wood. Place the corresponding jars, mixed in order, in front of the child and ask him to place the jars on the correct lids.

3. To teach the letters of the alphabet, cut out each letter in sandpaper, felt, or some other textured and durable material. Let the child trace over the letter while he names it, then ask him to visually pick out the same letter printed on a piece of paper with several other letters. If he has difficulty with this, let him trace over the letters on the paper to reinforce the movements he made when he traced over the original letter. Numbers may be taught the same way.

4. Have a series of four similar objects in a row with one object placed at a different angle or made of a different color. Ask the child which object is different from the rest and why. Trace over the objects if necessary to show that one is placed at a different angle from the rest.

5. Make several copies of the same line drawing using an object in the drawing that the child is familiar with. Mix the copies up so that in each series one of the pictures will be different. Ask the child to tell which pictures do not belong in each set. Then ask him to make each set all the same by taking out the different pictures and replacing them with the correct ones.

6. Place three related pictures on one card. Ask the child to pick the fourth related picture from a series of other cards. Ask him why he selected the card he did. Card games may be developed to encourage this type of matching activity.

7. Card games such as "Old Maid," "Authors," and "Go Fish" may be used with a small group of children to reinforce their learning of likenesses and differences.

OBJECTIVE

To increase the rate of visual discrimination.

Suggested Teaching Techniques

1. On a card write four words that are similar such as "in," "an," "on," and "no." Place the card in front of the child and read the words with him. Then show him a card that has only one of the words on it. Ask him to find the same word on his card. Initially tell him the word on the stimulus card, later let him read it for himself. Work for speed as well as accuracy (a stopwatch may be used to time his speed).
2. Use a tachistoscope or similar equipment to flash pictures, digits, letters, and words at varying speed. Begin by presenting a set of figures and asking the child to find the one that matches the figure on the screen. Later ask him to identify what he saw on the screen without giving him any prior clues. Use grossly different figures to encourage speed, then go to more similar figures for him to match and/or identify.

Related Instructional Materials

All About Me Boy's Book (Frank E. Richards Publishing Company, Inc.)
All About Me Girl's Book (Frank E. Richards Publishing Company, Inc.)
Animal Puzzles (Developmental Learning Materials)
Animal Stencils (Developmental Learning Materials)
Association Cards (Teaching Resources Corporation)
Association Pictures Cards I, II, III (Developmental Learning Materials)
At Christmas (McGraw-Hill Book Company)
At the Circus (McGraw-Hill Book Company)
At the Concert (McGraw-Hill Book Company)
Barnyard (Creative Visuals)
Basic Lessons for Retarded Children (John Day Company)
Boats (Creative Visuals)
Bowl of Fruit (Creative Visuals)

The Clown Family Speech Workbook (Charles C Thomas, Publisher)

Concept Clocks in Color (Teaching Resources Corporation)

Configuration Cards (Teaching Resources Corporation)

Discovering Opposites (Instructo Corporation)

Dubnoff School Program 2 (Teaching Resources Corporation)

Frostig Program for Development of Visual Perception (Follett Educational Corporation)

Geometric Shapes in Color (Teaching Resources Corporation)

Goldman-Lynch Sounds and Symbols Development Kit (American Guidance Service, Inc.)

Go-Mo Game Set (Go-Mo Products, Inc.)

Hayes Pre-Primer Non-Reading Activities (Hayes School Publications, Inc.)

Helping Young Children Develop Language Skills (Council for Exceptional Children)

Individual Word Study Cards, Set I (Scott, Foresman and Company)

In the City (McGraw-Hill Book Company)

In the House (McGraw-Hill Book Company)

Learning Lotto, Selection 2 (Creative Playthings)

Learning to Think Series (Science Research Associates, Inc.)

Little Picture Cards (Scott, Foresman and Company)

My First Picture Dictionary (Scott, Foresman and Company)

My Pictionary (Scott, Foresman and Company)

My Second Picture Dictionary (Scott, Foresman and Company)

Now I Look (John Day Company)

Observation and Memory: Jack-O-Lantern Has Lost His Hat (Sterling Educational Films)

On the Farm (McGraw-Hill Book Company)

Perception Puzzles (Creative Playthings)

Picture Stories (Allyn and Bacon, Inc.)

Ruth Cheves Program I (Teaching Resources Corporation)

See and Say Puzzle Cards (Teaching Resources Corporation)

Seeing Likeness and Differences, Levels 1-3 (Continental Press, Inc.)

The Sesame Street Learning Kit (Time-Life Books)

Shapes Puzzles (Developmental Learning Materials)

Small Form Puzzles (Teaching Resources Corporation)
Snail, Where Are You? (Harper and Row, Publishers)
Training in Some Prerequisites for Beginning Reading (Educator's Publishing Service)
Visual Discrimination (Eye Gate House, Inc.)
Visual Discrimination: Identification (Creative Visuals)
Visual Discrimination, Levels 1 and 2 (Continental Press, Inc.)
Visual Discrimination: Matching (Creative Visuals)
Visual Discrimination: Recall (Creative Visuals)
Visual Discrimination: Selection (Creative Visuals)
Visual Perception Skills (Educational Activities, Inc.)

Visual Memory and Sequencing

Associated Classroom Behavior

1. Often seems "too attentive" when involved in visual tasks.
2. Moves head or trunk excessively during visual tasks.
3. Does not seem to maintain interest and attention during visually presented lessons.
4. Fatigues easily while doing close work at his desk.
5. Cannot remember what he sees.
6. Does not know the alphabet by heart.
7. Is unable to learn the sounds of letters.
8. Has poor sitting posture while reading.
9. Holds head very close while reading books.
10. Points to words while reading.
11. Loses place while reading.
12. Reads in a word-by-word manner, and errors are of a visual memory type.
13. Has frequent visual perceptual reversals in both reading and writing.

Structuring the Learning Environment

1. Use audiovisual equipment to reinforce visual learning.

2. Allow the child to trace over words on flashcards when he is unable to remember the word in his reading lesson.
3. With younger children, use activities which will also develop the large muscles while working on sequencing.
4. Use auditory clues whenever possible.

OBJECTIVE

To teach visual memory.

Suggested Teaching Techniques

1. Have the children form two teams facing each other about four feet apart. At a given signal, each person looks carefully at the player opposite him. At the second signal, both lines turn around and each person alters one item in his appearance (unties shoes, takes off glasses, etc.). On the third signal, the two lines face each other again and the children take turns telling what their partner did to change his appearance.
2. While sitting at the lunch table have the child close his eyes and point to specific objects on the table or on his plate. If he makes an error, he may open his eyes to correct himself.
3. Send the child on simple errands around the room. Before he goes on an errand he must tell what the errand is and how he will complete it.
4. Have the child describe and locate specific items in another room without going there. If he makes an error, he may visually check himself by going into the other room.
5. Place several toys or objects on the table and have the child carefully look at all of them for thirty seconds. Ask him to close his eyes while one object is removed. When he opens his eyes he is to tell which object is missing. Gradually increase the number of items to select from the

table.

6. Place several familiar toys or objects on a table behind the child or under a cover on the table in front of him. Let him study the objects for thirty seconds, then have him try to name all of the things he saw on the table.

7. Show the child a page from a catalog or magazine which has in it several pictures of items with which he is familiar. Cover the page and see if he can remember the pictures he just saw.

8. Draw a simple form or pattern on the chalkboard while the child is watching. Erase the drawing quickly and thoroughly, then ask the child to draw exactly what he saw on the board before it was erased.

9. Print labels to place on furniture, toys, etc. around the room. Ask the child to go around the room and copy down the printed words from specific objects. Later remove the labels or parts of the labels and ask the child to fill in the missing words or letters.

OBJECTIVE

To teach visual sequencing.

Suggested Teaching Techniques

1. Arrange colored beads or objects in a sequence. Give the child the same number and color of beads and ask him to duplicate the pattern.

2. Line the children up in a specific order by sex, age, color of hair, etc. Verbalize the sequencing for the children. Rearrange the line of children and then ask one child to put the children back in the original order.

3. Start a pattern of pictures or designs on a bulletin board. Give the child pictures or designs to continue the picture or design and ask him to finish the pattern. Later put this same activity on a piece of paper for him to draw in the missing parts at his desk.

4. Start a paper chain in a pattern of colors, then ask the

child to complete the pattern using strips of colored paper provided for him.

5. Expose a simple pattern or design for a few seconds. Place it face down and ask the child to draw it from memory. Initally, the pattern should be geometric shapes, all the same kind, of various sizes. Later mix up the types of shapes used.

OBJECTIVE

To teach visual memory sequencing.

Suggested Teaching Techniques

1. Place three children in a row of chairs. Have another child observe where each child is sitting. While that child has his eyes closed, the other three move to other chairs. The child who is "it" must then try to put the three children back in the same chairs they started out in. Variations of this activity include telling where the three children should be sitting and drawing pictures of where the children should be sitting.

2. Arrange objects in a specific sequence in front of the child. Scramble up the order of the objects and ask the child to place them in the correct order again. Begin with only three or four objects and expand on these. Later use similar objects or even letters of the alphabet.

3. Ask the child to look carefully at a series of pictures in front of him. Let another child rearrange the pictures while the first child turns his head or closes his eyes. After the first child tries to complete the series as it was originally, the second child must tell him whether he was correct or not. The children may take turns playing this game.

4. Using wooden or felt letters and numbers will allow the child to use his tactile skills when learning to sequence. He can trace around the letters to reinforce his visual cues. In the beginning, have him arrange them in order,

using a stimulus to copy from. Later remove the stimulus or parts of the stimulus and let him arrange his letters from memory. A similar activity may be done later with paper and pencil at the desk.

5. Place five different objects in a paper bag. Take them out, one at a time and name and/or describe them. Then ask the child to name the objects that he saw and the order in which he saw them. This may be done also by having the child draw pictures of the objects or by having him write the names of the objects he saw, depending on his level of competency. In the beginning, use objects which are related to or in related categories.

Related Instructional Materials

Balloon 1 and 2 (McGraw-Hill Book Company)
Building Bead Patterns (Ideal School Supply Company)
Butterflies 1 and 2 (McGraw-Hill Book Company)
Clown 1 and 2 (McGraw-Hill Book Company)
Color Pattern Board (Ideal School Supply Company)
Design Blocks and Patterns (Ideal School Supply Company)
Dot-to-Dot Pattern Sheets (Developmental Learning Materials)
Dubnoff School Programs (Teaching Resources Corporation)
Erie Program (Teaching Resources Corporation)
Fitzhugh Plus Program (Allied Educational Council)
Flip and Build (Teaching Resources Corporation)
Frostig Program for the Development of Visual Perception (Follett Publishing Company)
Fruit and Animal Puzzles (Teaching Resources Corporation)
Geometric Shapes in Color (Teaching Resources Corporation)
Language Lotto (Appleton-Century-Crofts)
Large Construction Set (Media)
Large Form Puzzles (Teaching Resources Corporation)
Lift Off to Reading (Science Research Associates, Inc.)
Loops to Learn (McGraw-Hill Book Company)
Matrix Games (Appleton-Century-Crofts)
Peabody Language Development Kits, Levels P-3 (American Guidance Service, Inc.)

Pre-Writing Design Cards (Developmental Learning Materials)
Pyramid Puzzles (Ideal School Supply Company)
Readiness for Learning (J. B. Lippencott Company)
Readiness and Reading for the Retarded Child (John Day Company)
Reading Fundamentals Program (Continental Press, Inc.)
Sequence Puzzles: Building a House (Creative Playthings)
Sequence Puzzles: From Tree to Table (Creative Playthings)
Sequence Puzzles: Mailing a Letter (Creative Playthings)
Sequence Puzzles: Milk Production (Creative Playthings)
Sequential Picture Cards (Developmental Learning Materials)
Shapes Puzzles (Developmental Learning Materials)
Small Form Puzzles (Teaching Resources Corporation)
Speech Lingo (Speech and Language Materials, Inc.)
TRY: Experiences for Young Children (Noble and Noble Publishers, Inc.)
Two-Dimensional Color Block Designs (Ideal School Supply Company)
Visual Memory (Educational Activities, Inc.)
Visual Perception Skills Filmstrips (Educational Activities, Inc.)
Words Inside Words (J. B. Lippencott Company)

Chapter 8

HINTS FOR VISUAL PERCEPTUAL MOTOR LEARNING PROBLEMS ... YES I HAVE IT, BUT I CAN'T PUT IT ALL TOGETHER

$\mathbf{F}$IVE major areas of concern have been selected for the development of Hints for Perceptual Motor Learning Problems. *Gross Motor Coordination* problems involve the inability of the child to coordinate his visual perceptions with his large muscle movements. He may be able to observe others in the classroom who are making the correct motorical movements, yet he may not be able to correctly imitate these movements by himself. He may be a very clumsy child on the playground who either refuses to join the other children for vigorous athletic activities or who becomes the class clown because he knows he will look foolish in his attempts to participate no matter how hard he tries. He may become a loner who prefers to sit on the sidelines during playground activities or gym periods.

Laterality and Directionality problems are exhibited in the child who confuses left and right and other directional concepts. His reading and writing activities may show reversals of whole words or just letters. Concepts such as up and down are also confusing to the child, and may cause interference with his ability to complete simple classroom assignments, especially worksheets involving these concepts. Instead of putting his name in the upper right hand corner of a paper, he may put it in the lower left hand corner or even on the back of the page.

Spatial Awareness problems are evidenced in the child who is unable to print the alphabet in uniform-sized letters. Some of his letters may take up two spaces on the lined paper while others may take up three or more spaces. He has difficulty in planning ahead during his writing assignments and his letters may even go completely off the edge of the paper. When copying from the chalkboard or from a book, he may have all of his words running together into one continuous word. In reading, he may actually see the sentences as one long continuous word and thus he will have difficulty separating the words to make any sense.

Form Constancy problems are also related to other visual perceptual problems such as visual discrimination. He may not be able to transfer the visual learning from one situation to another when the task involves specific shapes unless the shapes are exactly identical on the original and on the reproduced copy with which he is working. He has difficulty in transferring one type of printed symbol to another, i.e. from the teacher's manuscript to the textbook's manuscript. This presents particular difficulties when the child tries to learn how to read because he may have learned only one form of the letters of the alphabet and when a different form of the letters is used he may not see any relationship between the symbols he learned originally and the symbols he is currently trying to read.

Eye-Hand Coordination involves the coordination between what the eye perceives and what the hand reproduces. The small muscles of the hand may not be coordinated enough to complete the task, even though the eye is able to adequately perceive the stimulus. Coloring and cutting activities may prove to be very frustrating to the child because he is unable to control the fine muscles of his hand to accomplish what his eyes are relating to him. When trying to write, the child may also experience difficulty with his ability to correctly grasp the pencil as well as with his ability to reproduce even simple geometric figures. He may become so frustrated that he refuses to even attempt these types of fine motor coordination tasks.

When a child is suspected of having perceptual motor learning problems, he should be carefully screened by a trained professional to determine his functioning level in the areas related to specific perceptual motor tasks. These skills are developmental in nature, and the young or immature child will normally have some difficulty in these areas. Age scales for specific tasks may be obtained from trained psychologists or others in the field of special education.

Gross Motor Coordination

Associated Classroom Behavior

1. Appears to be extremely clumsy for his age.
2. Often stumbles over his own feet or over no visible object within his reach.
3. Cannot march to the rhythm of music.
4. May refuse to participate in active sports and games on the playground.
5. Does not enjoy any organized athletic activities such as those employed during regularly scheduled gym periods.
6. Often bumps into furniture, people, etc. even though he tries to avoid them.
7. May get into frequent fights for pushing and shoving, yet he claims total innocence because he did not see the other child in time to avoid making bodily contact with him.

Structuring the Learning Environment

1. Make sure that all aisles and open spaces within the classroom really are aisles and open spaces by requiring that their floor areas be free from extraneous toys, classroom materials, etc.
2. Avoid cluttered areas within the classroom and place furniture in clusters or away from the main flow of traffic.
3. Involve the child in class or group athletic events, even if it means as scorekeeper (a vital role) or other functional roles which are not competitive.

OBJECTIVE

To teach motor coordination through the use of childhood games and activities.

Suggested Teaching Techniques

1. Hop Scotch may be played either indoors or outdoors. A

permanent playing area may be made with paint or colored tape. The size of the squares and the playing rules may be adjusted to meet the individual child's needs. For example, smaller squares may be used with a child who is hopping with both feet rather than with one foot during the initial learning phases of the activity.

2. Leap Frog may be played by two or more children. While one child crouches down, the other leaps over him, using his hands on the first child's back for support.

3. Fox and Geese is usually played in the snow, but the same playing area may be made with tape stuck to the floor. A large circle is made with six or eight pie-shaped wedges within it. The center of the "pie" where all of the paths merge, is the "free" area. One child is selected to be the fox while the other children are the geese. The fox chases the geese until he catches one of them. The goose that is caught then becomes the fox. At all times, the children must stay on the paths made around and within the circle by the tape. If actual snow is used, the paths are made by running along imaginary lines indicating the outer edge and inner lines which make the area look like a huge pie when all of the lines are complete.

4. Jump ropes may be used by individual children or by groups. Simple rhymes and songs may be used to help control the rate and rhythm of the jumping.

5. Scooters may be purchased or they may be made from discarded pieces of wood or crates and skate wheels. They may be made to operate from either a sitting or standing position.

6. Roller skates may also be used to help improve both gross motor coordination and balance.

7. Walking beams may be made from 2" X 4" boards, roughly 12' long. Have the child begin learning to walk on this type of board by first letting him experiment with the same type of activity using wide masking tape on the floor. When he is able to walk on the tape without any problems, have him walk on the board while it is resting directly on the floor. Gradually increase the distance be-

tween the floor and the beam by using supports at either end, plus one in the middle if necessary. A variety of activities may be incorporated into the use of such beams. Such activities might include walking forward, walking backward, walking sideways, and walking to a specific rhythm or beat. At first, both moral and physical support may be needed by the child for these activities. The ultimate goal is to have the child be able to perform these types of activities without the physical support of the teacher or other aids.

8. Simple stilts may be made from discarded and rinsed out cans. Smaller cans, such as soup cans, may be used with smaller children. Larger cans, such as fruit juice cans, may be used with larger children. By taking a nail and a hammer, two holes can be punched on opposite sides of the can, close to the top of the can (the bottom of the can should be removed with a can opener). A long piece of cord or twine can be used to make "handles" for each can by knotting the ends after stringing them through the holes. The child can then hold on to these handles while he places his feet on the tops of the cans and uses them as stilts.

9. Regular stilts can be made with 2″ X 4″ boards cut between 6′ and 8′ in length, depending on the height of the child and the distance desired between the foot braces and the bottom of the stilt. The foot braces may be made by sawing a piece of the original board into a rectangle approximately 5″ long. Saw the rectangle diagonally so that two triangles are formed. Nail each triangle to the 4″ side of each stilt, with the pointed end of the triangle toward the bottom of the stilt and the long part of foot brace facing away from the side of the stilt.

Objective

To develop gross motor coordination through the use of tires.

Suggested Teaching Techniques

1. Have the child climb through a tire while it is held for him by another child.
2. Have the child jump over the tire after getting a running start.
3. Have the child run around the tires placed in various weaving patterns so that the child will have to change directions while he is running.
4. Have the child skip around the tires placed in various geometric patterns.
5. Have the child stand inside one of the tires and jump inside of another tire.
6. Have the child jump from one tire to another using both feet, then one foot, to jump.
7. Have the child stand inside of a tire and jump to the left or to the right.
8. Have the child do a frog jump from one tire to another.
9. Have the child jump from tire to tire until every tire has been jumped through. Begin with only two or three tires, work up to eight or ten tires.
10. Have the child walk around the rim of the tire. Work for speed as well as accuracy.

OBJECTIVE

To develop gross motor coordination through classroom activities.

Suggested Teaching Techniques

1. Make a walk-through maze of the classroom furniture. Leave enough room at first so that the children will be successful in their attempts to walk through the maze without knocking over the furniture. Gradually make the path narrower and more complicated for them.
2. Arrange the classroom furniture so that the children will have to walk and crawl through the same maze. Have

musical noisemakers hanging from a box to be crawled through so that the children will receive auditory stimulation at the same time as they are receiving the motor stimulation.

3. Take six chairs, three in a row, and face them back to back. Drape an old sheet over them to make a tunnel for the children to crawl through.

4. For a more detailed maze, add a walking beam, a low table which the children must crawl under on their stomachs, and some steps and/or pattern walking. The pattern walking can be done with large colored squares or rope designs (tie the rope in a large "X" by looping it around the legs of four chairs). The children may be required to step in all four triangles made from the rope pattern or only in designated triangles.

5. Use a rope to play the High Water-Low Water game which starts with the rope on the floor and the children stepping or jumping over it. Gradually, the rope is raised off the ground, inch by inch. It can be held by two children, but for extra steadiness, it is better to attach it to permanent objects such as a desk and chair.

6. For Angels in the Snow, try using pieces of stryofoam to help the children see what they are actually doing. This may cause problems because it has a tendency to cling to clothes and hair, so keep a wisk broom handy. Also be sure that this is done in an area that can be easily cleaned up, such as the inside of an inflatable swimming pool.

7. Hop Scotch can be used in a variety of ways. The children can begin by jumping with feet together, gradually hopping on one foot at a time on the single squares. This activity can also be incorporated into learning colors, numbers, and letters.

8. Additional activities may include body rolls, somersaults, hopping on one foot, or jumping over low obstacles.

Related Instructional Materials

Due to the nature of the activities incorporated under Gross Motor Coordination, there are no commercial instructional materials listed in this section.

Laterality and Directionality

Associated Classroom Behavior

1. Has poor internal and external awareness of left-right and other directional concepts.
2. Tends to draw circles clockwise instead of counterclockwise.
3. Often begins a task with one hand and finishes with the other.
4. Is poor in activities requiring balance.
5. Tends to confuse "b" and "d," has other reversals.
6. Exhibits poor writing integration and closure.
7. Has problems in visual-motor activities such as copying.
8. Exhibits frequent visual perceptual reversals in reading, writing, letters, numbers.

Structuring the Learning Environment

1. Provide a left-right discrimination training program to help teach directionality.
2. Develop eye-hand coordination as a part of the readiness program to help the child firmly establish his knowledge of right and left and to improve his fine muscle movements. Choose hand and eye activities appropriate to the child's age and maturational level.

OBJECTIVE

To teach the concept of right and left.

Suggested Teaching Techniques

1. To teach the child right and left, have him make a red

"X" with a felt marker on his right thumb. With a green marker, have him do the same thing with his left thumb. Give him oral directions such as: Show me your left hand. Show me your left foot. Show me your right ear. Leave the color on the child's thumb for reading and other lessons until he has left and right clearly imprinted in his mind.

2. Have the child select an inexpensive ring to wear so that he will have a permanent clue to which is his right hand. Call his attention to the fact that the beginning sounds of "ring" and "right" are alike.

3. Point out to the child the common ways right and left are used in everyday life such as how we set the table, which directions boys' and girls' clothes button, which side of the street we should walk or ride.

4. Have the child count pennies while moving them from his left side to his right side.

5. Have the child name or count rows of objects from left to right. Count and name by pointing with the fingers, then count and name using the eyes. Finally, repeat the activity with the eyes closed.

6. Sit in front of the child and have four or five small objects or toys on a desk. Pick up one of these with your right hand and hold it over to the child's left side. Urge him to look at it only with his eyes (no head movement) and name it. While his attention is on the first object, pick up another object with your left hand and hold it over to the child's right side. As soon as he identifies the first object, ask him to look at the second one. While he is looking at this second object, repeat the initial activity with your right hand, the child's left side, and a new object. Keep the game going, building speed as his competency increases. As you observe more rapid eye movements and less head movement, hold the object in various positions away from the child so that his eyes will move in all directions.

OBJECTIVE

To teach directionality.

Suggested Teaching Techniques

1. Have the child find the odd picture within a group of pictures. Make cards using three identical and one odd picture on a card. The odd picture should be different only in its relation to the other objects. While three objects might be right side up, the fourth one might be on its side up side down, etc.
2. Replace manuscript writing with cursive writing if the child is able to maintain the flow required for this type of writing. The constant stops and starts in manuscript writing are often the cause for directionality problems with writing exercises.

Related Instructional Materials

Creative Dramatics for Handicapped Children (John Day Company)

Developing Learning Readiness (McGraw-Hill Book Company)

Dubnoff School Program I (Teaching Resources Corporation)

Fairbanks-Robinson Program, Levels I and II (Teaching Resources Corp.)

Finger Play I and II (Children's Music Center, Incorporated)

Frostig Program for the Development of Visual Perception (Follett Educational Corporation)

I Want to Learn (Follett Educational Corporation)

Lacing Cards (Developmental Learning Materials)

Move-Grow-Learn Movement Education (Follett Educational Corporation)

Readiness for Learning (J. B. Lippencott Company)

Remediation of Learning Disabilities (Fearon Publishers, Inc.)

Spatial Discrimination Workbooks (Follett Educational Corpo-

ration)
Text Manual for Remedial Handwriting (Interstate Printers and Publishers, Incorporated)
TRY: Experiences for Young Children (Noble and Noble Publishers, Inc.)

Spatial Awareness

Associated Classroom Behavior

1. Displays impaired size discrimination.
2. Is unable to judge distance.
3. Has difficulty with directionality.
4. Has distorted concept of body image.
5. Is impaired in ability to locate body in relation to other objects.
6. Exhibits frequent clumsiness.
7. Has difficulty understanding words designating spatial position.
8. Confuses letters such as "b" and "d" or "m" and "n."
9. Sees printed or written words as running together or even off the page.
10. Demonstrates poor writing ability, such as oversized letters and words for the space provided.
11. Writes words running together or off the page which may reflect an inability to accurately gauge spatial relationships.

Structuring the Learning Environment

1. Teach right and left; middle, first, and last; up and down; top and bottom; front and back concepts.
2. Use color cues to help with the association of words of relative position.
3. In training for spatial orientation, the teacher should attempt to help the child who is "lost" in space to find an "anchor," to stay within confines, to use judgment in spatial matters. The child should be taught to walk

halfway, all the way; to find which is nearer, which is farther away. He should be taught the concept of top, bottom, front, sides, and back. He should be taught to put things in, on, under, in front of, over, and behind. The teacher should stress relationships and sequences. At first, the teacher may need to structure everything the child does.

4. For children with perceptual problems involving the inability to judge positions in space, the teacher should provide some cues on the child's desk to aid him in making directional judgment. For example, a green marker might be placed on the left side of the desk to indicate *go* and a red marker might be placed on the right side of the desk to indicate *stop* for both reading and writing activities.

5. Guide his work if he has difficulty following the directions. Give him cues to aid him in following the directions.

6. A teacher who reminds herself that a child does not perceive things as she does will be able to understand the problems of such children. The teaching of the awareness of top, bottom, under, and over may be done through body movement as well as object placement.

7. The child often learns better if he has a concrete activity upon which to focus his attention. Rather than showing the child two blocks and saying that one is big and the other is little, let the child handle the blocks and describe them. The teacher may also point out the characteristics she wants the child to learn while he is handling the blocks. Such an activity focuses the child's attention while emphasizing the sensory training he is receiving.

8. Make allowances when giving assignments. If the teacher is primarily concerned with the quality of the thought that goes into an assignment, it is often self-defeating to hold the child with visual perceptual problems to high standards of neatness. If the problem is severe enough, the child may not really be able to write at all. Instead, he might dictate his report on a tape recorder or to someone

at home who can put it into written form for him to read.

To teach spatial awareness of forms and objects.

Suggested Teaching Techniques

1. With beginners, the teacher might use a color cone and a toy postal box which has the various shaped slots to initiate work in spatial relationships. A child with fine motor problems may have difficulty in handling these objects even though he understands the concepts and can visually discriminate them.

2. Use a great deal of drill to teach the concepts of first, middle, and last, since these are very important directions for the child and they are sometimes difficult to learn for them. Real objects should be used first. Use three objects: one red, one green, and one black. Place the red object first and the green object last. Show the child that one is first, one is middle, and one is the last. Ask him to repeat this sequence, first with you and then by himself. Gradually work toward fading out the use of the color cues so that he will not think that a specific color always indicates a particular place in space.

3. Letters that are spatially confusing for children with poor up-down and poor left-right directional sense, such as "m-w" and "n-u," are learned through repeated tracing, coloring, and cutting.

4. Rolling and shaping letters out of clay is often helpful. The color, depth, and texture of the clay produces forms that can be more easily identified both visually and tactily.

5. The use of pipe cleaners to make the individual letters is also very useful, especially for older children who might feel negative toward the use of clay. The letters can then be used to make words and perhaps even simple sen-

tences.

6. Have the child find odd pictures: pictures with baskets that have handles in the wrong places, tables that are in unusual positions, etc.

7. Help the child learn to judge size, length, height, and distance through the use of paired cards:

   a. Size: Pictures of small balls, large balls, small squares, large squares, etc.

   b. Length: Pictures of long trains, short trains, long sticks, short sticks, etc.

   c. Height: Pictures of tall men, short men, tall buildings, short buildings, etc.

   d. Distance: Pictures of objects that are close together, objects that are far apart, etc.

OBJECTIVE

To teach spatial awareness of own body.

Suggested Teaching Techniques

1. Before guiding the child through paper and pencil activities involving the concepts of up, down, under, etc. let him use his own body for similar activities. Let him crawl *under* a chair, *over* a rug, *between* two desks, etc. If he seems confused, play "Follow-the-Leader" and guide him through the activities. Verbally describe the actions being made and encourage the child to also verbalize his actions.

2. Other activities which help to orient the child in space include the following:

   a. Have the child hunt for an object that is hidden.

   b. Have the child hunt for many hidden objects, such as peanuts (he may eat the ones he finds).

   c. Play games in which one child acts out the teacher's directions, given either verbally or in writing, which involve spatial concepts and relationships. Have the other children judge whether the first child followed

the directions correctly.
d. Have the child listen to sounds, with and/or without seeing the person making the sound, and identify the sound and/or the source of the sound.

Related Instructional Materials

Cut and Paste (Jenn Publications)
Directional-Spatial Pattern Board Exercises: Dubnoff School Program, Level 2 (Teaching Resources Corporation)
Frostig Program for the Development of Visual Perception (Follett Educational Corporation)
Geoboard (Cuisenaire Company of America, Incorporated)
How? (Frank E. Richards Publishing Company)
Move-Grow-Learn Movement Education (Follett Educational Corporation)
Physical Fitness for Intermediate Children (Kimbo Educational Records)
Physical Fitness for Primary Children (Kimbo Educational Records)
See and Say Puzzle Cards (Teaching Resources Corporation)
Sequential Perceptual Motor Exercises: Dubnoff School Program, Level 1 (Teaching Resources Corporation)
Visual-Motor Perceptual Teaching Materials: Ruth Cheves Program 1 (Teaching Resources Corporation)
Visual Perception Skills (Educational Activities, Incorporated)
What's Inside-What's Outside (Hudson Photographic Industries, Incorporated)
What's on Top-What's Underneath (Hudson Photographic Industries, Incorporated)
What's Warm-What's Cold (Hudson Photographic Industries, Incorporated)
When? (Frank E. Richards Publishing Company)
Where? (Frank E. Richards Publishing Company)
Why? (Frank E. Richards Publishing Company)
Words and Movement about Myself and Musical Games (Rhythm Record Co.)
Zig-Zag Stacking Tower (Childcraft Educational Corporation)

Form Constancy

Associated Classroom Behavior

1. Is unable to identify and recognize like and unlike forms and/or objects.
2. Is unable to transfer forms from actual objects to pictures or from pictures to actual objects.
3. Confuses words that look similar; has difficulty with all symbols.
4. May learn to recognize a number, letter, or word when he sees it in a particular form or context but is unable to recognize the same symbol when it is presented in a different manner.
5. Displays impaired size discrimination.

Structuring the Learning Environment

1. Structure the classroom activities to include matching, sorting, pasting, and coloring experiences.
2. Supplement visual perceptual training with tactile perceptual training. The inability to recognize objects through the sense of touch might be a tactile deficiency. This is not a very common problem, but there are some children who need training in this area. Educating this modality to its fullest capacity will further the total learning process and will provide a basis for subsequent techniques designed to help with various visual-receptive problems.

Objective

To teach the awareness of like forms and objects.

Suggested Teaching Techniques

1. Have the child trace around blocks and cutouts or trace the outlines of simple, heavy line pictures. This furnishes

a definite visual pattern for the child to follow while allowing freedom of direction and mobility of the hand. It also creates a need to use the nonpreferred hand in a supportive role while it holds the pattern being traced.

2. Tear off the labels from cans and small boxes and have the child take these to the "market" set up in a corner of the classroom to choose the correct items by matching the labels. Whenever possible, say the name of the item as the child searches for it and finds it.

3. Have the child make pictures on the pegboard (acoustic ceiling tiles and plastic golf tees with the points cut off make excellent inexpensive pegboards). If it is difficult for him to create a design, cut familiar shapes out of light cardboard around which the pegs can be placed by the child. Remove the cardboard and have the child compare the outline of the pegs and the cardboard cut-out. This furnishes the opportunity for eye-hand activity to be followed by visual discrimination and inspection for similarities and comparisons. As the child gains skill in making "pictures" on the pegboard, urge him to use fewer pegs in his outlines. When he can illustrate a square, for example, by placing the corner pegs in the proper positions, he has learned to perceive form by using minimum visual cues.

4. Use educational toys and games to provide the child with the opportunity to match shapes. These furnish experience with visual comparisons, the visual relationship of size, shape, and solidity, as well as tactile comparisons of the same basic characteristics.

5. Have the child match and compare kitchen objects in cupboards or shelves set up in the classroom. Sorting dishes and silverware is a basic visual comparison activity. Canned goods can be stacked according to their labels. Colors, numbers, words, etc. on cereal boxes can be used for visual comparisons.

6. Matching colors. The teacher and the child have an identical set of blocks (start with two colors). The teacher puts one on the desk and asks the child to match it. Add

one color at a time until he can match all of the colors quickly and with ease.

7. Matching forms. A pocket chart may be used. A sample of each geometric form is pasted on a pocket at the left. The child picks up a form from a pile of assorted forms placed in front of him and places it in the correct pocket. If the child has difficulty in identifying the form, the teacher may hold one of his fingers and guide it along the edge of the shape while describing how the shape looks and feels. A comparison of the two shapes may be made visually, tactily, and verbally.

8. Matching sizes. A pocket chart with three different sized circles pasted at the left may be used. The child is asked to select the correct sized circle to place in each of the three pockets on the chart. Other shapes or forms may also be used for this type of activity.

9. Matching objects. A box containing duplicates of several objects is presented to the child. The teacher places one of each of the objects at the top of the desk, one at a time, and asks the child to match them. Similar but not identical objects may be used later to help with the teaching of categories.

10. Sorting forms. Geometric forms (cut-outs) are put into separate boxes according to shape. Place two (later three, four, etc.) open boxes on the child's desk. Each box should have a geometric cut-out pasted on it. The child is asked to sort a pile of cut-outs placed in front of him by putting each one in the correct box.

11. Sorting sizes. A shoe box containing pairs of several articles is emptied on the desk in front of the child. He is asked to put all of the little articles in one part of the box labeled "Little" and all of the large articles in the other section labeled "Big." A teacher example may be used initially to teach the child what is expected of him. Start with two or three objects of each size and continue increasing the number of objects. At first, be certain that the objects which are big are in direct contrast to those which are little. Sorting of heavy and light, hard and

soft, long and short objects may be done in this same way.

12. Place the following objects on the table and ask the child to match them according to shape: clock, ring, ball, saucer, box, toy chair, square, picture frame. Other combinations may be used later on.

13. Cutting, coloring, and pasting are done in increasingly more difficult steps, similar to those outlined below:

   a. The child is given two sheets of paper with a single, large identical geometric form on each sheet. He is asked to cut one of them out and then paste it on the second form.

   b. Duplicate papers containing two forms are presented with color cues being used. One form on each paper is black and one is red. The child is to cut out one set and then paste the forms on the second set, matching both color and form. When he is first presented with material where he has to make a choice, the child should be given as many clues as possible.

   c. Cards containing four forms are presented to the child. The forms on one set are outlined in black, those on the second set are outlined in four different colors. The child is asked to color each black outlined form to match one of the colored forms on the other set of cards. He is then asked to cut, match, and paste his forms on the other set of forms.

   d. When the child can read the printed forms, the outlines on both sets of cards are made in black. The second set of forms has the color words printed inside of each form. The child is asked to read, color, cut, match, and paste his forms onto the second set of forms.

OBJECTIVE

To teach the differentiation between unlike forms and objects.

Suggested Teaching Techniques

1. Have the child identify blocks of different shapes by

touch. The child looks at and feels each of the several different shaped blocks (start with two). With his eyes closed, he feels one that has been placed in his hand by the teacher. She then places the block back on the desk with the others. The child is asked to open his eyes and identify the block he just felt. If he cannot do this, he should be encouraged to feel the block again, but this time with his eyes open. An alternative to this would be to have the child identify the block while his eyes are still closed since the visual stimuli may be confusing to certain children.

2. Have the child identify other objects by touch. Use a ball, a doll, a top, a toy train, etc. and use the directions given in #1 above. Also, the use of form boards may be beneficial. Here, the child traces his finger (possibly guided by the teacher) around a form and then points to the matching space on the form board. Evaluation of his success is accomplished by having him place the form he is working with into the space he has just identified on the form board. This should be done with the eyes open and then with the eyes closed.

3. Have the child identify one of several textures by touch. Small pieces of fur, glass (but no sharp edges), sandpaper, velvet, and satin should be pasted on rectangular blocks of wood or sturdy cardboard. The child feels them while looking at them and then tries to identify them by touch alone. Also have the child identify materials of different consistency. Cans or pails may be filled with sand, flour, sugar, gravel, or soap flakes and the same procedures should be followed.

4. Use a Surprise Bag to hide the objects. The child reaches in the bag and tries to identify an object by touch alone. He then pulls the object out of the bag to check his answer.

5. Have the child compare two pictures from a magazine, two photographs, two leaves, etc. Progress to comparing two words or two objects that are different. Begin with dramatically different pictures, leaves, words, etc.

6. Use furniture, pictures, magazines, books, and other classroom objects for the child's visual comparisons. Ask him how two chairs are alike and how they are different. Ask him to describe the likenesses and differences according to size, shape, weight, and texture. If he makes unreasonable errors, let him check his visual judgments by touching or lifting the objects in question.

7. Sorting colors. Use beads or blocks of different colors, beginning with two and increasing the number as the child's ability increases. Start by placing a red bead in one box, a yellow bead in the second box, and asking the child to repeat this process. Color cues inside of the boxes may be used initially, along with word cards depicting the colors. Gradually phase out the color cues and use only the word cards.

OBJECTIVE

To teach the recognition of simple forms and objects when presented in a different manner.

Suggested Teaching Techniques

1. Begin by teaching the child basic figures such as circle, square, rectangle and triangle. When he knows these well, add detail to the figures to form objects. A square could become a window, a rectangle could become a door, a triangle could become a sail, and a circle could become a wheel. These details, at first, should be added in a different color from that used with the basic figures. When the child has mastered the identification of these, the details can be added in the same color as the figures.

2. Show the child a picture, very simple and uncluttered, from a magazine or coloring book. Let the child point out or trace with his finger or crayon the basic figures which the objects in the picture suggest. A picture of a church should suggest a rectangle (the walls or doors), a square (the windows), and a triangle (the steeple). Do not

start with the picture and attempt to work backwards. The child must know and be able to recognize the basic figures before he can progress to the identification of these shapes as a basis for other objects.

3. Give the child practice in copying simple forms such as those reproduced below:

When the child can copy these well and without error, use them for training visual memory. Present one and let him study it for a moment, then remove it and have him reproduce it. Reversals, inversions, and omissions here will reveal potential reading difficulties, and will indicate the need for more intensive training.

Related Instructional Materials

Alphabet Cards (Developmental Learning Materials)
Buzzer Board (Educator's Publishing Service)
Clear Stencils (Developmental Learning Materials)
Daily Sensorimotor Training Activities (Stanley-Bowmar Company)
Design Cards for Large Parquetry (Developmental Learning Materials)
Fitzhugh Plus Program: Perceptual Learning and Understanding Skills (Allied Educational Council)
Frostig Program for the Development of Visual Perception (Follett Educational Corporation)
Games Make Spelling Fun (Fearon Publishers, Inc.)
Large Parquetry Blocks (Developmental Learning Materials)
My Kindergarten Program (Follett Educational Corporation)
Mystery Box (Scott, Foresman and Company)
Parquetry Insert Boards (Developmental Learning Materials)

Pre-writing Design Cards (Developmental Learning Materials)
Readiness in Language Arts (Behavioral Research Laboratories)
Reading Fundamentals Program (Continental Press, Incorporated)
Shapes Puzzles (Developmental Learning Materials)
Small Parquetry Blocks (Developmental Learning Materials)
Small Parquetry Design (Developmental Learning Materials)
TRY: Experiences for Young Children (Noble and Noble Publishers, Incorporated)
Visual Perception Skills (Educational Activities, Incorporated)

Eye-Hand Coordination

Associated Classroom Behaviors

1. Is unable to hold a focus and to use both eyes for binocular vision. Closes one eye, tilts head, etc.
2. Demonstrates inability to control focus for all distances and for changing distances. Holds book too close or too far away and tends to move book closer on difficult words.
3. Has poor ability to look accurately and smoothly from one object to another. Loses place, uses finger to point to each word or needs a paper marker.
4. Moves head along a line instead of holding head still and moving only the eyes. This often causes him to lose his place.
5. Shows inadequate ability in following a moving object smoothly with his eyes.
6. Has an inability to fix vision at the place where it is most likely to give a total view.
7. Looks at the end of a word and guesses by using minimal clues.
8. Combines the ending of one word with the beginning of the next word when reading.
9. Has difficulty finding key words.

Structuring the Learning Environment

1. Teach eye movement patterns to develop visual skills. How well a child sees his world and the objects in it is determined by how well he learns to visually inspect the contents of the space which surrounds him. The control of eye movement is essential if the visual inspection is to be effective and efficient.

OBJECTIVE

To develop large muscle hand/arm coordination.

Suggested Teaching Techniques

1. The child who demonstrates any degree of rigidity in his arms (which is usually present to some degree in every child having difficulty in school) should work on circular movements first using both hands in unison. These can be varied through developmental directions also:
   a. Right hand moving clockwise while left hand moves counterclockwise.
   b. Left hand moves clockwise and the right hand moves in the opposite direction.
   c. Both hands moving clockwise.
   d. Both hands moving counterclockwise.
2. The child cannot fully perceive a straight line unless he can also draw one. Bilaterally drawn lines at the chalkboard give the child the opportunity to feel and see the lines that he will use in his workbooks in the primary grades. The child stands at the chalkboard with his nose against the board. He extends both arms as far as he can in opposite directions. Moving both arms at the same time, he draws a line from the farthest point right to the center of the bullseye (where his nose is against the board). He continues drawing the lines from the outside of this imaginary circle to the center of it until he has

made what looks like spokes of a wheel.

3. A variation of the above activity is to make two parallel lines of marks (an X will do) on the blackboard that are equal distance from the center of the child's body. The child stands against the board and draws parallel lines in to the center of the imaginary circle. The final product should look like a ladder rather than a wheel.

OBJECTIVE

To develop eye muscles and eye coordination.

Suggested Teaching Techniques

1. Attach a string to a rubber ball (about two inches in diameter) so it can be hung from a light fixture or a doorway. Have the ball at about the child's nose level when he stands facing it. Do the following exercises:
   a. Swing the ball gently back and forth and have the child watch it.
   b. Swing the ball from side to side again and instruct the child to watch it move without using his head, only his eyes.
   c. Hang the ball about three feet off the floor. Have the child lie on his back directly underneath of the ball. Now swing the ball in a rather large circle and have the child watch the ball with his eyes until the ball comes to a complete stop.

2. Have the children help each other in developing eye movement patterns. Attach a small cut-out of an airplane to the eraser of a pencil. One child holds the pencil and makes the airplane "fly" for the other child. The second child is the "plane spotter" and must keep his eyes on the plane at all times. The "pilot" of the plane is instructed to watch the "spotter" to see if he is really watching the plane as closely as he should be. Points may be kept according to how many times the pilot catches the spotter not following the plane. This type of activity

should be used with the understanding that not all players will give one another the benefit of the doubt! "Jobs" (roles) may be exchanged.

3. Have the child hold his right and left forefingers erect, about twelve to fourteen inches apart and about twelve inches in front of his eyes. Have the child look quickly from left to right, and from right to left. Urge the child to move his eyes as quickly as possible, but be sure that both eyes land on his finger tip each time. Work to achieve rhythm, speed, and smoothness of the "jump" between fingers and to make immediate "landings" with both eyes. Some children may have difficulty in developing the rhythmic fixation from finger to finger. If so, use your index finger to pace him from left to right, touching his fingers each time.

4. Have the child hold a pencil erect about ten to twelve inches in front of his nose. Have him look from the pencil to numbers on a calendar across the room as quickly as possible. Now look back at the pencil, then to the numbers on the calendar, etc. Have him make ten to fifteen "round trips" with his eyes in this manner. Be certain that he is sitting down for this activity.

5. Using the basic directions from the activity listed above in #4, gradually move the pencil closer and closer to the child's nose. The distance between the child and the calendar should be increased and decreased so that practice will be done for a variety of distances which surround the child in everyday life.

6. Suspend a small, bright or colorful object on a piece of fine thread about two feet long. While standing a few feet in front of the child and after directing him to watch the toy, swing it slowly back and forth in a small arc at his eye level. Note his ability to follow it visually. Are his eye and head movements coordinated? Increase the length of the arc as his ability increases. Hold the object above and below his eye level and repeat.

Objective

To develop eye-hand coordination.

Suggested Teaching Techniques

1. Have the child keep his eyes on a ball that two other children are tossing in a game of catch. It may be necessary to structure this activity by standing next to the child and moving his head gently from side to side as the ball moves. This encourages ocular movement and synchronization of eye and head movements. Work toward having him move his head independently.

2. Begin by using three-hole form boards and increase training level by using more complicated form and matching boards. During this training it may be necessary to guide each step by saying, "Pick it up, look at it, where does it go?" The grooved spaces in the boards set the limits for the child. He has no real choice, he must put the object in the proper space. Matching cut-out forms of different colors to identical forms pasted on a board would be the next step. Since the grooves have been eliminated, this becomes a much more difficult task for the child.

3. Have the child fit objects together, nested cubes of various sizes, simple jigsaw puzzles, etc. Many of the cans that are discarded from the kitchen at home can be prepared so that nested sizes can be obtained. Duplicate this activity for older children by having them stack dishes, set a table, sort silverware, etc.

4. Have the child cut out simple forms. In the beginning have him cut out the outline of the picture by following simple lines that encircle the actual picture. For example, it will be very helpful to him to have a black crayon line shaped around the picture of a dog, similar to a frame. This allows him to cut out pictures by keeping the directions of his scissors simple and within his ability. As his cutting skill increases, the crayon lines should be drawn closer to the contour of the actual picture. Thus, his skill increases with the increasing complexity of the task, until he no longer needs the crayon outlines and can cut on the actual picture lines. This develops the highly important eye-hand skills wherein the visual judgments

are the specific guides to his hand activities.

Related Instructional Materials

Animal Puzzles (Educator's Publishing Service)
Colored Inch Cubes in Perspective (Developmental Learning Materials)
Dubnoff School Program I (Teaching Resources Corporation)
Fairbanks-Robinson Program I (Teaching Resources Corporation)
Fitzhugh Plus Program: Perceptual Learning and Understanding Skills (Allied Educational Council)
Lite Brite (Educator's Publishing Service)
Now I Look (John Day Company)
Parquetry Insert Boards (Developmental Learning Materials)
Pre-writing Design Cards (Educator's Publishing Service)
Shape Puzzles (Developmental Learning Materials)
The Reading Fundamentals Program (Continental Press, Incorporated)
The Useful Language Program (Continentl Press, Incorporated)
Visual Perception Skills (Educational Activities, Incorporated)

Chapter 9

HINTS FOR SPEECH AND
LANGUAGE LEARNING PROBLEMS
... YES I KNOW IT,
BUT I CAN'T SAY IT

SPEECH and language are the primary forms of communication between human beings. Speech is the vocal production of symbols, and language is the understanding or meaning of these symbolic formulations. Speech is not necessary for language, but language is a prerequisite for speech.

Both the vocal and the auditory channels are utilized for the development of speech. A deaf child may be unable to speak distinctly because he is receiving inadequate auditory feedback. However, he may be able to integrate symbolic language which does not require sound, i.e. the sign language which is often used by the deaf. The mentally deficient child functions at a retarded symbolic level, but symbolic formulation is not his only area of deficiency. The development of symbolic language in this child is assumed to develop in proportion to his mental age. The emotionally disturbed child may reject sound and not use speech to communicate with others. His problem is not that of symbolic formulation, either. He has the ability to produce the sounds and to use them in connected speech, but he may deny this ability because he has no desire to communicate.

Speech and language therapy is an educationally oriented procedure that is similar to the educational processes designed for all children. Specific therapeutic procedures, however, are more closely identified with those used for children with specific learning and language problems.

There are three primary areas of speech and language development covered in *Hints for Speech and Language Learning Problems*. *Articulation* is the actual production of the speech sounds. A young child who is just beginning to speak may be unintelligible because of his faulty articulation. His immature speech mechanisms, including his tongue, lips, and jaws, may cause him to substitute, distort, or omit certain sounds. As he grows older, these mechanisms develop more fully and he learns to imitate the speech models he is exposed to during his formative years.

If these mechanisms do not develop properly, the child may continue with his immature speech patterns. Or, if the speech model he is using is inadequate, he may continue his faulty articulation. Until he becomes aware of this inappropriate speech pattern, he will not be ready for any corrective therapy.

Voice Quality is fairly uncommon, yet there are children who do not use the correct pitch or intensity while speaking. If the child forces air through the larynx in an abnormal manner, his voice may sound hoarse or husky. Prolonged forcing of the air in this manner may result in tiny growths on the vocal cords called nodes. Constant friction of these nodes causes them to grow and become hardened somewhat like a callus. Complete vocal rest or surgery may be necessary to control their growth.

Language Use and Comprehension is basically semantics. Before a child can properly use the symbolic system of his language, he must first be able to understand its meaning. Young children often use words in an inappropriate manner because of their limited vocabularies. Older children may display this same type of language behavior for the same reason: limited vocabulary. Auditory discrimination and auditory comprehension are also important in this phase of language development (see Chapter 6). The child must be able to discriminate similar speech sounds and comprehend the meaning of these sounds as they form the words used in connected speech.

Minor speech and language problems can often be remediated within the structure of the classroom. Before such remediation is begun, the child should first be examined by a physician or a speech therapist to determine the extent and possible cause of the faulty speech pattern. If the problem is caused by a physiological deformity or inadequacy, then appropriate measures should be considered prior to any classroom activities.

When no physical problems are apparent, the teacher should still confer with the speech therapist concerning specific corrective techniques. The activities listed in this chapter should be undertaken in conjunction with a conference with a speech therapist or other qualified professional. For this reason, many of the techniques suggested are geared toward structuring the learning environment. Several of the techniques mentioned may be used with an entire class, especially at the primary levels, for general speech improvement activities.

Articulation

Associated Classroom Behavior

1. Has many speech errors.
2. Omits, distorts, substitutes, or adds sounds to words while speaking.
3. Displays tension in the speech organs during the production of particular sounds.
4. Has a physical defect which is interfering with proper speech production.

Structuring the Learning Environment

1. Begin by teaching the use of basic sound elements. Teach the production of simple consonants, vowels, blends, etc. rather than whole words or phrases.
2. Corrections in articulation should not be attempted until the child uses verbal language rather freely.
3. Present ear training materials through the use of stories which emphasize particular sounds.
4. Provide opportunities for tongue, lip, and jaw exercises through games or structured drill.
5. Use the sense of touch to help the child recognize specific movements required for speech sounds.
6. Encourage the children to speak clearly when speaking by setting a good speech example which is clear and precise.

OBJECTIVE

To provide relaxation exercises.

Suggested Teaching Techniques

1. Pretend that the body is a rag doll, letting the head and trunk drop and the arms hang heavily at the sides. Practice this exercise both in standing and in sitting positions.
2. Fall gradually forward until the hands touch the floor by beginning with the head and letting one spinal vertebra at a time relax. Rise gradually with a reverse motion of the body.
3. Let the head droop to the chest and then rotate it completely, letting it fall as far backwards as possible.
4. Lie flat on the floor and let the body become completely relaxed as if floating on top of a wave.
5. Practice stretching the entire body with the arms stretched first above the head and then extended at the sides. Yawning during the exercise helps in producing a more relaxing effect.
6. Bend the trunk first to the right and then to the left with the arms extended at the sides. This is generally called the sideways stretch.
7. Rotate the trunk alternately to the right and to the left with the arms above the head in a clasped position.
8. Practice raising one arm or leg at a time and then letting it droop.
9. Turn the head sideways to the left and to the right, looking as far backward and downward as possible. Relax the muscles of the neck each time the head returns to the initial position.
10. Rhythmic dancing may also be used to accompany the movements just described.

OBJECTIVE

To provide exercises for improving posture.

Suggested Teaching Techniques

1. Practice standing tall and sitting tall.
2. Practice walking with a book or similar object balanced on the head.
3. Practice walking while an imaginary string is pulling the chest outward and upward. Pretend that the puller of the string is moving farther and farther away.
4. Take long steps and pull the legs well up into the pelvis.
5. Lie on the floor and raise the knees until the feet rest on the floor. Roll the pelvis inward until the middle of the back is flat on the floor.
6. Repeat the pelvis roll while standing against a flat surface. Try to hold this position while standing and walking.
7. Practice deep breathing, letting the air out very slowly.

OBJECTIVE

To provide breathing exercises.

Suggested Teaching Techniques

1. Lie on the floor and completely relax. Take long, deep breaths, noticing the movement of the ribs as they go in and out.
2. Breathe gently in and out through the nose with the mouth closed.
3. Breathe in deeply through the nose until the chest is filled like a vacuum cleaner bag. Slowly breathe out the air until the bag is empty.
4. Breathe in the nose and out through the mouth, pretending to blow a small windmill. A feather or small cotton ball may be used to demonstrate this activity. See how long the child can keep the object in the air by using a second hand on a watch or clock. Work toward a steady stream of air coming out through the mouth.

5. Breathe in deeply and see how many steps the child can take while holding his breath.
6. Breathe in and out to the rhythm of music.
7. Practice whispering simple sentences. Begin with one sentence and work toward short phrases of connected speech.

OBJECTIVE

To provide jaw exercises.

Suggested Teaching Techniques

1. Let the lower jaw drop quickly.
2. Let the lower jaw drop very slowly.
3. Drop the lower jaw open and protrude it forward.
4. Move the lower jaw slowly from the left to the right.
5. Close the front teeth so that they are touching.
6. Say all of the vowel sounds slowly, beginning each sound with the long "ee" sound.

OBJECTIVE

To provide lip exercises.

Suggested Teaching Techniques

1. Open the mouth wide, then close it.
2. Blow through the lips while they are held together very gently to make a fluttering sound. Do not use the voice.
3. Form the "oh" sound with the lips, but do not use the voice.
4. Make the lips protrude in a pucker.
5. Spread the lips by making a big smile.
6. Say all of the long vowel sounds, exaggerating the movement of the lips during the production of the sounds.

7. Make the upper lip go forward as far as possible.
8. Make the lower lip go forward as far as possible.
9. Make the upper lip go downward as far as possible.
10. Make the lower lip go downward as far as possible.
11. Raise only the right side of the upper lip.
12. Raise only the left side of the upper lip.

OBJECTIVE

To provide tongue exercises.

Suggested Teaching Techniques

1. Stick out the tongue as far as possible without touching the lips.
2. Point the tip of the tongue and touch the upper lip, the lower lip, the left corner of the mouth, and the right corner of the mouth.
3. Point the tongue and try to touch the nose.
4. Stick out the tongue and alternate between trying to touch the nose and trying to touch the chin.
5. Use the tip of the tongue to produce the "lah" sound. Try to repeat the sound quickly. Do the same with the "t" and "d" sounds.
6. Take the tip of the tongue and sweep the roof of the mouth, moving from the front of the mouth behind the teeth to the back of the mouth near the soft palate.
7. Lick the lips with the tip of the tongue, going in a circle all the way around the lips.

Related Instructional Materials

Animal Adventures (T. S. Denison and Company, Inc.)
Better Speech Can be Fun (Expression Company, Inc.)
The Big Book of Sounds (Interstate Printers and Publishers, Inc.)
Building Good Speech (Stanwix House, Inc.)
Carryover Articulation Manual: A Language Approach to the

(s) and (r) Phonemes (Charles C Thomas, Publisher)
The Clown Family Speech Book (Charles C Thomas, Publisher)
For Speech Sake (Fearon Publishers, Inc.)
Galloping Sounds (Expression Company, Inc.)
Initial Sounds (Steck-Vaughn Company Publishers)
Listen-Look-Say (Educator's Publishing Company)
Snoopy's Secret Code Book (Holt, Rinehart and Winston, Inc.)
Speech Correction Through Listening (Scott, Foresman and Company)
Speech Improvement Sound Cards (Steck-Vaughn Company Publishers)
Speech Improvement Through Choral Speaking (Expression Company, Publishers)
Speech Lingo (Speech and Language Materials, Inc.)
The Speech Tree (Mafex Associates, Inc.)
Stories for Quiet Listening (Children's Music Center, Inc.)
Talking Time, Sets I and II (McGraw-Hill Book Company)
Tell Again Story Cards, Levels I and II (McGraw-Hill Book Company)

Voice Quality

Associated Classroom Behavior

1. Speaks too loudly or too softly.
2. Speaks in an unnatural pitch, one that is too high or too low.
3. Has a voice quality that is hoarse, husky, thin, tense, nasal, harsh, breathy, monotonous, etc.
4. Does not have a strong production of consonant sounds, especially when they are at the end of a word or with other consonants.
5. Has exaggerated movements for the speech organs.
6. Prolongs a sound after producing it in such a manner as to distort the word being spoken.

Structuring the Learning Environment

1. Provide opportunities for the child to experiment with

various voice qualities, pitches, and intensities.
2. Develop the idea of sound quality through comparison of different sounds.
3. Call attention to the various qualities of sounds in the classroom.
4. Encourage the imitation of sounds of animals, airplanes, trains, etc. The ability to imitate these sounds helps the child prepare for the imitation of good voice quality.

OBJECTIVE

To provide voice building exercises.

Suggested Teaching Techniques

1. See the breathing activities under *Articulation* for specific activities related to the development of breath control.
2. Practice saying the long vowels by adding the "h" sound to the beginning of each vowel.
3. Repeat the long vowels, one, two, three, and four times. Use the lips and jaw to form these sounds.
4. Prolong the production of each long vowel sound by beginning very softly and continuing in a very soft voice. Also try beginning the vowel sound with a soft voice and gradually build to a louder, more intense voice.
5. Hum up and down the musical scale.
6. Repeat sounds such as "n," "d," "k," and "p" very quickly, using one sound at a time.

OBJECTIVE

To set an example of a pleasant, well-modulated voice.

Suggested Teaching Techniques

1. Provide ear training exercises to develop awareness of

sounds.

2. Use a mirror to demonstrate the presence of visible sounds such as "p," "v," and "th."
3. Slightly exaggerate the final sounds of words.
4. Provide special drill on words which contain the most commonly mispronounced sounds in the classroom. This may be done in imitation or game form.
5. Provide opportunities for all of the children to observe the speaker's face during conversation.
6. Be articulate, yet do not overexaggerate the visible movements of speech except when the child is attending to the correct production of specific sounds.
7. Use a tape recorder to help identify any faulty speech in the classroom by the teacher or the students. Be careful when using a small tape recorder because the sounds are often somewhat distorted when they are played back.

Related Instructional Materials

Due to the components involved in voice training, there are no instructional materials listed for this area. A qualified speech therapist is the best resource the classroom teacher has for voice problems in the classroom.

Language Use and Comprehension

Associated Classroom Behavior

1. Displays a limited vocabulary, both in speaking and in comprehending.
2. Frequently uses words which do not make sense. May even have his own vocabulary.
3. Seems unable to receive, integrate (as in inner language), and/or express verbal symbols.
4. Has conceptual difficulties.
5. Avoids speaking, especially in group activities.
6. Uses words inappropriately.

7. Reverses or substitutes sounds in words.
8. Has difficulty with prepositions.
9. Has difficulty with tenses.

Structuring the Learning Environment

1. Remember that there is a developmental hierarchy for the development of language. First comes sounds, then words, then phrases and simple sentences.
2. Use the child's vocabulary, including his nonverbal langauge, to communicate with him initially. Build on the existing vocabulary and language system he already possesses.
3. Translate gestures into simple, concrete words. Be consistent in your use of these words.
4. Let the child know you are interested in *what* he is saying more than *how* he is saying it.
5. Use activities which are motivating to the child. Individualize to meet his language needs.

OBJECTIVE

To help the child develop inner language.

Suggested Teaching Techniques

1. Take the child by the hand and lead him through a maze or around the room, verbalizing his actions as he does them.
2. While the child is completing a play activity, verbalize his actions for him. Provide specific play activities if necessary.
3. Ask the child to repeat simple verbalizations which describe specific actions that he is to imitate or initiate on his own.

OBJECTIVE

To teach receptive language.

Suggested Teaching Techniques

1. Ask the child to perform a specific task such as getting out of his chair and walking to the door. Repeat the directions while bodily leading him through the movements.
2. Place several familiar objects in front of the child. Name the objects and have the child repeat the names. Give simple commands such as, "Show me the _____" and "Give me the _____." If the child is unable to follow through on these directions, guide him through the required actions while verbalizing the movements for him.
3. Provide multisensory experiences to help the child incorporate what he hears with what he sees, feels, does, etc.
4. See Chapter 6 for further related activities.

OBJECTIVE

To teach expressive language.

Suggested Teaching Techniques

1. Begin with simple words which the child can produce easily. Make simple sentences from these words and have the child imitate these. It is best to use color or action words with nouns to help identify specific words.

2. When using action words, help the child imitate the action being described.

3. Play a game of Give. The teacher places several familiar objects in front of herself and in front of the child. She initiates the activity by saying, "Give me the _____." The child then takes a turn and asks for an object which the teacher has in front of her.

4. Using the principles outlined for the activity in #3, reverse the response. Instead of asking for a particular object, the players take turns handing each other objects while

saying, "Here is a _____ for you."

5. Give the child opportunities to express himself by telling about activities in which he has participated. Use classroom activities initially, then progress to outside activities such as family trips, sporting events, etc.

6. Use simple puppets to act out stories which have just been heard. Let the children trade puppets and switch roles to retell the story.

7. Let the children act out simple stories or plays after hearing or reading them. With older children, role playing activities may be used. The situations may be related to a special event that has taken place in the community or a contrived situation related to something which the child is familiar with.

8. Read or tell part of a story and let the children tell the ending. Suspense stories are especially good for this type of activity.

9. Let the children make up a story by having each person add a sentence to the story. The first person begins with a simple sentence which introduces the story. The second person makes up a sentence which is related to what the first person said. Continue until the last person completes the story by giving a logical ending to the entire series of events.

Related Instructional Materails

Caption Cards (Educational Design Associates)

Expressive Language Cards (Educational Design Associates)

A Functional Basic Word List for Special Pupils (Stanwix House, Inc.)

A Headstart Book for Looking and Listening (McGraw-Hill Book Company)

Helping the Child to Listen and Talk (Interstate Printers and Publishers, Inc.)

Language Experiences in Early Childhood (Encyclopedia Britannica Educational Corporation)

Language Instructional Activities (Love Publishing Company)

Language Motivating Experiences for Young Children (Children's Music Center, Inc.)

Multi-Story Sequence Cards (Educational Design Associates)

My First Picture Dictionary (Scott, Foresman and Company)

My Pictionary (Scott, Foresman and Company)

My Second Picture Dictionary (Scott, Foresman and Company)

Peabody Language Development Kits, Levels P-3 (American Guidance Service, Inc.)

Speech Through Pictures (Expression Company, Publishers)

The Sesame Street Learning Kit (Time-Life Books)

Story Stimulus Cards (Educational Design Associates)

Talking Time (T. S. Denison and Company, Inc.)

Training in Some Pre-requisites for Beginning Reading (Educator's Publishing Service)

ADDRESSES FOR PUBLISHERS OF INSTRUCTIONAL MATERIALS LISTED IN CHAPTERS SIX, SEVEN, EIGHT, AND NINE

Abingdon Press
Nashville, Tennessee 37202

Academic Therapy Publications
1543 Fifth Avenue
San Rafael, California 94901

Allied Educational Council
Distribution Center
Galien, Michigan 49113

Allyn & Bacon, Inc.
470 Atlantic Avenue
Boston, Massachusetts 02210

American Guidance Service, Inc.
Publishers' Building
Circle Pines, Minnesota 55014

Ann Arbor Publishers
611 Church Street
Ann Arbor, Michigan 48104

Appleton-Century-Crofts
440 Park Avenue South
New York, New York 10016

Barnell Loft & Dexter Westbrook, Ltd.
958 Church Street
Baldwin, New York 11510

Behavioral Research Laboratories
Box 577
Palo Alto, California 94302

Childcraft Education Corporation
P.O. Box 94
Bayonne, New Jersey 07002

Children's Music Center, Inc.
5373 West Pico Blvd.
Los Angeles, California 90019

Classroom Materials Company
93 Myrtle Drive
Great Neck, New York 11021

Continental Press, Inc.
Elizabethtown, Pennsylvania 17022

Council for Exceptional Children
1920 Association Drive
Reston, Virginia 22091

Creative Playthings
P.O. Box 1100
Princeton, New Jersey 08540

Creative Visuals
Box 1911
Big Spring, Texas 79720

Cuisenaire Company of America, Inc.
12 Church Street
Rye, New York 10580

245

John Day Company
P.O. Box 2028
Vaughn Building
Austin, Texas 78767

T. S. Denison and Company, Inc.
5100 West 82nd Street
Minneapolis, Minnesota 55431

Developmental Learning Materials
7440 Natchez Avenue
Niles, Illinois 60648

Dimensions Publishing Company
Box 4221
San Rafael, California 94903

Educational Activities, Inc.
P.O. Box 392
Long Island, New York 11520

Educational Design Associates
P.O. Box 915
East Lansing, Michigan 48823

Educator's Publishing Service
75 Maulton Street
Cambridge, Massachusetts 02138

Encyclopedia Britannica Educational
 Corporation
425 North Michigan Avenue
Chicago, Illinois 60611

Expression Company, Publishers
P.O. Box 11
Magnolia, Massachusetts 01930

Eye Gate House, Inc.
146-01 Archer Avenue
Jamaica, New York 11435

Fearon Publishers, Inc.
2165 Park Blvd.
Palo Alto, California 94306

Filmstrip House, Inc.
432 Park Avenue South
New York, New York 10016

Follett Educational Corporation
Follett Publishing Company
1010 West Washington Blvd.
Chicago, Illinois 60607

Garrard Publishing Company
1607 North Market Street
Champaign, Illinois 61820

Go-Mo Products, Inc.
P.O. Box 143
1441 Headford Avenue
Waterloo, Iowa 50704

Harcourt Brace Jovanovich
757 Third Avenue
New York, New York 10017

Harper and Row, Publishers
School Department
2500 Crawford Avenue
Evanston, Illinois 60201

Hayes School Publishing Company,
 Inc.
321 Pennwood Avenue
Wilkinsburg, Pennsylvania 15221

Houghton Mifflin Company
1 Beacon Street
Boston, Massachusetts 02107

Holt, Rinehart and Winston, Inc.
383 Madison Avenue
New York, New York 10017

Hudson Photographic Industries,
 Inc.
Irvington-on-Hudson, New York
 10533

Ideal School Supply Company
11000 South Lavergne Avenue
Oak Lawn, Illinois 60453

Instructo Corporation
Cedar Hollow Road
Paoli, Pennsylvania 19301

Interstate Printers and Publishers,
 Inc.
19-27 North Jackson Street
Danville, Illinois 61832

Jenn Publications
815-825 East Market Street
Louisville, Kentucky 40406

Kimbo Educational Records
Box 55
Deal, New Jersey 07723

Knowledge Aid
6633 West Howard Street
Niles, Illinois 60648

J. B. Lippincott Company
East Washington Square
Philadelphia, Pennsylvania 19105

Love Publishing Company
6635 East Villanova Place
Denver, Colorado 80222

Mafex Associates, Inc.
111 Barron Avenue
Johnstown, Pennsylvania 15906

McGraw-Hill Book Company
330 West 42nd Street
New York, New York 10036

Media
P.O. Box 2067
Van Nuys, California 91404

Charles E. Merrill Publishing Company
1300 Alum Creek Drive
Columbus, Ohio 43216

Noble and Noble Publishers, Inc.
750 Third Avenue
New York, New York 10017

Prentice-Hall, Inc.
Englewood Cliffs, New Jersey 07632

Research Press
2612 North Mattis
Champaign, Illinois 61820

Frank E. Richards Publishing Company, Inc.
324 First Street
Liverpool, New York 13088

Rhythm Record Company
Oklahoma City, Oklahoma 73120

Science Research Associates, Inc.
259 East Erie Street
Chicago, Illinois 60611

Scott, Foresman and Company
1900 East Lake Avenue
Glenville, Illinois 60025

Society for Visual Education, Inc.
1345 Diversey Parkway
Chicago, Illinois 60614

Speech and Language Materials, Inc.
P.O. Box 721
Tulsa, Oklahoma 74101

Stanley Bowmar Company
4 Broadway
Valhalla, New York 10595

Stanwix House, Inc.
3020 Chartiers Avenue
Pittsburgh, Pennsylvania 15204

Steck-Vaughn Company Publishers
P.O. Box 2028
Austin, Texas 78767

Sterling Educational Films
241 East 34th Street
New York, New York 10016

Tapes Unlimited
13113 Puritan Avenue
Detroit, Michigan 48227

Teacher's Publishing Corporation
School and Library Services Division
Box 2000
Darien, Connecticut 06820

Teaching Resources Corporation
100 Boylston Street
Boston, Massachusetts 02116

Charles C Thomas, Publisher
301-327 East Lawrence Avenue
Springfield, Illinois 62717

Time-Life Books
Time-Life Building
Chicago, Illinois 60621

University of Illinois Press
100 University Press Building
Urbana, Illinois 61801

AUTHOR INDEX

SUBJECT INDEX

A

Access centers, 103-104
Agraphia, motor, 21
Alexia, 21
  developmental, 21
Allied service centers, 105-106
Annexes, 103
Aphasia, 3, 20, 65
American Association on Mental Deficiency, 8
American Asylum for the Education and Instruction of the Deaf and Dumb (Conn.), 18
American Breeders Association, 11
Association for Children with Learning Disabilities, 25, 120, 143
Association of Medical Officers of American Institutions for Idiotic and Feeble-Minded Persons, 8
Association, poor, 123-124
Attention control, 24
Auditory attention, 155
  classroom behavior, 156
  learning environment, 156
  instructional materials, 158
  teaching techniques, 157-158
Auditory comprehension, 155
  classroom behavior, 158-159
  instructional materials, 165-167
  learning environment, 159-160
  teaching techniques, 160-165
Auditory discrimination, 155
  classroom behavior, 167
  instructional materials, 173-174
  learning environment, 167-168
  teaching techniques, 168-173
Auditory learner, 66, 122
Auditory memory and sequencing, 155
  classroom behavior, 174-175
  instructional materials, 181

  learning environment, 175-176
  teaching techniques, 176-181
Auditory perceptual learning problems, 155-181

B

Binet-Simon test, 10
Blindness, 7, 15-17
Block or departmentalized classes, 97-98
Braidwood, Thomas, 17
Braille, Louis, 15
Braille system, 15
Brain dysfunction, minimal, 23, 120
Brain injury, 3, 23, 120
  conceptualization, 21
  emotional control, 21
  etiology, 22
  language, 21
  perception, 21
Bureau for the Education of the Handicapped (1966), 52

C

California School for the Deaf, 34, 35
Cascade system, 93
Chicago Juvenile Psychopathic Institute, 12
Cerebral palsy, 19
  ataxia, 20
  athetosis, 19
  mixed, 20
  spastic paralysis, 19
    high spinal, 20
  tremors and rigidity, 19
Classification of children, 41-42 (*see also* Labeling)
Columbian Institution for the Instruction of the Deaf and Dumb and the Blind, 18, 50

253